Big 54

p6

THE SUBJECT REVEALED

    Displaying classic Southern hospitality, Janet Dailey ushered me through the marble foyer, down the pillared hallway to the kitchen table, which was littered with everything from Neiman-Marcus catalogues, art supplies and fan letters to the standard utility bills and birthday cards. After shoving an ice-cold Snapple into my hand, she sat down on the chair across from me and began to talk . . .

Novels by Janet Dailey

THE JANET DAILEY COMPANION

A Comprehensive Guide to Her Life and Her Novels

SONJA MASSIE AND MARTIN H. GREENBERG

HarperPaperbacks
A Division of HarperCollins*Publishers*

HarperPaperbacks
A Division of HarperCollinsPublishers
10 East 53rd Street, New York, N.Y. 10022-5299

ISBN: 0-06-108473-5

HarperCollins®, ▦®, and HarperPaperbacks™
are trademarks of HarperCollins*Publishers*

Cover design by Michael Sabanosh

A hardcover edition of this book was published
in 1996 by HarperCollins*Publishers*.

First HarperPaperbacks printing: May 1997

Printed in the United States of America

Visit HarperPaperbacks on the World Wide Web at
http://www.harpercollins.com

❖ 10 9 8 7 6 5 4 3 2 1

*This book is affectionately
dedicated to Janet Dailey
On behalf of millions of fans whose lives and
hearts have been touched by her work
And all the female authors who have passed
through the doors she opened*

CONTENTS

ACKNOWLEDGMENTS

The authors would like to thank:

*Kathy Lyerla—for her generous contributions
and love of Janet's work*

*Rob Ward—for hours of transcribing audio tapes
and resulting neck and shoulder cramps*

*Larry Segriff—expert shuffler of massive
amounts of paperwork*

Richard Curtis—for bringing us all together

*The Dailey Enterprises staff: Mary Dailey,
Char Harner, and Belinda Maples—for all that research!*

THE
JANET DAILEY
COMPANION

A Comprehensive Guide
to Her Life and
Her Novels

INTRODUCTION

Sonja Massie

When my agent, Richard Curtis, offered me the enviable job of interviewing Janet Dailey for this handbook, I experienced the predictably high levels of elation, closely followed by twangs of anxiety. What would she be like, this celebrated author, this icon of women's fiction?

Upon arriving at the wrought-iron gates of her imposing mansion, my stress level slid upward several degrees. My assignment was to spend a week or so with the best-loved living female author in the world and to somehow convince her to reveal her heart's deepest and dearest secrets to me and her public. I had labored over my list of questions, knowing that if she chose to guard her privacy and give me one-word answers, this interview could last all of four and a half minutes.

My first clue that everything might work out better than I had hoped was when the massive front door (with its sparkling, leaded, beveled glass) opened. I suppose I had expected a maid in a black and white French costume, or a butler with a stiff collar and cummerbund, but it was the mistress of the manor herself . . . wearing a sweatshirt, jeans, and a warm smile of welcome.

Displaying classic Southern hospitality, she ushered me through the marble foyer, down the pillared hallway to the kitchen table, which was littered with everything from Neiman Marcus catalogues, art supplies, and fan letters to the standard utility bills and birthday cards. After shoving an ice-cold Snapple into my hand, she sat down on the chair across from me and began to talk.

For the next five days, I was charmed by this warm,

sensitive, witty, and wonderfully sage woman. If she held anything back, it wasn't obvious. As you will see when you read the following interview, she answered every question with honesty and candor, far more than I could have hoped for. She told me stories that made me laugh, brought a tear to my eye, and made me think, long after I had left her presence . . . a better and somewhat wiser woman for the contact.

Since the interview, I have been asked countless times, "What is she like?" Whether out of adoration, envy, or simple curiosity, everyone wants to know the key to this phenomenal woman; what makes her tick?

If I could sum up Janet Dailey in one word, I suppose it would have to be "love." Not the gushy, schmaltzy, sentimental kind of love that might be expected of a woman who has penned nearly one hundred romantic novels. Janet is down-to-earth and practical, and so is her idea of what constitutes "love."

In spite of all those romantic scenes, written over the years, Janet's interpretation of "true love" has less to do with candlelight and roses, and more to do with loyalty and commitment.

Janet loves life. She loves writing, reading, her family and friends, her Yorkies, her horses, her art, gardening, Branson, Missouri, and her home, Belle Rive. A passionate woman, she pours an astonishingly high degree of energy into everything she "loves." And when, as everyone does from time to time, she runs low on energy, discipline takes over and she finishes the job.

By reading *The Janet Dailey Companion*, you will discover that Janet has led a rich and full life and continues to do so. As with any life, hers has been a complete spectrum of dark and light, highs and lows. But her dedication, discipline, and courage have enabled her to fulfill dreams that even she would not have believed.

Millions of fans worldwide have loved Janet's heroines, exalting with them in their triumphs, feeling the pangs of their sorrows. Now they will have the opportunity to know the woman who created those incredible heroines, a woman who embodies those qualities of intelligence, wit, and wisdom.

I'm grateful to have been given the chance to "get to know" Janet Dailey. Once you've read this chronicle of a remarkable life well lived, I'm sure you will be, too.

PART I

Janet Dailey, Up Close and Personal

FACTS AND FIGURES

BORN: Janet Haradon, May 21, 1944, Storm Lake, Iowa, in northwest Iowa, population 8,800.

> *JANET: I was born on the cusp between Gemini and Taurus. Most astrologers disagree about which sign I'm under, so if I read the daily horoscopes, I generally read both signs and pick the one that sounds the most exciting.*

CHILDHOOD: Grew up in Early, Iowa, population about 727. Her father, Boyd Haradon, died when she was five years old. When Janet was thirteen, her mother, Louise, married Glenn Rutherford, and the family moved to Independence, Iowa, population 5,500. Janet has three older sisters and four stepbrothers.

SCHOOLS: In the sixth grade, in Early, Janet wrote her first story. Called "Toby, the Bad Teddy Bear," it was followed by "Willie, the Bookworm." She attended Jefferson High School in Independence, Iowa, and graduated in 1962. At Jefferson she was a cheerleader, a member of the Writers' Club, and editor of the yearbook, *The Wapsie.*

FAVORITE AUTHORS: Edna Ferber, Louis L'Amour, James Michener.

ADULTHOOD: In 1963, she moved to nearby Omaha, Nebraska, attended secretarial school, and then worked for thirteen years as secretary and assistant to Bill Dailey, fifteen years her senior. Bill and Janet were married in 1965 or 1966. They don't remember the exact date.

In 1975 Janet started writing on a dare from Bill. Her first book, *No Quarter Asked*, was published in January 1976 by Harlequin Books. She was their first American author. During the next six years, Harlequin published fifty-seven romance novels by Janet Dailey.

She is now the number one female writer in America and the third-best-selling living author in the world. One hundred and eighty million copies of her romance novels and other books have been sold in nineteen languages in ninety-eight countries.

THE SILVER STREAK TOUR: In 1974, Janet's mother and stepfather sold their home and traveled in a trailer. A few months later, Janet and Bill Dailey decided to retire. Both had worked so hard that they found a life of leisure incredibly boring. In the search for "adventure," they bought a 1975 31-foot Airstream pulled by a 1975 Lincoln — and traveled 100,000 miles. On a dare from Bill, Janet wrote her first novel and didn't stop until she had written a book set in every U.S. state. The second trailer, a 33-foot Silver Streak pulled by a 1978 Lincoln is now in the carriage house at Belle Rive.

PUBLISHING HIGHLIGHTS: In 1978, while still writing for Harlequin, Janet began to write other types of books for other publishers.

Touch the Wind, published in 1979 by Pocket Books, was set in Mexico, Janet's first locale outside of the U.S. *The Rogue*, published in 1980, included the first oral sex in a romance novel. Surprisingly, it was done to a woman by a man. Sales of each of these two books were close to one million copies. Her twelve Pocket Books include the Calder series, set in Montana.

The Daileys were instrumental in forming Silhouette Books, which is now a subsidiary of Harlequin Enterprises. In three years, from 1981 to 1984, Silhouette published twelve books by Janet Dailey at the same time that other books by her were published by Harlequin,

Pocket Books, and Poseidon Press (a subsidiary of Simon & Schuster), a unique and prodigious record in the publishing industry.

MAINSTREAM FICTION: Janet wrote sixty-nine novels of the romance category, a type of escapist fantasy. Then she evolved into "mainstream romance," which is more realistic, and now writes "women's fiction," though she has many male readers.

According to Janet, her most challenging book was *The Great Alone*, published in 1986 by Poseidon, about seven generations of an Alaskan family from eighteenth-century Russia through American Indian cultures to modern Alaska.

In 1987, Janet signed a multimillion-dollar contract with Little, Brown and Company. Her books for Little, Brown include *Heiress* (1988), *Rivals* (1989), *Masquerade* (1990), *Aspen Gold* (1991), and *Tangled Vines* (1992). Her last sixteen books have been bestsellers. *Tangled Vines*, set in New York and California, was a Literary Guild Main Selection and a Reader's Digest Condensed Book. The audio edition of *Tangled Vines* was narrated by actress Adrienne Barbeau.

Janet's favorite states include Missouri, Texas, Alaska, and Kansas. Her favorite book: the one she's writing now.

PHYSICAL DESCRIPTION: Janet is 5'4", has a slender, athletic figure, is a brunette, and has green eyes. Most of her clothes are purchased by phone from catalogs (Nieman-Marcus, Spiegel, Saks Fifth Avenue).

HOBBIES: Horseback riding, gardening, painting. Although she has an abundance of talent in many fields and an avid interest in almost anything and everything, she readily admits, "I'm not much of a cook. When they were passing out cooking skills, I thought they said 'book' and went back for a second helping."

MISCELLANEOUS: She types on an Adler electric typewriter (does not use a computer) in her office, adjacent to her kitchen and dining room, with a view of the lake. She and Bill drink many cups of coffee each day (Folger's made on a Bunn coffeemaker). She carries a Bic pen with which she jots down reams of notes.

The Daileys take vacation trips between books, notably a safari trip to Kenya in November 1992 with country music performer Boxcar Willie and his wife, who live in Branson, and a Caribbean cruise in February 1993 aboard the Norwegian Cruise Line's m/s *Seaward*. Janet hosted a reception, gave a talk, and answered questions from the passengers on the Janet Dailey Appreciation Cruise.

Janet Dailey's literary agent is Richard Curtis of New York.

GOALS: "To be the best I can be."

THOSE "EARLY" YEARS

J: I grew up in Early, Iowa, a town with more trees than people.

S: Early? That's where you got it . . . this thing about getting up at four in the morning to write.

J: There were only about 500 people. Back in the fifties, the little town still had country stores, a clothing store, a hardware store. Saturday nights were so busy, people coming into town to shop, the real Beaver Cleaver type of thing.

Growing up in a small town, I feel I have an advantage that lends to my writing today: In a small town you not only *know* everyone, where they work, what they do in their off time, who their parents were, who their grandparents were, their family history. You don't meet just a person who likes horses.

You see the full, rounded picture of them—wh.
they came from, who they married, what good times
they've had, what hard times they've had, when they
were in trouble, what they were in trouble over. You
see it all, and you see that nobody is all good, and
nobody is all evil.

I think you get that full sense of people, to give
them all of their different dimensions, and all their
many layers. Whether it's the arrogance, the cockiness that covers the insecurity, that covers the,
"Well, I don't think I'll really be able to do this."

You'll see the struggle and the pulling together.
You'll see that "neighbor helping neighbor" spirit
that draws them together. I think you see it in a com-
posite of the small area.

When you get into a larger city, you tend to look
at them just from what you know of them. They
work at this place; that's what they are.

S: You only see the one facet of their life that you
observe.

J: Exactly. Without seeing *why*.

S: Are you saying it helps to understand and accept people because you see their frailties?

J: Yes. It helps you to draw characters. When you are
creating characters, you're not just saying, "Oh . . . I'm
going to create *this*." Once you start creating that character, you see more than just a character. You see all
the things that went into molding them, so that
maybe they feel different. Like the ugly duckling, they
don't feel as though they belong to that family. They
are a product of all these elements. You can play it any
way you want, but you get a better feel for who they
are, and you see the whole.

S: That's what loving people is all about, don't you think?

J: Yes, I do.

S: In a small town I suppose you grow up seeing the relationship between sowing and reaping.

J: Yes! I think that's especially true in the Midwest. And you grow up seeing the relationship to the land, seeing how much we get from our environment, how much we have to put back.

S: In your childhood, what do you feel you got from the land?

J: Oh . . . what didn't I get? All the food came from the land.

S: All of *your* food? You actually saw this?

J: With the exception that Mother would sometimes go to the store to buy something, but usually she would buy it from my grandparents. We had our own garden in the back yard, so we grew everything and canned everything. You took care of the garden. You didn't let weeds grow to take away the food and the water and the nourishment of those plants.

S: So, your gardening wasn't done just for the beauty, for the flowers, it was sustenance?

J: Yes, and you learned that a bite of that tomato, that fresh carrot pulled straight out of the ground . . . the food came from the land. You learned to appreciate the sunny days and the smell of the rain. Of course you always laid back, you always stored away your foods for the winters in cellars. We did all of that:

being around farmers, putting up hay, walking the bean rows, pulling out all of the weeds, and walking the pastures. Grandpa would always pay you to walk the corn and wheat fields, walk the pastures, looking for thistles. Grandpa was *death* on thistles in the pastures. You worked, you planted, you created with that work.

There's a strong connection between me and the soil. There's no time that I enjoy more than when I'm actually digging in the soil. I can remember my grandfather would always grab a handful of soil and taste it with his tongue.

S: He could probably tell the mineral content that way.

J: Exactly. And I'm sure he did this to shush us up, but after supper at night, we'd be sitting outside and the corn field would grow right up to the house yard, and he'd say, "Sh-h-h . . . you can listen to the corn grow. Sh-h-h." And we'd sit there and shut up and just listen. Although at times you could swear you could hear it crackle as it was growing.

S: Really?

J: Yeah. If you've ever planted some corn, you watch it and when you go to bed at night it'll be "this" tall. And when you get up in the morning it'll be *this* tall.

S: Well, I have planted corn, Janet, and that was not my experience at all.

J (*laughs*): It died, didn't it?

S: Very quickly, yes. Hearing mine grow was not an issue.

J: But those memories of sitting outside, being really quiet and listening to the corn grow . . . good memories.

J: My cousin David and I always wanted to be up before the dawn. We wanted to see them milk the cows, and there were calves you had to take care of. You always had chores when you were a kid.

S: Speaking of the calves . . . was it hard to raise something that you knew was going to be slaughtered?

J: No, it was so accepted. I know my mom used to tell stories that when my daddy was alive—I must have been about three or four—the vet would come to castrate or whatever. I was always out there, because I had to make sure he was doing it right. I was right there in the thick of it. She said I would grab my coat, and go out the door, and say, "He's gonna cut the pigs today, and I gotta be there to make sure he does it right."

S: Do you like reading James Herriot?

J: Uh-huh. I love him. I *love him*.

J: Early is a neat little town. A very structured town. Wednesday was the day that you did much of your baking.

S: Excuse me . . . why did you do it on Wednesday?

J: That's just the way it was.

S: Oh, of course. Sorry.

J: Thursday was "ladies' card" day. That's when you played cards with your friends and neighbors. Friday you cleaned for the weekend. Saturday you went to town and you did your shopping. Sunday you went to church, came home, and had Sunday dinner. And it was either roast beef or chicken. Monday you washed your clothes. If you didn't have your clothes on the line by nine o'clock in the morning, your neighbor would come over and see if you were sick.

S: Are you serious?

J: Absolutely. And Tuesday you ironed.

S: What if you were lazy and you didn't iron until Wednesday? Would it ruin your reputation in the town?

J: You couldn't do it on Wednesday . . . Wednesday you're supposed to bake! Maybe it was because you had to bake something special for ladies' card day on Thursday.

S: What type of baking did you do?

J: Whatever Mom told me to do.

S: Desserts?

J: Yes, and breads. You didn't buy that much bread. I remember walking into Grandma Haradon's house. She always made these great rolls, dinner rolls. They had a floor register and that's where the bread would be left to rise. And you'd walk in and you'd smell it through the whole house.

S: Nothing smells as good as bread being baked.

J: That's true, and nothing smells so bad as chickens being singed.

S: I have to admit, I haven't sniffed a lot of singed chickens in my time, but I can imagine it would be pretty gross. Did you guys have to have to butcher your own meat?

J: Yeah, but I have never killed a chicken. I figure I should probably learn to do this. I'll have to go to Evie's, my sister, sometime when they're killing chickens. Mom would wring their necks or just use a broomstick.

Have you ever listened to Garrison Keillor's Lake Wobegon? I can't even begin to tell you which tape it's on, but he has one part that talks about butchering hogs. And it's so very true, in the midst of all his humor, he captures the farmers' truth, and that's the respect they have for the animals they kill.

You don't take pleasure in their pain, you don't find humor in them running around "like a chicken with its head cut off." This is death, which is part of life. And you must honor and respect that this animal is giving something to you. And that respect—especially with farmers—is very, very subtle, very, very quiet, and if you don't look for it, you'll never see it. But it's there.

JANET: Both my parents came from big families, so I grew up literally surrounded by family.

MOM, DAD, STEPDAD, SISTERS, STEPBROTHERS, AND GRANDPARENTS: KINFOLK AS FAR AS THE EYE COULD SEE!

J: My recollection of my father is minimal—mainly what my sisters and mother told me about him. My mother remarried when I was thirteen. By then, all my sisters were married or gone, leaving me the only one home. My stepdad is really the only father I can remember. He made my mother very happy, and I'm glad about that. I love him, too.

When my mother remarried, we moved from Early, Iowa, to Independence, Iowa. From a small town of 727 to a "big city" of 5,500. It was quite an adjustment, more exciting than traumatic. I graduated from high school there, was a cheerleader, editor of the school newspaper and yearbook, and was in any other organization there was to join.

S: Tell me about your sisters.

J: I was the youngest of four: Shirley, Marilyn, Evie, then me. Evie I always felt closest to because she was closest to me in age. Shirley was married by the time I was five. My niece Sherry is only six years younger than me.

Evie didn't move far away. When she got married she still lived within the area, so I would go out to her farm to spend the summers. And even after my mother had remarried and moved, I would go back to that section of Iowa near Early and spend three or four weeks with Evie. Initially, it was when she was getting ready to have another baby and I would take care of the other kids.

S: Did she do this often?

J: Yes, yes, she did. So, obviously, I've always been close to her and to her kids.

And Marilyn, her husband worked for the HyVee grocery store and he was always getting transferred and they were always moving.

S: That makes it difficult.

J: And Shirley, my oldest sister (*laughs*), she's always been Shirley and we love her dearly. But her husband was a truck driver and he was always on the road and that left her home with a little girl and she just stopped doing a lot. When your husband drives a truck, you're never sure when he's going to be home, and you want to be there when he gets there. And you have to take care of the home and there's all those other things to do.

But we've always been a close family. And we were always there for each other. On my fiftieth birthday we had the house full to overflowing. Between my house and Mom's, I think we were sleeping twenty-nine to thirty-three people.

S: How many bedrooms do you have?

J: We have four upstairs and one downstairs, but there were a lot of them on the floor.

S: In other words, all horizontal spaces *were* covered.

J: Yes. And we were talking about the fact that these were our best memories, when we'd get together and you'd have to walk over people so that you could go out the door. We like those kind of gatherings.

S: And you like your relatives, don't you?

J: Oh, yeah, I *love* them. I look at my sisters and they are all so talented in their own individual ways.

Shirley needlepoints and . . . anything . . . she can touch her hand to anything and make these beautiful works of art. She drove a truck with her husband for years after her daughter was grown.

S: One of the big rigs?

J: Yep, the big ones. And I love the boldness of that. I love the adventure. And my sister Marilyn, God has blessed her with a beautiful voice. Unfortunately, she's very shy and it's tough for her. She'll only sing in church. And she cooks like a dream. Anyone who isn't a good cook can recognize the talent when they see it. She'll try anything, and she just *loves* it. She has three boys and a girl. Extremely talented. I think she could paint. Her husband does some woodcraft things and she's been painting some of those for him. And I think, boy, turn her loose with a brush and she'll find out she can paint.

And Evie, Evie is this modern woman marvel to me. You can go into her house when she's five minutes away from putting dinner on the table for six people and six more can walk in and she just touches it, and there will be enough for twelve. She can feed the multitudes! And never turn a hair.

S: How many children did she finally have?

J: She has four, a boy and three girls. She had five, but she lost a little girl.

Her place is where everybody goes. All the neighbors show up, all the relatives show up. I think this last year they didn't have one weekend where they didn't have at least five or six people staying over.

S: And she likes this?

J: Yes. Obviously it gets tiring for her sometimes. She works a full-time job at a grain elevator as the book-keeper, taking care of all the accounts and the government reports. Plus, her husband's a farmer, which means she's a farmer's wife, which means she has to help with the farm and pulling the pigs and pulling calves and putting up all her own food.

S: I'm not a farm girl; do you mean pulling pigs and calves into the world?

J (*nods*): Uh-huh. And gardening and cleaning and putting things up, and butchering her own hogs and raising four kids and going to church and working for the church. . . .

S: Where does she get so much energy?

J: She *loves* life, just *loves* life! When Evie comes, she's got a smile on her face that just lights up. . . . Happiness, just genuine happiness.

I remember one time when we were there, and she had just got home from work. And after getting the food on the table, she had no more than got the dishes done, when she picks up her baskets to head for the garden. And I couldn't believe it. I said, "Evie, can't you make your kids weed the garden? You're tired and your kids are old enough to weed. Make them go out there."

And she said, "Little fool, if I'm in the garden pulling weeds, they aren't going to come near me. It's the only peace I get!"

S: What a smart lady!

J: And I never forgot that. I recognize now that there's

nothing I enjoy more than going out there and pulling weeds in my own yard.

S: How about your mother? You two seem to be very close, good friends.

J: My father died when I was five years old, and when I think about it, it daunts me . . . my mom had four girls that she had to raise on her own. And women's liberation I never understood when it happened, because I had never thought of a woman as being limited in any way. My mother was always the head of the household. If the sink drain wasn't working, you fixed the sink drain. When it came time to put the storm windows on, we'd do it. We mowed the lawn, she did everything there was to be done in the family. If the door needed to be fixed, we did that. She was the one who worked. I mean, this was life.

S: Where did she work?

J: In *my* memory, she worked in a little mercantile store in Early.

My sisters were gone when I was growing up and it was mostly just Mom and me. Evie, the one next to me, she got married in '57, I was only twelve or thirteen. And even though Mom had remarried, my stepdad worked nights, so it was still only Mom and me. His name's Glenn.

S: Do you see your mother often?

J: Yeah, we do yoga three times a week. And they live in the little cottage here on the property, the gate cottage.

My mom has always taught by example. When Bill and I were talking about selling the businesses we owned and retiring to travel, he suggested selling our home and all our belongings as well. I couldn't imagine doing that. Then, to my amazement, I learned that my mom and stepdad were selling their home, their furniture—nearly everything they had acquired over a lifetime—and buying a travel trailer. I wondered how she could do it at the age of sixty-two, when there I was at thirty, agonizing over the decision. Finally I realized she was right. The house was just a building, and all our possessions were just things. So in 1974 Bill and I sold out, too. That decision was literally the start of a new life because it was after we started traveling that I began writing. So my mom has been my mother, my friend, and the best teacher anybody could ever have.

S: How about your stepfather?

J: He's the only father I've ever known.

S: And he came into your life when you were . . . ?

J: About twelve or thirteen.

S: That's an interesting time for a girl.

J: Well, I thought it was cool. I was going to get a dad! I thought it was really neat. He had four sons, all grown, and I had always wanted a brother. Of course, they didn't visit that often, but that was all right too.

S: How old were they, compared to you?

J: They were all completely grown. His youngest is Evelyn's age. I remember the first or second year that he and Mom were married, Mom got mad at him for

something. He had won some money and he had
bought a fishing reel. And she just thought that was
a terrible waste of money because he already had five
fishing reels. She didn't think he needed another
one, so she didn't speak to him for two days. I used
to razz her endlessly, which I'm sure never made it
easier.

S: Did you want her to be nicer to him so that he'd stay
around?

J: Probably. He was a good father.

S: What did he give you that you really needed at that
time?

J: I suppose just by being a male force there. I can't say
that I ever ran to him for advice or had long talks or
any of that.

S: Did you feel that he loved you?

J: Oh, yeah.

S: Did you have his approval?

J: Sure. Obviously I did things that he *didn't* approve
of. He was very strict. One time I got caught after curfew. Our town had a curfew . . . I think it was ten
o'clock. But I had gone to a movie with my boyfriend,
double dated, and you could only drive through town
twice. On the third time you got stopped.

S: The police would stop you just for going through
town three times?

J: It was to keep you from cruising.

S: They had nothing else to do but sit there and count how many times each kid went up and down?

J: (*Nods*)

S: Boy, those were the days!

J: Yep. So we had left the movie, and we had taken the other girl home; it was a double date. We had to come back to take her date home, then we had to go through again to take me home. And by the time we were taking me back, it was after curfew. So the cops picked us up. When my dad found out, he said, "Oh-h-h-h . . . it's going to be on your record, you're going to go to jail." And I'm thinking, *Oh, god, Dad!* He said, "You've got a criminal record now." And I said, "Okay, I've got one then."

COWBOYS

J: In Early we had a little community building that had a theater. And on Wednesdays and Saturdays they had matinees. For ten cents you could see Roy Rogers, Gene Autry. . . .

S: Were you in love?

J: Yes!

S: Who were you in love with?

J: Roy Rogers, definitely Roy Rogers.

S: Did *Dale* bother you?

J: Nope, no, I didn't think about Dale at all. Actually, I was in love with Gene Autry for a long time, but then Roy came along and, fickle person that I am, I fell for him.

S: How old were you at the time?

J: Oh gosh, oh please . . . seven or eight.

S: I guess you were entitled to be fickle then. How long did you stay with Roy?

J (*laughs*): What do you mean? I'm *still* in love with Roy. If I find out that Roy's going to be on anything, I have to see it. I got to meet Dusty Rogers, his son. Boxcar Willie is here in town and he knows Roy. I told Box that if Roy ever comes to town and he doesn't introduce me to him, he's in trouble. Of course if he did, I'd probably just sit there and stare at him with goo-goo eyes and look silly.

S: I know what you mean. I was in love with him, too, but I didn't know how we were going to get around that obstacle of Dale.

J: I never even thought about Dale, never crossed my mind. I guess I just thought that our eyes would meet and. . . . (*sighs*)

THE LIBRARY . . . AND BOYS, BOYS, BOYS

J: We had a little library there in Early that was open Wednesday and Saturday afternoons. I got my library card when I was five years old. Elsie Bettin was the librarian there. I became such a fixture at the library. You were limited on how many books you could take out. So I'd go on Wednesday and check out as many as they would let me. As soon as they'd open on

Saturday, I'd be back with those books all read. I'd return those, take out my limit, then I'd race home and read as many as I could that day so that I could run back on Saturday night and take out more to read until next Wednesday. I was what you'd call a tomboy bookworm.

S: What does that mean? Did you read books while hanging from fence posts?

J: When I wasn't reading, I was outside playing football, baseball, basketball, cowboys and Indians, cops and robbers.

S: You must have had a few boys to play with.

J: I *only* had boys to play with. My sisters were all grown, and in Early, in my class of twenty-eight, there were only five girls. And of those five girls, only I and another girl lived in town. But she was on the other side of town, and of course, when you're little, that's still too far for your mom to let you go to play. So the only ones in my neighborhood were boys to play with. Which didn't trouble me a great deal.

S: How were you at baseball?

J: Oh, I was good. I was very sports-oriented. I *am* very sports-oriented.

S: What position did you play?

J: Anything. I wasn't picky, just let me play.

S: How did they feel about that? Did they just accept you as one of the guys?

J: Well, yeah . . . I mean, I beat up the local boys.

S: You had a *reputation*, huh?

J: Yeah. My cousin and I used to wrestle all the time. So wrestling and fighting came natural for me.

S: Your cousin, mmm-m-m . . . was he cute?

J (*grins, nods*): Uh-huh.

S: So, wrestling with David was an interesting pastime?

J: David and I had so much fun. He lived in another town, but because there are only ten or eleven months' difference in our ages, at the family get-togethers, David and I were the only ones of that age group. Everybody else was older, so David and I always loved playing.

If David was going to get to spend time at the farm, then *I* would get to go to the farm. My grandparents and my uncles wouldn't have to entertain one individual child, they could just invite us both out at the same time and we'd entertain each other.

As a matter of fact, when we had a family reunion—just this last week—David and I were talking. Each of us had gone back separately to the family farm recently. And we both said the same thing. We both remember digging our worms, getting our cane poles, and walking wa-a-a-y down to the river, down this lo-o-o-ng hill. This was a big adventure.

What a disappointment! It isn't even as far as that lake (*points out the window*) and that big hill is just this gentle little slope. I was in such shock. I remember it being such a long walk. It took us *forever* to get back.

David and I were great raft builders; we never had one of them float. We had visions of floating down the Boyer River to the Missouri. And we built tree-houses together.

Our favorite story was something we did that we

both just confessed to recently. My great-grandfather
Eli Haradon was a blacksmith and the town of Early
built up around him. The old town cemetery was
across the farm road from the house.

When the railroad came through two miles to the
north, they picked up the town and moved it to the
railroad.

S: Literally? Houses and everything?

J: Houses and everything. And then the farm just
became the farm, but they didn't move the cemetery.
So it was everybody's favorite playground. My older
cousins played in it as well.

But David and I were trying to fend off some
Indians who were attacking us. And we realized we
needed a fort. So we moved all the tombstones to
make our fort, without knowing that all the records
had been destroyed. They didn't know where anybody
was buried. There was this terrible hoo-rah when the
centennial came, and they went into the old cemetery
to fix up and clean up and found the tombstones were
all mixed up.

S: Had you even attempted to put them back?

J: No! I mean, we wanted our fort! We kept it right
there.

S: How did you two move them?

J: It wasn't easy! But David and I are very ingenious and
we decided that we could figure it out, and we were
going to have us a fort that *no* arrow would get
through.

S: So, tell me . . . how many tombstones does it take to
make a fort? Sounds like a bad joke, huh?

J: I don't remember for sure, but we had to have moved at least eight. To this day I don't know if Uncle Lyle figured out that David and I did that.

S: Well, he'll know now, because we have to put this in the book.

J: Oh, that's okay. We 'fessed up long ago that we were the guilty party.

S: You know, that's probably what happened at Stonehenge . . . it was just some kids playing cowboys and Indians.

S: Your cousin Dave, what's his last name?

J: Freeman.

S: Do you remember . . . did you ever have a little bit of a crush on him?

J: Oh, yeah . . . I think so. I remember wondering, "Well, how *come* first cousins can't marry? They did it in *Gone With the Wind!*"

But you know, David and I did it perfectly innocently, and we never had any fear in that cemetery. For me a cemetery was never a place of fear or ghosts.

I remember growing up as a girl in grade school and walking to the cemetery to my daddy's grave. It happens to be fairly close to the road, and there used to be a tree near his gravesite. I'd just walk up there and sit under the tree and talk to Daddy. I'd tell him what was going on.

S: You felt that he was there?

J: Yeah, and I'd just talk away. So a cemetery was a place I could talk to my daddy.

Another funny story that came out. . . . On my great-grandpa's grave, there used to be this great big, mammoth headstone. It wasn't fancy or anything, but it was just *big*. And on it were engraved the names of all three of his wives. Although they were buried in other places, he wanted them remembered because he had children by each of them, and they were living in the area.

S: So, was it sort of like, "Husband of . . . and . . . and . . . ?"

J: Yeah, and a year ago in June, Mom and I had gone looking for all the graves: Daddy's grave and Grandpa's grave and Grandma's grave, and all the family. But so many of the trees had died, at first, we couldn't place the locations; our landmarks were gone.

So we were really looking and wondering and roaming around. Finally, we came to Grandpa Eli, and the stone wasn't there.

I said, "What happened to the stone? I remember there used to be a big old stone here."

And she said, "I wonder too."

So, at the reunion I asked Aunt Vira, David's mom, "What happened to that stone?"

She said, "Your Aunt Margaret was so embarrassed that Eli had three wives—it didn't matter that they had died, and he had married again—that she had the stone removed and had a new one made."

S: Seems like it would have been easier to have just engraved on there, "And they all died . . . of natural causes. . . ."

BEST FRIENDS

S: Who was your best friend?

J: Oh, gracious. That's probably my one tragedy. A tragedy in the sense that sooner or later I'm going to have to get off my rear and find out what happened. Nancy Megonigle. Her name was originally Nancy Lee, then she was adopted by a man whose last name was Megonigle. We were best friends all through high school, Nancy, Cathy Reed, and me.

In our senior year, Nancy moved to California and we kept up this long-distance correspondence. I mean, we would write these *books* to each other.

She got married and eventually moved to Firestone, Colorado. We maintained our "book" correspondence, and we'd call each other once a year. About three years ago, my Christmas card came back. Her phone was disconnected, and I never heard what had happened to her. That was three years ago this Christmas.

S: Do you have mutual friends you can contact?

J: No, I have nobody to call. Her daughter Sherry lives somewhere in Colorado. I've called every place that I know to see if they have a new address. I've called other Andersons to see if they know or are related . . . and nothing.

S: Maybe we can get a lead for you when this book comes out.

J: Maybe, I hope so.

CATHOLICS, BLACKS, AND THOSE WANDERING JEWS

J: Talk about growing up in a small town in Iowa. . . . Until my sister Marilyn went to Omaha to secretarial school—up until that point I was convinced that all the Jews were dead, because I didn't know any of them.

S: Oh, no . . . did you think they all died in the Holocaust?

J: No, I'm not even sure I knew about that. I guess I thought they all died in the Old Testament.

S: What? You hadn't heard that they got out of the wilderness? You thought they were still wandering around in the desert, trying to find the Promised Land?

J: Yeah, I guess so. Until my sister went to stay with a Jewish family in Omaha and took care of their children—they gave her room and board while she went to secretarial school—until that point I wasn't even aware that Jewish people existed.

S: Isn't it astonishing how . . . uninformed . . . we can be if certain things aren't a part of our surroundings?

J: Of our upbringing, yes. If we're so sheltered.
   My senior year and my junior year, we had our first black student, because a black doctor had moved to the hospital. And I could never understand what all the hooplah was about. I liked him. I suppose he felt different, but I never did. He was just the new student. There wasn't any prejudice, other than against Catholics.

S (*laughs*): There are always prejudices. It's just a matter of against whom.

J: It wasn't all that overt. It was just understood that if you married a Catholic, you might have to join the

Catholic religion and you don't really want to do
that.

S: Any explanation as to why?

J: No.

S: Just, "Trust me, you don't want to do that"?

J: Yeah, but my mother worked for Catholics, and she
adored them. I played with their kids, and their
daughter Jeanne was my age. But she went to a
Catholic school and you just didn't socialize, even if
the town *was* only five hundred people. Which, looking back I find that strange, but you just didn't do it.
I don't think it wasn't allowed, you just didn't know
them.

S: Isn't it interesting that sometimes an attitude is
unspoken, but it's there. It's one of those things that
no one talks about, but everyone knows.

J: But I don't recall an unkind word being said against
anyone.

S: Speaking of the need to be informed . . . do you think
that what you read shaped your attitudes toward life,
relationships, goals?

J: No, no, I really don't. I'm not sure how much books
can shape your attitudes. If they really could shape
your attitudes, I'd look at those beginning years
when I was reading *The Black Stallion* and all those
books. Yes, he was good to the horse, and yes, he
established the relationship with the horse, but I
never once believed that there would be this magical,
mental union between me and this horse. I wanted a
horse, but . . .

S: You did a good job of being able to separate fantasy from reality?

J: And I'm not sure if books are that formative. I think your own life has to form it.

S: For me they did. I was raised in the South during the height of the civil rights movement, and at one point I read a number of books like *To Sir with Love, Black Like Me, A Patch of Blue*, and it really helped me to be far less closed-minded. Those books opened up a new way of thinking. In my narrow, sheltered upbringing I had never even known that there were people out there who thought differently than I did, than my parents had. And those books had a lot to do with broadening my perceptions of the world.

J: From that standpoint, yes, probably. But for me, I grew up in the fifties and graduated by '62, which was way before any movements of social awareness.

S: I see what you're saying. That's just one of the differences in growing up in the fifties or the sixties. If I look back on the Nancy Drew series or Jack London books, I can't say that any of my attitudes were shaped by those. Different times, huh?

THE PLEASURES OF A YARN WELL-SPUN

J: My favorite story is . . . a good one.

S: Picky, aren't you.

J: I guess. But it's as simple as that. I love Tony Hillerman, his Jim Chee and his mysteries. I really enjoy mysteries.

S *(laughing, Tally Ho, Janet's Yorkie, bouncing up and down like a yo-yo, ears flapping, trying to get up onto Janet's chair):* I'm sorry, but she's so funny. Can't she make it?

J: She doesn't think so.

I'll pick up anything, anything that even remotely looks like it's going to be a good read.

S: What, to you, is a good story?

J: The same thing as it is to anybody else, if I can't put it down. If I just have to keep reading, the old page-turner. Like everybody else, I read *Bridges of Madison County.* Give me a good book.

It's harder for me now to read romances than it used to be.

S: Are you more critical?

J: I'm more critical. Invariably, unless it's a really dynamite book, I think, *I wouldn't have taken it that way. I would have taken it in a different direction.*

S: That makes it harder, doesn't it?

J: It does. It ruins the pleasure that I used to get. But it also makes the ones that are good, the ones that you just don't care. You're going to go wherever they take you. It makes them eighty times better than they ever were.

S: What's the last really good romance that you've read?

J: I can't remember the name, but it was one of Karen Robards's books, a historical.

And another one was—and I know I'm preju-
diced—but it was my friend, Melody Adams, her
Silhouette romance, *What About Charlie?* I would *kill*
to have written a character like Charlie. I just turn
green with envy every time I think about Charlie.

Of course, there's Nora Roberts's books. Nora
Roberts is an excellent writer. I always pick up her
new book, whatever it is.

And Sandra Brown, same thing. I always buy
Sandra's books. I loved *French Silk.*

There are always authors that I trust, that I know
I'm going to get a good story, and I'll buy it. But
there are others who I wait until somebody says,
"Wait until you read *this* book!"

S: Do you finish every book you start?

J: No. I don't have time. And especially my reading time
   is limited.

J: I love to read everything. I've never been hung up
   about one kind of book, where that's the only kind I'll
   read. Romance, adventure, mystery, I read everything.

S: Can you tell me some of your favorite authors when
   you were a kid? I know you read everything in the
   library. . . .

JANET'S ALL-TIME FAVORITES

Giant, *by Edna Ferber. "This is by far my favorite
story, setting, and cast of characters. It has it all."*

Hawaii, *by James Michener. "Who could possibly
forget the volcanic creation of the islands?"*

> Ben Hur, *by Lew Wallace. "If it is possible, the*
> *chariot race in the book is even more memorable*
> *than the film version."*
>
> My Friend Flicka, *by Mary O'Hara. "Every mem-*
> *ber of the family can identify with the characters*
> *in this classic tale."*

J: I did. I read everything they would let me read. I
   ended up working there, and sometimes I'd be able to
   steal books that they thought were too old for me,
   like Frank Yerby. Of course I shouldn't have read
   them.

   First, I read all the horse stories, all the Black
   Stallion, the Walter Farley books, and Nancy Drew
   and the Hardy Boys, Cherry Ames, and everything.
   Everything!

   I went from the horse stories to the dog stories.
   Then I would go into what I suppose you'd call the
   categories. Although we didn't use that term back
   then. Like the mysteries, I'd read all the Mike
   Hammer. I remember discovering Yest. Lloyd C.
   Douglas. *Magnificent Obsession. The Robe. Magnificent
   Obsession* totally intrigued me. And then I read west-
   erns. Then I got into World War II. I read *God Is My
   Co-pilot, Four Jills in a Jeep.*

S: You must be a fast reader.

J: Uh-huh. I would just devour a section of the library
   and then move on and devour another section. Then
   I'd get into the epics, the Michener books, historical
   biographies. I read biographies of Andrew Jackson,
   Lincoln. I never zeroed in on any one thing for long.

S: How long were these phases? How long did you stay with one type until you moved on?

J: That would depend on how much that particular library had to offer. Hey, "I've exhausted the supply, I must move on."

FISHING—FAKING IT

J: I was never a fisherman. I don't like fishing. But give me a cane pole and a bobber and a book, and I'm into that.

S: Okaaay . . . let me ask a foolish question. If you don't want to catch a fish, why do you need the cane pole?

J: So that you have an excuse for sitting on the riverbank, reading a book.

S: Oh, I see. You don't need a hook or any bait. You just stretch that pole across the water and float that little bobber, and they think you're doing something besides just reading a book?

J: That's right.

S: Did you do a lot of that kind of fishing?

J: No, David usually made me put a worm on the hook. And if I caught something, he knew what to do with it.

S: Did you eat it?

J: Oh, yes. You had to. You had to clean and eat whatever you caught.

SCHOOL DAYS:
THE AWAKENING OF CURIOSITY

S: Did you enjoy being a kid?

J: Yes, I used to love school, before we moved, the Early school. In that school, you participated. They were small classes, personal, and you wanted to please the teacher.

When we moved from Early to Independence, Iowa—from a town of seven hundred and twenty-seven to fifty-five hundred, from a class of twenty-something to thirty-something—it was difficult. Of course, I was the new kid. I was used to wanting to be the best in the class and learning everything.

Each classroom had a set of library books, and I was through them in about a semester, because as soon as I was finished with my work I'd take a book and read it.

I never liked recess. I wanted to learn. I just wanted to learn.

But when I hit Independence, if you raised your hand, you were made fun of. They would say, "What are you, a brown-noser?" It wasn't cool to raise your hand.

The Early school was part of the work ethic; a small town is very oriented toward that.

TEACHERS

S: Any favorite teachers?

J: Teachers? Pick a teacher, any teacher. I was blessed with some wonderful teachers. I don't remember my first teachers, my kindergarten teacher. I can't tell you who was fifth grade and who was sixth grade, but there was Miss Farber and Mrs. Swan. But Mrs. Swan had two different colored pairs of glasses. She had a red pair that she would wear with her outfits where she needed red and a blue pair that she wore with blue.

S: Was that the height of fashion in Early?

J: Well, I thought it was cool.

And that was about the time when I started to get writing assignments in class, where *I* was actually doing the writing. For me, that was the first time I had to put words together and tell a story.

Mrs. Kreft was my seventh grade teacher, and we were always reading what I wrote in class. Which was cool. It wasn't embarrassing; it was wonderful!

When I moved to Independence, Mrs. Peters was my freshman English teacher. I wrote a short story, a mystery, and she read part of it in class to teach the other kids how to write.

S: You must have felt like a million dollars.

J: Oh yeah. And Mrs. Turgason was my journalism teacher. I was on the high school paper all four years of high school. I wanted to do sports; I wanted to do it all. The first year that I was on the paper, we actually set type. You got to *set type!* And then after that, it was just running them off on the mimeograph.

My junior and senior year, I had Mrs. Helt for creative writing. One thing I can say, of all my teachers: I wanted to write, I loved writing, and I was always writing. And anything I wrote, I turned in, whether it was an assignment or not. If you can imagine how much work a teacher has to do, how many papers to correct, to grade . . . and here I am, throwing in extra work! But it was always returned to me, covered with red lines and blue lines and all these little side notes and *always* the encouragement.

S: Was the criticism positive rather than negative?

J: When there was criticism, it was justified.

I remember this one time—it was when the Berlin Wall went up, so you can see how old I am—I wrote this one story. I haven't read it for a long time, and I would probably just shudder. But it was this whole literary thing about this soldier walking his patrol along the wall in the rain, and the people on the other side of the wall. And I titled it, "The Immortal Bullet." As opposed to the "shot heard round the world," this is the immortal bullet.

S: Well . . . it's a great title.

J: That's what she put. Great title, has nothing to do with the story.

S (*laughs*): She didn't know much about the publishing industry, did she? Sometimes a great title is all you need!

J: To this day, the title had better have something to do with the story or I just freak out. Nothing upsets me more than to pick up a book where the title has nothing to do with the plot. If I pick up *Promise Me Tomorrow* it better have something to do with the story.

S: Then she taught you well, didn't she?

J: Yes, she did. And interestingly enough, after the first few of my books had been published, I got this letter from Mrs. Helt, and it was such a precious thing.

S: What did it say?

J: Just how proud she was, that in all of her years of . . .

I remember her telling me in class that she loved to read mysteries. She would save her weekends to read more involved novels. But everyone needed an escape, and that was her escape.

It was in English Lit class and we were complaining about all the stuff we had to read. She would say, "These are good, you should read these." But there was always encouragement.

I never wanted to be restricted by the subject. I hated it when she would say, "Write something about salt." I *hated* that. Don't tell me what to write. I hate being told what to write! Which is why I never tried to go to work writing travel articles for a newspaper. That's why I didn't go to college. I didn't want to be told what I could write.

S: Does it amaze people when you tell them that you don't have a master's in English or literature?

J: Oh, yes. But they learn to construct, not create.

S: Teachers . . . any more you want to talk about?

J: Ah, Mr. Mills. He was my American history and government teacher. From the time I hit school, I had heard about Mr. Mills. He was someone you looked upon with absolute terror, and you were sure that when you got to his class it was going to be pure hell. He was this short little stumpy man, bald head, sort of a leprechaun. On the first day, he walked in, sat down in front of his class, and said, "Okay, I'm going to tell you all right now, nobody in this class will ever have any excuse to miss this class unless you're dead. I don't care how sick you are, you *will* be in my class. And I want you to know that *nobody* in this class is *ever* going to get an A because none of you are that smart. And none of you are going to get an F because if you're that dumb, I don't want you back."

Then he passed out the books, the American history books, and told us to read the first chapter.

The next day, he asked if we had read the chapter, and of course, we raised our hands. Some went up and some didn't.

He said, "Okay, good."

Then he started lecturing, and he *never* cracked the book. He just taught history. Through him, history lived. He knew *everything* about *anything*. He knew things like: Paul Revere didn't really make the ride—

S: Oh, don't tell me that! I could have gone my whole life without knowing that!

J: He was stopped outside of town by the British. He was never able to make the ride.

But history was alive for Mr. Mills, and he made it alive for us. He began with the American Revolution, and we went clear through to the frontier. We'd talk about red-light districts . . .

S: To high school students? Boy, that must have gotten your attention.

J: That's when I fell in love with history.

S: He gave you that, didn't he?

J: Yes, he did.

S: And look at what he gave the world by giving it to you.

J: He graded you by what you talked about in class, how much you participated. You had a test at the end of the week that was an essay and then at the end of each semester, you were given a one-question essay test. That was your grade.

S: What grade did you get out of his class?

J: An A–.

S: He wouldn't give you that A, just on principle.

J: That's right.

S: Then congratulations on your A–.

J: But I adored him. I absolutely did.

S: Did the other kids think you were nuts?

J: Most of them were terrified of him. I was never terrified of him, and I couldn't understand why they were terrified of a man who *loved* what he was doing. You talked, by George, or he'd hassle you until you spoke. He made you participate. And I suppose that for the ones who were shy or self-conscious, they probably dreaded it.

S: What to you is a good teacher?

J: A teacher is one who will awaken that need to learn. Because I think we all want to learn. None of us want to be ignorant. But they can awaken that need and make you realize that you can learn anything. Anything!

S: Then why do you think so many people have problems in school?

J: Because, sadly, I think our school systems and our whole attitude toward teaching is: You're ignorant.
    Instead of awakening what you know, expanding

on it, and making it grow, they're saying, "You can't know anything until I teach it to you."

And I think we approach teaching from a negative instead of a positive. Instead of awakening the love of learning, we punish it.

S: How do we punish the love of learning?

J: By making it a miserable experience. To this day I love research, I love reading the material, I love finding out something I had no idea about before. Whether it's about a given area, a given subject, it doesn't matter. I don't mind useless information. I'm full of so much trivia . . . lots and lots of trivia. And the sad part of it is, when you research, you can only use about twenty percent of what you learn.

S: So, you were a kid who made good grades.

J: Oh yeah, I made straight A's through most of my school years, until the latter part of high school where I just sloughed off.

S: Come on, you didn't slough off. You were on the school paper, playing baseball and . . .

J: Okay, I did pretty well. On a 4.0 scale I graduated about a 3.7 or 3.8.

S: Bummer! Your favorite subjects I suppose were English and history and your least favorite math?

J: Yeah.

S: How about science?

J: Biology! I loved biology. I *loved* cutting things up. Cutting the frogs up and —

S: You did? Yuck!

J: I really enjoyed that.

S: Why?

J: I don't know. Maybe it was the tomboy coming through.

S: Was it the curiosity?

J: Yeah, to actually see the organs.

S: Didn't you see them on the farm?

J: No, because you were just disemboweling, you weren't trying to keep them intact. You weren't cutting with the intent to see how they were lying or how they worked. And also, I was going through the "Maybe I'll be a veterinarian" stage.

S: How long was that phase?

J: It lasted about as long as it took me to realize that I'd have to study everything else. A vet is much more skilled than an M.D. And I realized, I don't want to know all of that. It wasn't *that* fascinating.

COMING "OF AGE"

S: I understand you were in the drama club in high school.

J: My freshman year I tried out for a lot of plays, and there was always some reason why they never put on the play. They couldn't get the money or whatever.

Then one year I tried Dramatic Readings and Speech. I did one, and I realized, I *never* want to do this again. I have no desire to act again.

S: Not a thespian, huh?

J: *Not* a thespian. My senior year I had a secondary part as an assistant director or something like that. I worked behind the scenes, and I really enjoyed that. *Much* preferred that. I like the illusion of control.

S (*laughs*): Don't we all!

S: Was adolescence a big deal for you?

J: Not really.

S: Did you just sli-i-ide through?

J: I must have. I dated . . . a lot . . . as a matter of fact. If I have any regrets, it's having dated so early. When I was a freshman in high school, I went steady with a senior and when I was a freshman, I went to the senior prom.

S: Why is that something you regret?

J: Because by the time I got to be a junior and senior, it wasn't so special.

S: You had your dessert before your dinner, didn't you?

J: Yes, yes. And I wish now that they hadn't allowed underclassmen to go, although I would have been furious at the time and thought it totally unfair.

But anyone I ever went steady with, I never, never . . . I knew I didn't love them.

S: You didn't try on the last name for size or . . . ?

J: Oh, I might do some of that stuff because the other girls were doing it, but I never wanted to marry any of them.

S: Really? Just didn't cross your mind?

J: Nope. And it used to irritate the holy devil out of me if a boy started getting serious, because I had no interest in it. I wanted nothing to do with it.

S: I wouldn't think that would have been the norm at that time.

J: No, and when some girl would get the "crush" on somebody or was wildly in love—planning the wedding while they were two years away from graduating—I thought, *Ugh, grow up! You can't know what you want now!* And sometimes I'd think, *What's wrong with me? Why don't I ever feel that way?*

But I never did, because I didn't want to feel that way.

S: Sounds like you were pretty happy with the way you felt.

J: Yeah. And I liked going out and having fun and doing things, and being involved and being active.

JANET: When I graduated from high school, I did what any good farm girl would do. I went off to the big city: Omaha.

DECISIONS, DECISIONS

S: Considering your scholastic abilities, why did you decide not to go on to college?

J: In a small town you have to rely on your imagination. None of my teachers could convince me I needed a college education.

At eighteen, I knew it all. I didn't want to write news stories. I didn't want to teach, and I didn't want anyone telling me what to write. So with my nose out of joint, I said, "If I can't go to college and become a novelist, I won't go and I won't write ever."

S: Would you like to talk about secretarial school?

J: Naw ... it was just learning basic skills that I already knew. Ninety percent of it was common sense. I had gone to Omaha, because that's where my older sister Shirley had gone and it seemed like a safe thing to do. And again, I hadn't gone to college. What was the point? They couldn't guarantee me that going to college would make sure that I'd be able to make a living as an author.

DRIVING

J: My stepdad worked nights, and we only had the one car. So when I was fifteen and could have taken Drivers' Ed, I didn't have a car. I was deciding whether to sign up or not for the Drivers' Ed class and when I got around to doing it, I was too late. The class was full and I couldn't join.

Plus, I lived directly across the street from the school. So it was no big deal. I wouldn't have had a car to drive to school anyway. I wasn't about to take Drivers' Ed the next year because I'd have to be with *underclassmen*!

S: Well! You couldn't have that!

J: God forbid! And since I was a cheerleader, I went to all the games anyway. Besides, I always had a boyfriend and girlfriends who could drive. I'd just buy the gas. So I never got around to learning how to drive in high school.

When I went to Omaha, to secretarial school, I lived on the bus line, so what was the point in learning to drive? I still didn't have a car and I still couldn't afford a car.

And when I went to work for Bill, again . . . bus line or taxis. I could go anywhere I wanted to, and I never felt the need to learn to drive.

Which is why everyone got such a kick when I got my pilot's license and still didn't know how to drive a car. They said it was probably easier for me.

I didn't learn how to drive until we moved here to Branson and were living here on this side of the lake. At the time we moved here in '79, '78, there was only one taxicab for the whole town.

S: You're kidding! What did you guys do on Friday nights when everybody got snockered?

J (*laughs*): You called *the* taxi. If Bill was gone and I wanted to run into town to the grocery store or something, I'd call the cab. I might have to wait forty-five minutes. Or if traffic was bad, they might just never show up.

S: A good time to learn how to drive!

J: Yes, and I was always saying, "Jimmy, will you take me?" And you hate imposing.

   So I said, "Bill, I'm going to learn how to drive."

   And he said, "Well, I'm not going to teach you."

S: Smart man. People have gotten divorced over driving lessons.

J: True. So he had his secretary call the College of the Ozarks and arrange for the man who instructs driving instructors to teach me.

S: So you learned well.

J: I learned very well. I *finally* learned how to drive. Got my license and . . . TURN ME LOOSE!

S: Do you enjoy driving?

J: I *love* driving! And I've always loved to fly; I love being up there, but I like being up there alone, just me and God.

BILL DAILEY

S: Back to secretarial school . . . isn't that where you met Bill?

J: Secretarial school *is* Bill. The school had taken an old hotel in downtown Omaha and renovated it to where it was like a dormitory. I had two roommates. Myself and these two girls shared a large room in the back.

   They were friends from Minnesota, and they both happened to be Catholic. They would go to Mass every Sunday, and after Mass I would meet them and

we'd go out for Sunday dinner. And on our way
home from Sunday dinner one time, we were walking
up to the hotel, and there was this man standing outside. He looked our way and saw the Bibles.

He said, "Looks like you've been to church. Did
you say a prayer for me?"

Being the good girls that they were, my roommates ignored him entirely. I, on the other hand,
had never learned to keep my mouth shut. So I said,
"Yes . . . you look like you needed one."

S: You didn't! Those were your first words to Bill?

J: Yep! Then we just walked on in.

S: Was it true? *Did* he look like he needed a prayer?

J: Naw, I was just being a smartmouth.

There was a little drugstore on the corner. One
with a counter. A couple of days later, I walked up to
the counter, and the only seat available was the one
next to this man. It was after school, and I had been
washing clothes.

I walked up, sat down, and he recognized me. He
asked me what I was doing, and I told him I was
going to secretarial school.

He said, "One of my secretaries just quit. Instead
of going to school, why don't you go to work? Go
apply."

Well, I wasn't too keen on secretarial school . . .

S: So it didn't take a lot of arm-twisting?

J: Not at all. I thought, *I wonder if I could get a job*. And
they hired me, so I quit school.

What I didn't know was the reason he was at the
hotel that Sunday. They were getting ready to do
some remodeling, some construction, and he was

there to put a bid in on the work. Anyway, I went to work for him, became his secretary.

I'm sure he told you about how I fired one of his other secretaries . . .

S: No, he didn't tell me about that.

J: He was always on the road, on construction projects, out of state. This one secretary wasn't working, and I was having to do all of her work. She would just horse around when he was gone. So I got mad and I fired her.

She said, "You can't fire me."

And I said, "Yes, I can."

That was back when if you fired someone you had to pay them their wages on the spot. So I paid her out of my own money.

Bill came back, I told him what I had done, and he reimbursed me. At that point he's always said he had a right-hand man. (Which, considering that he's left-handed, it's appropriate.) From my standpoint, he was so much older than I was, and I couldn't imagine that he'd be interested in me. So I was really quite leery at first.

S: At what point did you become interested in him?

J: I think I was interested right away. He was probably the first person I had met who was actually smarter than I was.

S: Isn't smart sexy?

J: Yeah, and it was like, I could never get the best of him. I had always been able to maneuver, manipulate, but he was always outthinking me.

S: What a challenge, huh?

J: Yes, exactly. And that was quite a shock. It made me even doubly leery as to why he would ask me out.

JANET: Bill used to call me Sam. At first I couldn't find out why, but apparently he decided that if he thought of me as one of the fellas he could manage not to fall in love with me. It didn't work. I married the boss!

S: What was your first date?

J: The first time . . . we went out to dinner. It was after work because we worked late, and I enjoyed the challenge of his work. There were never any dull moments, anything anticipated. Even though you were always dealing with mundane things, there were always so many exciting things happening.

   Plus, he would have me draft his letters, so the writing was being used. And the first time I went out with him, it was like . . . this is probably the most fun I've had in ages!

S: Where did you go?

J: We went to Travata's. It's an Italian restaurant, has a little bar.

   When Bill's ex-father-in-law passed away, we went back for his funeral. We just happened to stop at Travata's. We were curious when we drove past.

S: Is it still named that?

J: Still named that. Yeah, it was really a date. We went in and had a drink for old times' sake. It was actually coffee, I think. And it was fun.

S: You had fun with Bill? Was he lighthearted?

J: Yes, most of the time. We were always working. There was always some project that we were trying to do, or we were working toward something. It was very much always a work together thing. That's been one aspect of our relationship that has stayed constant throughout the years. We've always worked together.

S: Business aside, what do you like about Bill as a person?

J: Oh, mercy. That would be a real toss-up; there's so many things.

S: You don't have to rate them, just in general.

J: He has a marvelous sense of humor. Generosity. He has a generosity that is amazing to see, because he comes off like the hardest man who was ever born. Yet he's the softest touch. He wants to help people, but he doesn't want anybody to know.

S: Why?

J: It embarrasses him. He'd rather just do it and then . . . shut up. I love that about him because it's genuine.

S: That *is* genuine generosity. The other kind is self-serving.

J: That's right, because he doesn't want anyone to know that he did it.

S: What do you believe is his payoff for doing it? Does he like people that much?

J: He does. He really does. He gets very impatient with people. See, he really believes that everybody has common sense. And I keep trying to explain to him that common sense is a rare thing.

S: Definitely a misnomer.

J: It is *far* from common. I mean, once it's presented to you, it's obvious. But until it's presented it isn't obvious to a lot of people. So he does tend to get pretty impatient with people.

S: We assume that other people have the same abilities we do.

J: Yes. And his absolute loyalty. Also, the honor. When Bill gives a man his word, or when he gives a woman his word, no matter what it costs him, he'll keep his word.

S: Do you believe that's true of you, too?

J: I'd like to believe it.

S: On a good day, huh?

J: Yes, it's one of those things . . . before, I never thought that my word was that important.

S: What do you mean?

J: Well, I guess I was used to idle words, where you could say, "Oh, I swear, I'll do that tomorrow." I was used to idle comments like, "I'll call you next week." Well . . . if you tell Bill you'll call him next week, he's expecting a phone call. So I thought, *I shouldn't, if I don't mean it. I shouldn't be inviting people.* And it was this awareness that certain things should be taken seriously and not casually done.

S: Can you take everything seriously, though?

J: No, you can't.

S: No one can do *everything* well.

J: But you would be surprised with Bill. You will not hear him say things like, "Let's have lunch sometime." He won't say it. If he doesn't want to have lunch with you, he won't say those words.

S: That came through so clearly when I interviewed Bill. He is just so ... Let's be blunt ... one moment I hear him saying something that seems so chauvinistic, like, "Well, when she gets off work, I expect her to be a wife and do what a wife's supposed to do."

J: Uh-huh.

S: And some people would consider that chauvinistic. Then the next minute he's talking about you as a business partner and there is not *one ounce* of condescension. There's just total respect, total equality there.

   He would never dream of telling you how to write a scene. Never. A *truly* controlling man draws no lines. *Everything* that is yours, is his. And I'm sitting there, during this interview, just going back and forth, back and forth with him. Does that make sense? Is that the way he is?

J: It is. He is. I've had more than one person in the course of my career—people usually involved in business—who meet Bill and me together, and they believe that he totally controls me, that I'm totally dominated by him. Occasionally they will tell me, "Well ... can't you think for yourself?" or "Can't you make a decision for yourself?"

But what they fail to understand is that it's this "working thing." I am well aware—and Bill is well aware—that I am *good* at what I do. And *he* is *good* at what he does. And I'm not about to tell him how to negotiate a contract, or how to promote, or what's good, or what's bad.

I will give input, but usually when he asks. And he gives input when I ask. To me, real liberation is recognizing where your true skills and your true talents are, and not trying to be what you aren't. That's stupidity to go over here and say, "I know better than he does."

Most people in my position would hire somebody like Bill. I married him. And I was lucky that I was married to him before the career ever happened. But he doesn't dominate. Now, he can't stand disorganization, but as he said, he can't *make* me sit at a typewriter, and he can't *make* me write the words. It doesn't work that way, and it won't work that way for anybody . . . not for long. So there's nothing he could make me do, and he knows that. And there's nothing I can make him do, and I know that.

S: Then where do you think this misconception that people have comes from?

J: Because I usually . . . and I do it for a purpose . . . I defer to Bill. If we're in a business discussion, I don't think fast. Now, it's just like writing; you give me a couple, three days to mull over and think through a thing, and I can probably reach the same decision.

S: But sometimes you don't have that luxury.

J: Right, or I reach that point and he's gone five paces beyond it. I have never, I have *never* seen his equal in any publisher, president, or anything. I've never seen his equal to this day. Because he can think farther than they can, he can see what they're offering, and immediately there's a little thing in his head that goes, "Here's the pros, here's the cons. The cons . . . let's do something . . . I don't like this data over here." And he'll immediately leap and say, "But what about this?" He makes that instant leap and it may take three days for them to think there was one.

I'm not going to step in. I'm going to say, "Well, what do you think, Bill?" 'Cause I'm not thinking that fast, and I'm going to defer to him every time.

S: It sounds as though you've been with him so long that you really trust his judgment.

J: Yeah. It's the same thing with promotion. I'm not going to try to second-guess the best way to promote my books. It's not my area of expertise. I can have opinions.

And it was the same when we started promoting the books and doing the interviews. One of the first things he said to me was, "You need to promote your books, and you need to learn how to do interviews if we're going to do this." And I made some comment. And he said, "Honey, you don't have to worry. I won't ever ask you to be anything other than what you are. You don't have to be fake. And you don't have to be phony. You just have to be you. And I'm never going to ask anything more than you are."

So I never felt like I had to put on a front, that I had to come across a certain way, or to be sophisticated, or to be nice, or to be a hillbilly or a hick. I never felt as though I had to live up to any other image. I just had to be me.

So when you're dealing with that situation, you're darned right, I'm going to turn to Bill and say, "You handle it."

If I'm making an appearance, I'll say, "Is this something that I should do? Is it good, or is the timing bad?" Unfortunately, in the entertainment field—

writing, recording, or movies—you have husbands who aren't qualified to do this, but their egos need stroking, and they need to feel in control. Husbands like that make it much more difficult for someone like Bill who *is* qualified to do it. Because Bill is equated with all the others who aren't. Which is one of the reasons why we have an agent, so that Bill has a buffer. But believe me, other than Richard calling to tell me this, that, or something else, he knows that when it comes to a point of negotiation, he's talking to Bill.

Now, Bill is the first one to tell Richard to keep me apprised if there's an offer. "Don't hide it from Janet." If there's an incident, or whatever, Bill wants me to know what's happening and to always be aware of that business side. And he always tells Richard the same thing. "Janet needs to know the offers. She needs to know what's happening, and why, and what these things are."

So it isn't as though Bill is trying to circumvent or stand between me and Richard. He never would do that.

S: What does Richard do for you that Bill doesn't do for you?

J: He's the buffer. He's the mouthpiece. When a publisher has to deal directly with the author and/or her husband any demand becomes personal.

S: Then you get into feuds and —

J: Feuds and pettiness. But when an agent makes it, it's treated like business. Like Richard wrote in his book, *Beyond the Bestseller*, the author says, "This is it! I'll never write for them again. You just tell them that!" So Richard calls the editor and says, "We need to have lunch."

JANET: I didn't like research. Bill said he'd take care of that. He organized my time so I could write. He took over everything I didn't like doing.

J: Bill handles the research. Sometimes he physically gets the material. Sometimes, for instance, when there's library research involved, he may hire someone to do the actual library research because, obviously, he has other things that he does as well. When we're in an area, he may call on the Agriculture Bureau, the Bureau of Land Management, the Weather Bureau, the Farm Bureau. Whatever background I'm needing, he will go to the sources. He may go to ranchers, if it's a ranching story. He will literally call on the necessary people and run down whatever information I need.

I like to have things at my fingertips, and I'm not the type that likes to nose it out, to go to five different sources before I find the one I want.

J: Another thing about Bill is, he tells me when to start a book, and that's because he knows me well enough ... he's seen my mind working, he's seen me playing with characters, he's seen me reading the research and he knows when I need that push.

BILL: At first, it surprised the hell out of me. But after I considered all the time and work she'd contributed to my businesses, it seemed only right that turnabout was fair play, so I became her researcher-manager. After all, Janet worked for me for more than twelve years. It seemed fitting

that I should work for her so she could attain the
success in her field that I had enjoyed in mine.
And as a boss, Janet isn't bad. Plus, you sure as
hell can't beat the fringe benefits. So in addition
to being married to a romance writer, I work for
one, too!

S: Do you?

J: I do.

S: It's scary, beginning a book. It's like diving into the deep end and not knowing if there's any water there.

J: Exactly, and sometimes I don't have any idea what that first page is going to be. It's like ah ... ah ... ah ... you mean, I have to decide where I'm going to start this story?

I'm sure this comes from being with a person ... but he instinctively knows the time when I'm saying, "Oh, God, honey, this just isn't the day. I'm just not getting anything done. I can't write today." He can look at me and know when that's all bullshit. And I'm really just copping out.

S: He told me that he can look at you and tell when it really *is* a bad day, and he'll say, "Come on, let's go out for a cup ofcoffee."

J: Yes, he can always tell.

S: Can you tell yourself?

J: No, but he's invariably right. I've been in here some-times, and I'm thinking, *If I just stay at it a little bit longer, I'll figure out how to work my way out of this.* And he'll walk in and see me, and . . . I don't know . . . maybe my eyes are glazed.

He'll say, "Having problems?"

And I'll go, "Yeah, I . . . ehki . . . eirjio . . . jkjh."

And he'll say, "Why don't you just knock off for the rest of the day?"

S: How does it go when it's the other way? When you're having a lazy day?

J: It's, "Shut up and just sit there!"

S: Oh, no! Doesn't that make you mad?

J: Uh-huh.

S: It does, it makes you mad?

J: Uh-huh. I feel like, "You should understand me. This is *awful*!" Except that, deep down, I think I know he's right.

S: I'm just thinking of what I would say if my husband said something like that to me.

J: Well, again, it's one of those things. For so long, the relationship wasn't just the writing. It dealt with business and I think it gives it a whole different aspect. I think if it had leaped in this way, it probably wouldn't have worked.

S: So, basically, I think I hear you saying that the reason why you, an independent and self-sufficient woman, find it possible, even preferable, to defer to him isn't out of fear or weakness, it's just out of time-proven trust.

J: Time-proven trust. Absolute respect for judgment. Trust and respect, those are almost interchangeable.

You can't respect what you don't trust; you can't trust what you don't respect.

S: What if he's wrong? He has to be wrong sometimes.

J: Oh sure, everyone is sometimes.

S: But you can live with it?

J: Of course. I've been wrong, many times.

S: So as long as his percentage is lower than yours . . . ?

J: Yeah.

S: How do you feel when an editor suggests that you defer to Bill too often?

J (*laughs*): My favorite story: Shortly after I had written *Touch the Wind*, and it had been published, there was an ABA* conference in Los Angeles. They had said come to the ABA, so I had gone out.

Simon and Schuster was giving a party at the Polo Lounge in Beverly Hills. Bill and I were standing in the cocktail area, talking to one of the sales reps for Pocket Books. This man came up, about my height, maybe a little taller than me, and started talking away. And I shook hands with him, but I had been doing interviews and shaking hands with a lot of people, and it didn't mean anything.

After he left, the salesman turned to me and he says, "Do you know who that was?"

And I said, "No."

"Well," he said, "I want you to know, that was Richard Snyder, the president of Simon and Schuster. You just met 'God.'"

---

*American Booksellers' Association

And I said, "He can't be God; Bill's God."
I guess that story made the rounds.

S: Okay, it's pretty easy to see how that was miscon-
strued. But, tell me, what did you mean?

J: I don't know. Again, we're dealing with Bill. He doesn't
use tactful means. He calls a spade a spade. If he thinks
it's bullshit, it's bullshit. And you aren't going to get
around it. He wants to go straight to business; he doesn't
want to go with all the other stuff that comes before.

S: Like the amenities?

J: The amenities. He's a bottom-line guy. If you want to
make the offer, make the offer. If you say you're
going to promote the book, you're going to promote
the book. If you say you're going to do it, do it.
Because that's the way he is. Whatever he tells you he
will do, he will do it!

S: That's a wonderful quality.

J: Yes, it is.

S: But why does that make him God?

J: Well . . . I . . .

S: I know you don't mean that. But I'm just trying to
find out what you meant when you said that.

J: Well, because that man might have been God in that
salesman's life. He might have been the power to be. But
he wasn't in my life, because there's no power that is
greater than Bill. And I think I also meant that in meeting him, he didn't impress me like Bill did. (*Laughs*.)
I thought that Bill could take him on right easy.

S: So it all comes back to trust. You're trusting Bill with . . . with a *lot* when you trust him with your career.

J: I prefer it this way. I prefer to write my books . . . and that's it.

S: How about on a daily basis . . . no pun intended . . . on a daily basis, who decides which television to buy, which restaurant to eat in, which picture to hang on the wall, which person to invite to do so-and-so, things like that? Just daily living decisions?

J: Mm-m-mm . . . it would all depend on our areas of expertise. Pictures to hang on the wall? No, that would probably be me. I'd decide that, although I'd ask him what he feels, because he can visualize quicker than I can. I'd pick the painting and say, "Do you like this? I like this." And ninety percent of the time, he does. Now . . . a television. I don't know that from beans. I'd probably send Jimmy, Bill's son, to pick that out for me.

S: I was wondering . . . the other night when we were getting ready to go out for dinner, you asked Bill if your pants were all right. And he said, "No." And you said, "Okay, I'll change."

J: Uh-huh.

S: You can't tell me you don't know which pants to wear.

J: Oh, well, you see it's a standing joke with us, because I don't like to dress up or put on makeup or do all those cruddy things. I always see how far I can go with it.

S: We have the same situation around our house, but it's my husband.

J: So I always say, "Hey, if we're only going to that place, we aren't going to see all that many people who we'd have to worry about. Maybe I can get by with maybe just a little . . ."

S: That's what it was?

J: Yeah. Can I push the envelope?

S: And once again, you defer because you believe he's right.

J: Uh-huh.

S: Was he right?

J: Yeah.

S: You needed to put on the better pants to go out that night?

J: Yes, absolutely. Without a shadow of a doubt.

S: So, what is this? You were just trying to be a naughty little girl, going out in your dungarees?

J (*grins*): Uh-huh. I don't think I'll ever grow up at heart. And I'm glad.

S: No, don't ever. Growing up is highly overrated.

S: What do you feel you and Bill have learned from each other?

J: Bill and I are definitely opposites. And I believe that opposites attract and opposites work. When it comes together, you build and you make stronger. There are many sides to Bill. He's very business-minded. He's very practical and he has a lot of common sense. He's a visionary.

S (*Bill walks in*): You aren't supposed to be listening. (*He grins.*)

J: I'm very creative. I live with the mind, and I play in the mind. I'm also very detail-oriented. I do the detail, whether it's the individual words in a scene or whether it's in the office. I'm still his secretary in the office.

S: So, as well as your writing career, you still work with him in his various businesses.

J: That's right. I'll play the numbers and see that everything is filed properly, that everything is filed when it has to be, whether it's government or whatever. I'll still handle those things because that's my part of the responsibility.

I don't tend to be practical. I can be. Sometimes the Scots ancestry comes through, and I won't want to spend a lot of money for some particular thing that I don't think is worth it.

At the same time, I tend to be terribly impractical. To me, to write a book when I don't have a publisher, to write a book on spec . . . that's impractical. But Bill will encourage me to write it. He sees it as having value. But to me, why invest three or six months of your time for something that you may or may not have a market for?

S: I would think that you could write a grocery list on a piece of toilet paper right now and sell it.

J: But it's still . . . I will still . . . we're talking previously and we're talking today.

> **BILL:** *It was a way to go into every state and publicize who we were and what we were doing. We made her a personality, not just an author. It was a gimmick for us.*

THE SILVER STREAK TOUR

S: Your Silver Streak tour. Would you like to share some of your fondest memories, your worst?

J: First of all, I had traveled very little when Bill and I sold our companies in Omaha and "retired." That was our ambition. Sure, I had flown to Florida. I have flown to Hawaii. I had flown to places, but I had not traveled the United States.

So when we set out, initially we didn't go very far because we wanted to see family. And we wanted to do the circuits that made the rounds to say goodbye to all the family before we headed off.

For the first time I started seeing the differences as we traveled from state to state. I had no idea. My image of Mississippi was cotton fields. Just big cotton fields everywhere you went. And the first time I saw those forests of lone pine, I said, "What are trees doing . . . what are *evergreens* doing in Mississippi? They're supposed to be cotton fields." And I just became fascinated with the differences, the changes in the dialects.

People will say, "Ah, one part of the country is just like the other part. You can't tell one from the other. Every street corner looks alike." And I'll admit, if all you do is go to a town and drive around and look for the Sears store and the McDonald's, the Pizza Huts, yes, you're going to see them everywhere. But if you just look a little bit further, you'll see that restaurant that's got the greatest food that's just in a really bad area. You can get the real local food and the real local flavor. It's there, but you have to stop looking at the surface and look beyond.

The other thing we loved about traveling is that once you go into a campground—now, we had lived for years with only nodding acquaintances with our neighbors—by George, when you pull into a campground, you're not there twenty minutes—usually you don't even get pulled in—but the people parked beside you are out saying, "You need some help with unhooking?"

S: Do you think it would still be that way?

J: I think so. We used to spend our winters, most every year, down in Rockport, Texas, just north of Corpus Christi. And there would be this same group of snowbirds that would come down every year. And it was like getting together with family. About the second or third year, you'd just be waiting. "Well, when's Earl and Marie comin'? Is Earl and Marie comin'?"

S: What does a snowbird look like?

J (*amazed*): What does a snowbird look like?

S: We don't have snowbirds in Southern California. We don't even have snow!

J: A snowbird is somebody who leaves the North when the snow flies and goes South where it's warm.

S: Oh, I thought you meant a particular *kind* of bird.

J (*even more amazed, but patient*): No . . . a snowbird is a *person*.

S: Oh! A person! (*Blush, blush.*) I thought you meant . . . oh, never mind.

J: They fill up that part of Texas and Arizona.

S: Were you guys considered snowbirds?

J: Yes. We just lived in ours all the time, that's all.

My favorite traveling story is, we were in upstate New York in the Thousand Islands area around Clayton, New York, camped there. There was this other couple camped there, and we'd been driving for a couple of years.

The woman and I got to talking. They were native New Yorkers, the state of New York. The woman said, "Where are you from originally?"

I said, "I'm from Iowa."

"You are?" she said. "Isn't that interesting. You have a really unusual accent." (I'm sort of a sponge; I pick up certain accents.)

I said, "We've been traveling a lot."

She said, "I'm serious. How did you say that? Where are you from?"

I told her, "I'm from Iowa."

"Now see there," she said, "that's what I mean. Here we pronounce it O-hi-o!"

She was positively, totally serious. I had to do a whole little geography lesson. That's my favorite traveling story.

I heard once that someone had a sweatshirt made up that said, "The University of Iowa at Idaho, Ohio." Those three states get confused so much.

S: I used to live in Washington when I was a kid. And it really ticked me off that if I said I was from Washington, everybody thought I meant Washington, D.C. Why do you have to say, "Washington State"? When I was a child, a lot of people didn't even know there *was* a Washington State.

J: That's the one word that will tell whether you're from the Midwest or not. You wash your clothes; I warsh mine.

S: I used to warsh mine, too, until the kids in Seattle schools teased it out of me.

J: We used to travel with our dog who was a German Shepherd. Dreist. It's German for "bold." His name in German meant, "The Bold One of Hess." He'd been police-trained.

S: Did you get him as a pup?

J: Five weeks old.

S: So, *you* had him police-trained.

J: Right. And Dreist was a gentleman. Absolutely the most well-mannered dog you've ever seen.

In a trailer, in close quarters like that, a tail can be deadly. But all you'd have to say was, "Dreist, I have hot coffee." And he'd stop wagging his tail. But in his police training he had also been taught to come out of windows, to break through the windows. And travel trailers—I'm sure it's more true today than it was then—have pop-out windows for emergencies.

We were in San Antonio at a campground, we were out walking, Bill and I alone. We had stayed there before at this particular campground and we ran into a couple that we had met at an air base there. Their son was with them; he was about fifteen, sixteen years old. He comes up to us and slaps Bill on the shoulder and says, "How the heck are ya?"

S: Oh no . . . Rin Tin Tin. . . .

J: Yep, the next thing I know, out of the corner of my eye I see this big black dog just coming out of nowhere. And I'm thinking, *Where in the heck is that dog coming from?* And the next thing I know, he's got this kid on the ground with his face in his mouth like this. He had been watching us and he had seen what—as far as he was concerned—was this guy "strike" Bill. The odd thing was, he and the boy had played together before this.

S: But nobody hits "Dad," huh?

J: *Nobody* hits Dad. And that was sort of our "momentary alarm."

S: Did he harm the boy?

J: No, he was trained to attack and hold. He was never trained to bite. If he holds, he holds, and if you don't fight him, you won't get hurt.

S: So it won't pierce, it'll just bruise?

J: Right. A German shepherd or any dog of that size, their jaw pressure can break an arm without ever breaking the skin.

And another time, in the same place but on a different occasion in San Antonio, I was walking him and it was late at night. We were doing our final walk before going to bed. And this woman was coming with her little poodle, not on a leash. Dreist didn't like other dogs who weren't on a leash. So I was walking him as close as I could to the other trailers, just to give the other dog all the room. And the woman was saying, "Come here, come here."

I'm walking along, not really paying attention, and as I get to the last trailer, and as I'm just level with the door of the trailer, it opens. It was something like a

Rottweiler, one of those *big* kinds. And that dog was coming! All I saw and all I heard was this roar and this face coming at me!

Dreist was there on my left, and I yelled, "Geez!" and threw my arm up to block. Dreist just flew over my head and met him . . . just like that! Fortunately, I still had my leash, and the other dog's owner was able to grab him!

S: Oh, good. You prevented what could have been a real tragedy there.

J: Oh, yes! But I still say, I couldn't have gotten away. I couldn't have eluded that dog.

S: I'll bet Dreist got petted really good that night.

J: He got loved good!

S: Did you have him the whole time you were on the trip?

J: We had him until he went through the window the fourth time and then we realized, this was not a wise thing. He had his territory set up; he had an imaginary line drawn around the trailer, and anybody could do anything, as long as they didn't cross the line.

S: Of course, they might not *know* they were crossing the line. . . .

J: Exactly! We realized that this just wasn't good. Two or three times a year we returned to Iowa. One time we were back visiting the vet who had always taken care of Dreist and loved him *to death*. We told him we were going to have to find a home for Dreist and . . . (*Laughs.*)

S: Look no further, huh?

J: Yep.

S: Did you go and visit him from time to time?

J: No. I couldn't.

S: I don't blame you.

J: It was just too hard. He was my m-a-a-n.

S: How old was he?

J: When we finally gave him away he was about eight or nine.

S: What do you think traveling like that gave you? What did you gain from the experience?

J: Ah . . . You gain an absolute and total awareness of the differences that exist. Not just here in the United States, but anywhere else, so that you realize that just because there are cardinals in Iowa, there may not be cardinals in California. Just because this tree grows here doesn't mean it grows somewhere else. The opening of awareness and the research for the fact that in a given area the plant life may be different. The animal and bird life may be different. The agriculture and the industry will be different. The food will be different. The customs—whether it's holiday customs—change. Dialect changes. Even the words that you're greeted with may be different, different phrasing, different terminology.

You learn an awareness of all these hundreds of different things. You realize that if you're going to set a book in a given spot, in the United States or elsewhere, you can't take for granted. Sure, I live in Iowa, so I know what it's going to be like in Illinois. No, you don't. *No, you don't.*

S: Was there anything that the tour cost you?

J: Oh, I don't . . . no, I can't see where it cost us a bloomin' thing. I grant you that it was more difficult for people to track us down when we were on the road. If the publisher wanted to get ahold of us or if we needed to be contacted it was more difficult. For a long time, nearly every manuscript, I had a different typist, because we would just get whoever we could get.

S: Of course, this was before Federal Express, fax machines, modems . . .

J: Exactly! From that standpoint, you didn't have an office. It cost me files and books. I would have bought a lot more books and had a bigger library of research materials. I just *loo-oove* accumulating those. Every time we'd go back to Iowa, I'd have to box up all my little stuff, and I'd have to take all these research books that I'd already used and trade them in for ones I needed. I'd store them at my sister's and bring another batch out. We didn't have a lot of space.

S: Didn't you long for a bigger bed, a shower that you could both shower in once in a while?

J: Well, most campgrounds provide you with a shower. And there were occasions when, once or twice a year, Bill and I would get to longing for a shower that you could do the elbows with or to lay in a tub, because we had a shower but we didn't have a tub in our trailer. So we'd go in and rent a motel, which was kinda fun.

S: That was your treat?

J: Uh-huh. But our trailer was a thirty-three-footer. My standing story of how much room we had in that trailer was: when we parked it for the last time in the driveway in Branson, when I took all the clothes that we had in the trailer and tried to put them in the walk-in closet, they wouldn't fit.

S: Because of the efficiency of the trailer's design?

J: Yes. I had so much on hangers that I couldn't get into the closet. It was *amazing*!

S: What did you pull it with?

J: We had a Mark, a Lincoln Continental. And we also had it equipped with a three-to-one gear ratio. Towing the trailer with the car, we could actually accelerate and pass people going *up*hill. That's how much power the car had.

S: Did you trust it enough to be in the trailer when Bill was driving?

J: No, it's illegal. Besides, I liked being in the car. You can think so much in a car. You can just daydream your life away, just staring out into the spaces.

S: Would you ever do it again?

J: Are you kidding? I'd give my eyeteeth to go on the road again!

S: Seriously?

J: I'd just *love* to take off for a year or more.

S: You would leave all this . . . ?

J: Yeah, I sure would.

S: Then why don't you?

J: Well, we've got so many business things going here. We're a little more tied. And it just isn't as easy to get away as it once was.

S: How long were you actually on that trip?

J: Six years.

S: What was it like, being together that much?

JANET: We were flying from Omaha to Delaware when we ran out of fuel. There wasn't anyplace we could glide to. We finally found a strip of land. There was a crosswind and Bill couldn't correct it, so we cartwheeled wingtip to wingtip. It was miraculous. We survived and didn't get a bruise. But the narrow escape did make us think seriously about our lives. It was shortly after the accident that we decided to retire.

J: Bill always understood that I needed my space. He would go out and do research, so he always kept himself occupied and gave me the space.

FLYING

J: In one week, I've been in towns like St. Louis, Columbus, and Philadelphia, places where the airline connections are not the best. Instead of waiting in

airports for airplanes, I like having the airplane waiting for me.

S: Aren't you afraid of small planes?

J: No. In a sense you're safer in a small plane, because a
small plane can glide. If it loses all power, it can
glide.

S: I just have a prejudice against them because my best
friend, her husband, and four others were killed in
their charter plane.

J: My instructor was killed. He was not only my instructor, but he was also the FAA flight instructor who
gave you your license. You had to do your check ride
with Frank. He was killed in a small plane.

   I don't know if Bill told you or not, but we totaled
an airplane.

S: No!

J: Yeah, yeah!

S: Both of you were in it?

J: Yep.

S: Oh, Janet! We almost didn't have this interview . . . is
that what you're telling me?

J: Yeah, we almost didn't have that first book. I was so in
love with flying. Actually, I had passed my written
test before I had ever gotten into an airplane, because
Bill was getting his pilot's license—I had no desire to
fly, I thought he was crackers—and I went along with
him to ground school so that I could help him study.

   Then it came time for him to take his written test,

I went along, and he said, "You might as well take it, too." So I took it too and passed my written test before I'd been in a cockpit. The instructor convinced me that I should go up and get at least a couple hours of instruction because I'd be riding with Bill. He said, "If there is ever an emergency you need to know how to land a plane."

This made sense to me. So I did. And the minute I went up . . . this was it . . . just give me power! It was *power!* At that point, it wasn't enough to get my private, I wanted to get my commercial license. I was going all the way. I passed my commercial written and one of the requirements, in addition to having two hundred hours logged, you had to have a long cross-country.

At that time, one of Bill's sisters was living in Delaware. Bill and I decided to go see her for the weekend, and that would be my long cross-country. We went out and rented the slowest airplane we could rent. We got a little 150. Most of the way we had a headwind, so we were only making about seventy-five miles an hour.

S: Did you have to get out and push once in a while?

J: Yeah, if the wind was too strong, we'd go backwards.

S: I don't know much about flying, but I don't believe that!

J: It was heck flying along over the interstate and watching the cars going faster than you are. Anyway, there's a whole, whole enormously long story on that trip, but let me start out with . . . first clue . . . see, I love flying at night. So we decided we'd take off at eight o'clock at night. Our first stop from Omaha was going to be Peoria, Illinois. We got our maps out, worked it all out, and figured that we could fly from Omaha to

Peoria before we'd have to fuel up. We'd have enough gas to make it to Peoria. So we take off from Omaha, and Des Moines is just a little less than halfway. We'd still have to go a little past Des Moines to be halfway. As we were flying along, I saw the Des Moines lights off my wing. I looked down at my gas gauge and it said half a tank.

I said, "Bill,"—he's my navigator—"are you *sure* we can make Peoria?"

So he calculates it all up again, and says, "Yep, we can make Peoria."

We were flying along, and I look off my right wing, and I can see the Burlington Airport tower at Burlington, Iowa. And I looked down and I had a quarter tank.

"Are you *sure* we can make Peoria?" I said. "Because I can land at Burlington."

Yeah. He calculates again, and he says, "Honey, you can make it."

I said, "Okay." So I fly on some more and I see the lights of the tower of the airport at Peoria.

I called in and it was midnight, so they said, "You're clear for a straight-in approach." I didn't have to enter a traffic pattern, nothing. All I had to do was fly straight in.

I was registering just a hair off empty. I landed, and taxied down the runway . . . and . . . that was it! No more! They had to come out and tow me off the runway! I was out of gas! This should have been the clue of what the trip would be like.

S: Oh, Janet . . . just how weak *were* your knees?

J: And I'm sitting there going . . . (*jaw hanging, eyes glassy*). Bill said, "I *told* you we could make Peoria."

S: I would have hit him! I would have just grabbed . . . whatever . . . and smacked him on the head with it.

J: So we took off from Peoria and flew to somewhere in Ohio. I think it was Columbus, I don't remember. And we slept. We had pillows and blankets in the back of the plane and we just slept there.

Then we take off the next morning and we had to cross the Alleghenies, I think it was Maryland or Kentucky or ... someplace, I don't know where ... maybe Virginia.

Our radio equipment went haywire, and we were lost. I mean the needles were just doing weird, cracky things and we couldn't find landmarks. So we called ahead, and we had to be radar-vectored into the airport where we were going, because we just weren't getting anything.

S: I'm not sure what that means, radar-vectored.

J: It means you depress your mike and talk for so long, so that they can figure out where you are. Then they say, "Turn so many degrees this way," and, you know, you get radar-vectored in. Again, we came in with just *barely* enough gas.

We took off again and this time I was just exhausted. Bill says, "I'll fly, and you sit in the right seat and you navigate, and we won't tell anybody. We'll go ahead and log it as your hours."

So we headed for Delaware. This was the last stretch, and it was Labor Day weekend.

We had crossed the Chesapeake Bay and we were over Delaware, not far from our destination. Five thousand feet, cruising along, and we started feeling that we were getting carburetor ice. And Bill pulled the carburetor heat control.

S: Do you mean it was freezing up?

J: Yeah, evidently all the temperatures and everything must be right. So Bill pulls the carburetor heat control.

And the cable crystallized and just snapped. And what we thought had happened was that it had opened up and it was letting heat into the motor. We had to be able to get it turned off, or we'd be landing with a real hot motor. Bill said, "Not to worry."

It sounded right to me; I thought it was logical.

Well, we were wrong. It didn't open the valve, and the engine froze up, so we lost all power.

On Labor Day weekend the roads are *loaded* with cars. Bill said, "Let's look at the beaches."

We looked at the beaches, and the beaches were lined with people. In Delaware there's no big pastures, and we couldn't make the airports, we couldn't make anything!

So he said, "Honey, we'll have to do it offshore, in the ocean. It's the only place I can think of that's halfway safe."

He set up to do that, and as he banked to make his approach there, I looked down and I said, "Honey, there's a piece of land right there! It's long enough! I'm *sure* it's long enough! We can land right there!"

He took a look and he sees it and he says, "Yep, we can make it."

So he whipped around and made his approach. As he was coming up from the south landing in the north, and we were coming in, I said, "Oh, God, honey! There's a power line on this side!"

S: *Now* you tell him!

J: Yeah! So he dove to pick up speed and he just hopped the power line. He sat down and we rolled maybe . . . I don't know . . . not far. But then we hit a crosswind. It caught us and we cartwheeled from wingtip to wingtip. And when we stopped, we were upside down. We had no wings.

S: No wings!

J: No tail. It had taken off the nose gear. Everything. All that was left was the fuselage. The pillows and the blankets that we had slept in were all around us ... and we were hanging upside down.

   His door was crunched in, so he kicked out my door. He crawled out and helped me out. We sorta crawled along the ground over to a tree. We were laughing and crying and shaking.

S: Did it occur to you that you might be badly hurt?

J: We could see that we weren't hurt. As a matter of fact, as we were cartwheeling, I remember thinking, *Is this the way you die?* I couldn't think of one prayer.

S: Was the crash just a blur or did you know what was happening?

J: Oh yes, the minute I felt the flip. I felt the wind catch the wing. I knew that without power we couldn't correct. It felt so ... slow-motion ... which I'm sure it wasn't. But then it all came to a scrunching halt.

   So this farmer came running out—and of course, we thought, *He's coming out to see if we're okay.*

S: You *would* think so.

J: But the first thing he said to us wasn't, "Hi, how are you? Are you hurt?" He said, "Who's going to pay for the damage to my strawberries?" We had landed in his strawberry patch.

S: Did you say, "We'll pay for your strawberries, you old coot, and we're fine, thanks for asking"?

J:(*sighs*): But anyway our instructor flew out with another plane—'cause we had rented that one—and he had Bill and me check out in a 210 on the way back.

I said, "I don't want to fly."
And he said, "Yes, you will. You'll fly."

S: Bill said that, or the instructor?

J: The instructor. He said, "It's like a horse, Janet, like a horse. You just get back on."
   I still went for the commercial a little while later, but by then I had basically lost interest. I'd done it all. Been there, done that.

S (*laughs*): You sit here and tell me how safe small planes are, and then you tell me stories like that?

J: But think of the time we had and think of all we had to do. We picked out *two* landing areas!

S: Yeah . . . sure.

J: Now, if you lose power in one of those jets you just drop.
   Boy, we got really sidetracked there, didn't we?

S: Ah, it's okay. A good story.

CHILDREN

S: Is there anything else about your personal life that you would like to share? Your horses, the kids, the grandchildren?

J: I feel extremely fortunate when it comes to the kids. When I met Bill, he and Judy were separated. Linda and Jim were small. When I say small, Jim was four and Linda was just getting ready to turn six. So I've known them, virtually, all their natural lives.
   I never saw Judy as a threat; Bill had already left

her. I never saw her as a rival or competition. And Judy never saw me that way.

S: Bill and I talked about that today ... being friends with your ex. It's really nice when it can be that way.

J: It is. And it makes all the difference in the world, and of course, Bill believes that divorce is hard enough on children, and I never wanted them to feel that if they loved Judy, they couldn't love me.

As a matter of fact, once Bill and I decided to get married, I thought the kids would be really excited for us. I thought they had gotten pretty close to me. And when I told them, thinking they would want to be in the wedding, both of them just got this stricken look on their faces. And Jimmy started to cry.

I said, "What's wrong?"

He said, "Does this mean I have to leave Mommy and come live with you?"

I told him, "No, Jimmy, that isn't what this means. This means that I'll always be here when you come to see your daddy."

S: That's a good "stepmama" answer.

J: I always told them, "I'm not your mom, I'm Janet." I didn't want a big wedding fuss, so there wasn't one. Why make the transition any more difficult?

JANET: When we were married, the justice of the peace told us to forget we'd ever been to see him. He said we should lock up the marriage license and pretend we didn't have one. That's just what we've done.

S: Do you want to talk about why you and Bill didn't have children?

J: If I hadn't had such a close relationship with Jim and Linda, if I hadn't felt and received that sense of children and children growing up, I probably would have wanted to have children of my own. But I also think—and Bill would be the first to tell you—Bill is not a father.

S: I asked him about fatherhood today when I interviewed him, and it was obviously tough for him to talk about it.

J: It *is* tough. He doesn't know how.

S: He seems to care —

J: Oh, he does! He cares very deeply. But Bill had his own expectations of what he should be. For instance, he isn't interested in any sports. He isn't interested in baseball or fishing or whatever.

Also, work came first. Work always came first. With me, I knew that if I had a child of my own living with us, the child would come first. I knew that would create problems. But I never had to choose. I *never* had to choose.

S: You got the whole package all at once?

J: That's right.

HORSES AND OTHER FUZZY FACES

With a great deal of satisfaction, Bill will tell you that he buys something special for Janet to commemorate each book she publishes. One of her most beloved gifts is an exquisite Arabian horse, appropriately named Heiress.

Heiress and several other equine beauties live on a fourteen-acre site of lush pasture and forests across the road from the Dailey mansion, Belle Rive.

Bill's son Jim, Jim's wife Mary, and their son Maloy live and keep their own horses there as well. Both Mary and Jim work on various projects for Dailey Enterprises.

J: I always loved Arabians. We previously owned quarter horses, but when we started traveling so extensively, we sold all our horses.

While I was researching for a book, which I wanted to write using Arabians as background, I met Joanne Puckett of Oasis Arabians and saw her stallions. I immediately wanted to get back into horses again. When you love them, you can't stop.

Like a lot of people, I grew up reading Walter Farley novels, and I loved the magic and mystique of the Arabian horse.

As well as the horses, a number of other furry faces have adopted the Daileys. And who can blame them?

When you arrive at Belle Rive, enter those ornate wrought-iron gates, and drive down the circular roadway leading to the house, you are greeted by the two deadly sentinels of the estate—a couple of Yorkies named Sissy and Tally-Ho.

The jaunty red satin bows on top their heads do little to dispel the menacing image, fangs gleaming, eyes flashing, growls, barks, yips, that let you know they are on duty!

Sissy, the older and larger of the pair, is a particularly fearsome sight. In contrast to her immaculately groomed coat, her mustache is perpetually bedraggled on the left side, pointing in every direction, exposing those glistening incisors. Of course, once you spend some time with the terrible twosome, you discover that this fashion faux pas is due to the fact that the overly maternal Tally-Ho is forever kissing and licking her friend's mustache until it stands straight up!

Sorta spoils the "killer" guard dogs routine.

A TYPICAL DAY IN THE LIFE OF AMERICA'S FAVORITE LADY AUTHOR

S: Your fans will want to know, what is a typical day in the life of Janet Dailey?

J: Boring! Aw, it is, really . . .

S: Come on, they want to know how you live.

J: I get up at four and put on coffee.

S: The chickens aren't up by then! It's dark out, isn't it?

J: Bill calls that the crack of dawn, because you have to be cracked to get up at that hour. But you know, it's redundant, I'm a writer, so I have to be cracked.

S: We already established that.

J: Yeah, it's established, and I do ten pages a day, however long that takes. On the average, it's ten to fourteen hours, but it has its own built-in rewards and punishments. If I have a productive day, I'm done early, and I have the rest of the day to fool around, which also gives me time to plan the next day's writing.

S: Well now, let's see. If you're getting up at four, ten hours would be two o'clock in the afternoon. Right? So, that's a short day.

J: That's a short day.

S: If it goes into a long day, that would be eight o'clock at night or whatever . . .

J: Uh-huh. I have worked 'til midnight.

S: Are you stopping and eating, and things like this during the day?

J: Well, I only eat one meal during the day, I take the dogs out, or on occasion I'll fix Bill something, but that's rare . . .

S: Are you in here (*office*)?

J: Uh-huh.

S: Do you close the door?

J: No.

S: Do people drop by and say "Hi" . . .

J: No. They call first. Actually, it's been a little more difficult here to isolate. You know, I've been threatening to get an answering machine on the telephone.

S: I'm so surprised that you don't have one.

J: At the same time, in the other sense of the word, I've always had distractions; there's always more that could happen. As a writer, you need to learn to get that concentration level where you can write in the middle of a train station. It's one of the things you need to learn.

The asset of getting up at four o'clock is that you can get into the concentration level so when all the distraction occurs, it doesn't bother you.

I've always been a morning person. I love the mornings best of all. What time I finish dictates what I do afterwards. I may hit the tennis court, or I may go out and pull some weeds. If it's too hot, then I'll putz around the house and do things in the house. On some evenings I paint or do my watercolors.

S: Do you ever watch TV?

J: I watch TV.

S: What are some of your favorite shows?

J: I love *Picket Fences.* I loved *Northern Exposure* when it first came out, 'cause, God, all those weird characters were in Alaska. They were there. The whole plotline later wasn't as fun as it was. I like *Lovejoy,* on A&E. And I *love* football. I *adore* football.

S: Which team?

J: Oh, doesn't matter. I don't care.

S: You don't have a team?

J: Aw no! I'll watch anything. I'll watch it if the score is forty-eight to zero. I'll watch it. Just to see that one little play that's magic. Yeah, I love football.

  Obviously, I root for the Kansas City Chiefs, but I don't care. I really don't care who wins and who plays. I just want to watch football, pro football. I'm not so big on college games. I am a poor sport. So I don't watch college sports, because I know on a college level that these players aren't having a continuing career. This is the last call; every game means something.

S: It's too serious?

J: It's too serious for me, and it means too much. I used to follow college games. I had my teams, and if they lost on Saturday, the whole rest of the week I was just . . . I was just down.

S: Oh, Janet.

J: I'm such a poor loser. And I can't stand that, which is why I have learned to compete with myself. To go up against myself. I don't like to lose. I just *flat, don't like to lose*.

S: Not into board games, huh? Is that why you play solitaire?

J: Well, no, I like board games, but I like to play games for the sake of games. I play them because I enjoy it. And if I lose fifteen games of Pitch in a row, or if I lose Trivial Pursuit or Scrabble, or whatever, it doesn't matter, 'cause I just love playing with the words.

And I just enjoy playing the game, the fun. We make up our own little rules when it's family, and you're with somebody who doesn't mind. In our Trivial Pursuit you're allowed to get clues.

S: Hmm.

J: They can be weird clues, but you're allowed to get clues.

S: How about the evenings? Do you see friends? Do you go out to dinner? Do you have dinner with Bill?

J: Sometimes, it depends.

S: We know you don't cook.

J: I'll cook on rare occasions, but we'll usually go out. It depends on his schedule. A lot of times he has activities in the evening.

For me, it's usually tennis, or I'll go up on the hill and mess with the horse. Sometimes my friend, Melodie Adams, and I will get together and have one of our marathon conversations. And, of course, living here in Branson there are opening nights or charity functions that we go to. The women's crisis center here always has special things. I try to participate.

S: Sounds like a good life.

J: It is! It's really a good life. And, of course, family, my mom and dad. We go down to the orchard and pick fruit. Then we have to take care of all the stuff we pick. We used to have peach trees when we moved here, but they all got a disease. We had to pull 'em all out and this fall we'll plant more peach trees. That's on the plans.

JANET DAILEY, THE WOMAN

S: What do you like about Janet Dailey, the woman?

J: I think I have a good sense of humor and I like challenge. I like to challenge *me*. I don't like playing it safe. There's never anything to be gained by playing it safe.

S: What are some examples of you challenging yourself?

J: Oh, I could easily write the same book over and over. I mean, that would be real easy, but I always want to try something new. The only way to learn is to keep trying something new. Keep pushing the limits. Sometimes you make something work. Sometimes you don't. Whether it's in my writing . . . when I did *Silver Wings*, I had never dealt with female relationships and how they interrelate . . . and how it works or doesn't work. I loved exploring that. I loved juggling the history and the great love. I loved, through fiction, telling the history of Alaska.

As a matter of fact, someone criticized the book by saying, "All it is, is an overblown tale of Alaska," and

I thought, *Well, you're right. You got it right on the nail. You finally got the message.*

So I like trying something new. I like exploring new things.

S: It does take courage, doesn't it?

J: Uh-huh, yeah, 'cause it's easy to play it safe. It would be easy to just keep rewriting the Calders. And it gets boring if you do. It gets boring for the reader, no matter how much they think they like it.

So I like that about me.

S: What else?

J: I guess I like liking people. I think that's a good thing. I love people; I love being with people.

I spend so much time alone at the typewriter that when I'm not writing, I say, "*Give me real people*, that talk and walk, and act, that laugh and demand, you know."

S: As a writer, you have to be around people, or you'll have no grist for the mill.

J: Uh-huh. Yeah. What did I miss? I love the god-like qualities in animals. The absolute forgiveness. I read somewhere that if you spell dog backwards, it's "God," because they're always happy to see you, and they never ask where you've been.

S: You're a good friend to people . . .

J: Oh, I try to be . . .

S: I've noticed . . .

J: Being friendly, being friends, is important. If there's

anything that I'm concerned about, it's that sometimes you get so involved in your career—and I'm
sure that's true with anybody—you get so involved,
you don't have time for friends. Friends have to be
cultivated, the same as a crop does.

S: That's true.
    If you could just wave a magic wand and suddenly
just change one thing about yourself, what would it
be?

J: I'd get rid of the procrastination. I'm such a procrasti-
nator. I'm the kind that, "I'll give up procrastinating
tomorrow."

S: Do you honestly think you'll ever get over it?

J: No.

S: Come to live with it, huh?

J: It irritates me, it's . . . it . . . just irritates me.

S: Do you hate it in other people, too?

J: No.

S: No? You forgive *them* for it, but you can't forgive *you*?

J: Yeah.

S: Well, there's another quality. You're very forgiving.

J: Yeah, well, somewhere I read that sometimes you
have to forgive what you can't forget. You just have
to forgive it.

S: Good point.

J: It's perfectly all right not to forget . . . but forgive. For yourself, too—but that's harder. It's harder to forgive yourself.

JANET: I'm glad we did all the traveling we did when we did it. I'm becoming quite a homebody. I love being here on the lake. We have twenty acres right here on the lake, and it's very quiet. I have the horses, my son has horses, and I can go riding anytime I want. It's become very nice just to be at home.

BRANSON, MISSOURI

J: The great thing about living in Branson is it reminds me that the world doesn't revolve around my writing. Half of the people we know don't even care what my next book is going to be. Your world doesn't get self-centered that way.

I hear all the problems in life and try to understand the common bonds among people. If I lived in a place like Hollywood or New York, I might end up living at a level where you lose touch with the most important things in life.

No one makes a fuss over me. All our friends have business projects, so they just accept that writing is my business, that's all.

This is the other thing I love about Branson. Harold Bell Wright's *Shepherd of the Hills* was probably what you call popular fiction. This book was such a huge seller that people came to the area to see Uncle Matt's cabin. People came to stay and see the place . . .

S: How do you feel about Branson's growth?

J: It's geared to family entertainment, it's modestly
   priced. It amuses me because a lot of people haven't
   visited areas where the traffic is so much worse.

Janet and Bill Dailey moved to Branson, Missouri, in 1980.
In recent years, this area in the Ozark Mountains has become
a tourist mecca. About 4.5 million people a year travel by car
and bus to visit the 27 country music theaters.

JANET: *I remember telling Bill goodbye and Bill*
saying, "I told God that if you go then I go. And
He told me He didn't want me up there messing
things up. So, because of that, you get to stay." I
think I remember laughing a bit.

JAPAN, THE TURNING POINT

Janet: On October 17, 1982, I became ill while we were
   in Kyoto, Japan. Within two hours I was on the operating table of the nearest hospital for an appendectomy.

   Because I have a congenital floating upper colon,
   complications ensued from the initial surgery when
   the upper bowel twisted and strangled itself.

   From then on, it became like dominoes falling.
   The appendectomy caused a strangulated bowel,
   which necessitated excessive and prolonged dosage of
   antibiotics, which caused the blood infection, which
   led to transfusions, which caused the yellow jaundice
   and hepatitis, which caused . . .

   You get the idea. If I ever wrote a story and had all
   this happen to the heroine, no one would believe it!

For the first twelve days of Janet's ordeal, she remained
mostly unconscious and remembers very little. Thankfully, she

*was unaware that her heart had stopped during surgery and
the physicians had been forced to perform heart massage to
save her life.*

*On the other hand, Bill Dailey recalls the frightening details
of that period all too well.*

Bill: It was a hospital for the poor. Facilities were inadequate and hardly anyone on the staff spoke English.
When I called the American Embassy in Kyoto for
help, they offered none—zero. They didn't even have
the courtesy to say they were sorry my wife was ill.

It was amazing. The only thing nurses did in that
hospital was insert IVs and giggle. You had to do
everything else.

I didn't know about the Japanese concern for
honor and when they realized that I had brought
over an American doctor and nurse, they became
very upset.

In all the trauma of the situation and with her
weak condition in mind, I promised Janet that I
would get her home. Of course, I wouldn't have
moved her without the help of a doctor.

They wouldn't let me transfer her to another hospital, like the very fine and nearby Kyoto University
Hospital. When I wanted to move her to the States,
neither the doctors nor the administrators would
allow her release. After all, they wanted the rich
American author to walk out totally recovered. But
Dr. Hirsch felt that her condition warranted returning her to the U.S. as soon as possible.

I fibbed a bit and told them that Janet wanted to
go home. I told them that she was merely recovering
from an appendectomy and the state people there
gave me her release.

Japan Airlines wouldn't allow air travel for anyone sick enough to still be on IVs, so we cheated
some by removing them until we were airborne.
After we were in the air, they weren't likely to return

to the field when we placed the needles back in. But it turned out that the airline people were wonderful and very helpful.

Our next step was to clear Janet through customs in L.A. and quickly board her on another connection to Kansas City. Time was of the essence because of her condition and because we had only so much medication.

Senator Tom Eagleton and ex–Missouri governor Joe Teasdale had previously arranged for Janet to be cleared immediately at customs in L.A., but we weren't prepared for what happened next. They had no room where Janet could lie down. I was afraid they would not let her board, so Janet sat in a chair for several hours.

Janet: They lost me on the operating table, brought me back, and I spent two months recovering. For the first time in my life I had to cope with the fact that, besides everything else I thought of myself, I could be scared, too.

They told Bill I was dying every day for three weeks. When I finally got back to this country, I was in the hospital for another month. Let me tell you, almost dying made me think about what was important.

There was a time when I would have been more greatly concerned about the readers' perceptions and the readers' expectations than I am and than I have been. After Japan, I realized that I didn't know how much time I had to write a book. If there was something I wanted to write, I'd better be writing it. You do have to satisfy your inside.

S: That changed your priorities, didn't it?

J: It changed my priorities totally. You come to terms with your mortality.

I do want to live up to my readers' expectations and the loyalty they've shown me; I don't *ever* want to thumb my nose at it. That's not what I'm doing. What I prefer to think is, *They don't know, they might just like this! Let me show them.*

The situation has changed our lives. We decided to slow down and write a different sort of book, not our typical Janet Dailey romance novels.

Flying into the Los Angeles airport after no one had expected me to return home alive, I experienced a midlife crisis. The dramatic illness forced me to ask myself what I planned to do with the rest of my life. I knew the book I wanted to write, *Silver Wings, Santiago Blue*, wasn't the type my readers expected, but I couldn't put off writing something for myself any longer.

One afternoon at the St. Mary's Hospital in Kansas City, the mailman left a bundle of cards in my room. A nurse came into my room and commented about all the mail I had received.

When she asked who they were from, I explained they were from you, my readers.

"All this mail from strangers!" she said.

"No, from friends," I replied.

I finally realized how many friends I have and how many people cared. I'll never get over it.

The Writing: The Joys and the Trials

THOSE CORNY LITTLE BOOKS

J: Funny, I remember the library had the little nurse/doctor romance section, and I read a few of those, and I thought they were the corniest pieces of junk in the world. Never could read those things.

   Then after high school, I'd still go to the library religiously every week to get my books. I discovered Phyllis Whitney and Victoria Holt and started reading them. Then I had gone to my sister's farm for a weekend vacation and all she had to read were these stupid little Harlequins.

S: And you were forced to either read them or the cereal boxes.

J: Yeah, I decided to read some of these dumb little books. I picked one up and it was called *Dark Star*, by Nerina Hilliard. She wrote very few books for Harlequin before she died. And it was probably like . . . "These are pretty good! They aren't so bad after all."

GETTING STARTED . . .

JANET: My life was great and I tried to shove fictional writing aside. But something was missing. I constantly came up with story ideas, often writing whole scenes with descriptions and dialogue in my head.

While we were on the road I finally had time to catch up on my reading. I began buying romances because they gave me a positive feeling when I was done with them. I felt a complete identification with the books and knew there was a natural link. Then I kept up with ideas for plots until I was convinced I could write them.

In 1974, I began to talk nonstop until Bill, who has no patience with words that aren't backed by action, finally said, "Okay, then get off your duff and do it."

I remember when I sat down to write my first book, I didn't even know what a manuscript looked like. First I went through a Harlequin book and typed it so that I could figure out how long a book should be, and how long a chapter was, and I went through some of the books I really liked, trying to figure out how they did something and where they did it, and I had to find out things like—how many ways can you say, "Two weeks later . . ."

S: Bless your heart. Obviously you hadn't heard of tip sheets.*

J: You have to understand, back then they didn't have anything like that.

---

* Tip sheets are written guidelines given to writers by publishers—"tips" as to what they want in manuscripts.

JANET: When I finally started it was like a dam bursting. The first book took nearly eight months, but once I got the romance format down, I was turning them out in eight days. I cringe at the cliches of my earliest books, but another writer recently pointed out to me that at the time I wrote them, they weren't cliches — not until other writers copied them.

JANET: I stayed at the typewriter for six months and when the first story, *No Quarter Asked,* was finished I showed it to Bill and asked him what to do next. His advice: "Send it to Harlequin. If you're going to get turned down by somebody, it ought to be by the best and the biggest."

I wrote to Harlequin to say, "I have this manuscript, would you like to read it?" They wrote me back and said, "We don't publish original novels, only reprints from Mills and Boon in England. You may write Mills and Boon and see if they're interested."

I did, and they wrote back and said, "Yes, we'd be happy to read your manuscript." And I sent it in.

Ignorance is truly bliss. I didn't know that the first work of an unpublished author usually ends up in the slush pile. But my story was accepted without revisions.

I realize that I'm lucky. I was in the right place at the right time with the right product. Harlequin and Mills and Boon had decided that they wanted to test the market and try the work of an American author who used American backgrounds and settings. Until I arrived on the scene, they had only bought books with foreign backgrounds.

But there was no tip sheet, nothing that told you book length. Nothing! They would have sent it if there had been.

S: No printed guidelines about degrees of sensuality?

J: No, not at all. With those early Harlequins, if you kissed at the end of the book it was a miracle. And I don't think you could even use the word "passion." We didn't go below the neck! So if you think about the level of tension you had to create to maintain ... By the time I got done writing them we were *way* below the belt.

S: Yep, things have changed.

J (*laughs*): Yep, they have.

> **JANET:** *They called it everything, from trash to everything else. I always thought of it as fun entertainment.*

J: One of the wonderful things ... Harlequin gave me the cover art (the original painting) for my first book.

S: How neat. Any others?

J: Silhouette gave me the cover of my first Silhouette. And Pocket gave me the one from *The Rogue*.

S: Was this after you said you particularly liked it, or was it part of your contract?

J: No, it was just a really nice gesture, a gift of appreciation. I also got the *Mistletoe and Holly* cover.

NOW AND THEN

J: I don't know if I want to say this, but ... I really believe that those early Harlequins, the editorial controls were so tight. They published so few. I really think they published the best. Because I honestly believe that back then, when they only published eight titles a month, I think they were more selective. They really took the best. Now that they're doing so many titles a month, I don't think they always have that solidly plotted product.

S: You don't believe that every romance novel out there is good?

J: No, they aren't. And I think it's unfair to suggest that every book in the romance genre or every book in the Western genre, or that any book that gets published—just because it gets published—is a good book. In any genre or category, you will find some poorly written, poorly structured, poorly plotted books.

JANET: My paperback decade was a rehearsal for hardcover. I've often said I want to evolve into a writer that's a combination of James Michener and Edna Ferber. But writing romances has definitely not hurt me.

J: Category romances were very useful to me as a writer. They really taught me how to write; they were my college education. In the romance fiction market—or basically any category fiction market, whether you're dealing with Westerns or romance or mystery or science fiction—there are certain strictures that you have to set your story within. They're very much like the short story market, which has pretty much gone by the wayside. You learn to tell your story quickly, succinctly, draw your characters quickly, succinctly.

And it teaches you the basics of writing: timing, the tempo of the story. Your plot—is it tight, does it drag anywhere? It teaches you the fundamentals of writing. It's where you can perfect your craft.

JANET: A writer can begin with talent, then has to refine her skills. My style has lost some of its early immaturity. Subplots don't exist in a romance. It's strictly a love story.

In anything you always have to start out with a degree of natural talent. But if you don't refine your craft and perfect it, you don't go anywhere, you just keep doing the same thing. And I feel I was blessed. I became very successful writing romance novels, but it also opened up something totally new for me. It was like a stepping-stone, and I don't know where it's going to go from here. Hopefully higher!

JANET: It's different now, because when you hear the word "romance," you think it's a legitimate arm of the paperback industry. Back then, nobody admitted reading them, nobody admitted publishing them, and nobody admitted writing them.

S: What role do you think romantic fiction plays in our society?

J: Romantic fiction, or romance stories, will live forever. There will always be a place. Always, always, always. The song from *Casablanca* could not possibly be quoted enough to describe exactly the way it is, and the way it always will be. "The world will always welcome lovers." That's the absolute truth in a nutshell.

There will always be a market for brand-name romances. I said it from the beginning: No other medium is providing romantic stories. Television isn't doing it. The movies aren't making *Casablanca* or *Gone With the Wind* anymore. If you want romance, you have to buy a book.

S: What role do you feel romance novels play in the lives of the women who read them?

J: Romance novels allow women to see other women moving into jobs and careers, competing with men, having identity crises. But they retain their femininity. They find love—and that's what readers want. So the books are reassuring. I think teenagers read my books to find out what life is going to be like. In a way, romances deal with the realities of love and romance. In romance novels, love includes communication, emotional respect, comprehension. Not just sex.

J: The publishers' guidelines used to irritate me. There was that ridiculous rule that the heroine had to be a virgin. I think I wrote twenty books that never made it clear whether she was a virgin or not.... It wasn't essential to the story. And you couldn't have passionate kissing till the end of the book, and certainly nothing below the neck. I was going *way* below the neck.

Sometimes you get to the point where you say, "How many ways can you put a hand on a breast?" Nipples, rosebuds, peaks, and crests—oh, we were kept busy thinking of alternatives.

In the mid-seventies, romance writers could have

some passionate kisses, but they had to be at the end of the book, and you never went below the neck. Then things began to go lower. In seven short years, we were below the belt and lower. We started saying, "Let's be realistic. In this day and age, if we love a guy, we'll go to bed with him."

Sexual desire is a very strong element in romances—and in romance, too! And we writers certainly don't back away from it. But there is always a point where the man stops saying, "I want you—I desire you," and says, "Hey, I like you." The heroine becomes a person for him. He begins to appreciate her humor, her way of talking. It's that, not just the sexual element, that makes the romance work.

S: You've always been a rather controversial figure in this industry. You've always been inclined to break the rules.

J: True. According to the rules, you couldn't have children in a novel; they were thought to distract from "romance." So I wrote a book where the children played matchmaker.

The publishers said you couldn't have any form of handicap in a novel, and I thought, *That's silly. A heroine can be born blind and still find love,* as in The Ivory Cane.

PASSIONATE PROSE

S: Speaking of breaking the rules, how do you feel about writing all that sexy stuff?

J: The other day we were sitting around here and Melodie Adams and her mother, Diane, were here and somehow we got to talking about the love scenes. Diane said to my mom, "What do you think about it?"

Mom said, "I just hope she got it all out of her system. She just wrote a couple there, and I just couldn't wait until she got it out of her system."

S (*laughs*): And yet if you don't write those scenes some people are upset. They say, "I waited and waited and when they finally did it they were in the other room and we weren't there to enjoy it."

J: Yeah, and then you get the letters from the readers who loved your book, ". . . except for those love scenes. You didn't have to write those."

So I never know. I just write what the book says to write. If I feel their story would be natural to have the steamy love scenes, then I put it in. But if it isn't, if I have to force it, it just doesn't work.

I finished a scene last week where, and of course it's the 1860s and she's ready to go for it, and he doesn't. He didn't do it. He was a gentleman. And I thought, *Holy crap, do you know how long it's going to be before you get to do it? Honey, you didn't do it, now you've got to wait 'til Chapter Twenty-Three.*

I know the reader wants to be titillated, but subtly. That's why the dialogue is so important. It's filled with innuendo, double meanings, the kinds of retorts you often wish you could think of. To keep the sexual tension going, the love scenes must be sensual, not graphic. You use a word like "stroke" or "caress" without being too specific. You say "his roaming hand" without saying where it's roaming. The reader's imagination will supply that. To go too far in print is not romantic at all.

JANET: I don't get detailed, I get sensuous. I call it hard-core decency.

S: How do you feel about sexually explicit as opposed to sweeter romances? Steamy versus sweet.

J: A good story, whether it's steamy or sweet . . .

S: Which do you prefer to read?

J: Oh, I've got to be honest. Unlike so many other readers, I get to some of these love scenes, and I just flip to the next part of the dialogue.

S: Do you find it boring?

J: Yeah.

S: Why?

J: It's rare for me to ever find one that titillating or exciting. It's extremely rare. And I find, too often, that I don't agree that it would happen, so therefore it feels gratuitous. Therefore, I'm saying, "Well, okay. I know, now I want to see how the relationship becomes . . ."

S: They call them OSSs. Obligatory sex scenes.

J: Yes. Yeah. And I get very impatient with it, and I do tend to flip through, which makes me angry that I did that to another writer. I know what I would go through trying to write the thing and I feel guilty when I'm not reading every word. But, I have to admit, it's rare when I do.

   I really try when I write my love scenes. My opinion is that explicit love scenes deny the reader's imagination. My imagination will never offend me, but your writing can. Therefore, I try very hard, when I'm writing a love scene, to stimulate the reader's imagination. Not to paint pictures for them. Not to tell them where the hand goes. I'll never put the hand where they didn't want it to be.

Whatever stimulates them is what they will have happening and therefore becomes *five* times sexier than I could ever make it. I always work, when I'm doing a love scene, not to do (I beg your pardon) a blow-by-blow description but to make the reader feel the emotion more than the sensation.

When Rhett Butler carried Scarlett O'Hara up those stairs, we never went in the bedroom . . .

S: I know, and I have to admit that I was pretty bent about that!

J: But gosh, we saw her smiling the next morning . . .

S: And she was giggling. I wanted to know what he did, but that's the difference between you and me.

J: And the same thing with Burt Lancaster and Deborah Kerr, on the beach, in the waves. There is something to be said for the theater of the mind.

S: May I quote you on that?

J: Yes. It can be a definite turn-on, and boy, it can be the biggest turn-off.

S: Do you read love scenes that offend you at times?

J: Uh-hum.

S: Obviously, if they're gratuitous, you've made that point, what else offends you?

J: No. That's personal. I think everybody has their little idiosyncrasies, that to them, something is offensive. It's something they don't like. But it can be the opposite for someone else. It's obviously something that has to get into your personal life. So, that's my business.

S: Okay. Do you feel that they should not have written that?

J: No. No. I don't believe in censorship in any way, shape, or form.

S: It just isn't according to your taste?

J: Exactly. . . . It's all a matter of taste, and to censor somebody, now my censorship is in not reading it. My censorship is in turning the page. I'll censor personally, that's my right. My right is turning off the television. My right is walking out of something that is offensive to me.

S: A theater . . .

J: A theater, a movie, whatever. If it's offensive, and if I don't approve, I exercise my right, which is to not participate. And that to me is the wisest censorship. I have the freedom to do that.

S: Right.

J: And they have the freedom to write what they want.

S: And you don't think that it's morally wrong for them to write that?

J: I, no, I can't begin to say that. Everyone makes their own moral judgments and I don't think that a sexually explicit scene is immoral. God put us on the Earth with the intention to mate, to multiply. He gave us the enjoyment of the act of life. . . .

S: . . . to make sure we did . . .

J: Exactly. So this is something God gave us and for me to morally look down on it . . . Let's get real here!

S: You know why I'm asking. Because there are people who feel it's immoral to write about sexual matters.

J: If someone reads me and they don't like me, now I'm absolutely comfortable with that. But if they've never read me, and say they don't like me . . . no . . . no. You can read me and say you don't like me. That's fine. But don't judge me before you have read me. I won't accept that.

S: Do you ever get asked what your husband thinks about you writing sexy scenes?

J: He has a response that just breaks them up. He says, "I have to go out and research all these love scenes, then come back and show it to her." He always says, "You remember that rape scene in *Touch the Wind*? It took her three times to get that right."

S: How do you feel about "heroes" who are abusive, or domineering?

J: Dominating . . . domineering is mental.

S: Or who force sexual favors of any kind onto women?

J: No. I'm against it. No. I *totally* and *absolutely* and *positively* disagree. No woman wants to be raped. I don't want to read about a woman being raped. Rape is a violent act. A woman wants to read about being ravished.

S: Well. That's different.

J: It's *totally* different. For people to say that women have rape fantasies, that is not true. They have fantasies of being ravished, which is totally, totally different.

S: Where do you draw the line? Is a woman being abused if she is being kissed, when she says, "No"? The infamous bruising kiss that she does not want?

J: If she honest-to-God doesn't want it, yes, that's abuse.

S: What if she's saying she doesn't, but she does?

J: Then it's not.

S: I think she's a fool if she does that, because it perpetuates the idea that women say "No" and mean "Yes." I think some women say "No" and mean "Yes," but I think it's destructive behavior.

J: Yeah, Exactly.

JANET: I quit writing category romances with the publication of Leftover Love. *I was — and am— moving on as a writer. I concentrate on more historical or general fiction. But I stay with the strong love theme. Pick up any bestseller and you'll find it there.*

CATEGORY ROMANCE VS. MAINSTREAM FICTION

S: What is the difference between "romance" and "mainstream"?

J: While you may have a romance plotline in a mainstream

novel, the focus is A: What the woman wants. And B: What's she's going after.

In the case of *Heiress*, I have to find out who this woman is and that's number one. Who did Daddy love? Or in the case of *Tangled Vines*, she must find out whether her father is a murderer.

In *Masquerade* the hook was: She's trying to find out who's trying to kill her and shut her up.

THE ILL-AFFORDED LUXURY OF "WRITER'S BLOCK"

JANET: It's work. Words never flow. I never have creative urges. Inspiration never strikes. I have to work at everything. That's what writing is—work. It's discipline. I go to my office to write every day just like other people go to their jobs. It's that simple.

I don't think a writer deserves to have this so-called artistic temperament. I think it's foolish. You're just a writer, you don't have some great wonderful thing that nobody else has. There's a creative genius in all facets, whether you are a writer or a corporate executive for General Motors. You don't hear a GM executive saying, "I don't think I'll work today, I can't." It's stupid. I don't believe in the artistic temperament. It's what creates some of the eccentricities that some people feel like they have to have to write. I think that's a lot of nonsense.

Sure, there are times when something isn't coming together, or you haven't got the structure quite right. But you work it out. You don't just throw up your hands and say, "Oh, I'm going to have to wait two months—I have writer's block." I think the minute your concept of what a writer is allows you to put it on some other plane of existence, then you begin to create excuses. You allow yourself to have problems and justify it by saying, "Well, I'm a writer."

JANET: Where do my ideas keep coming from? I'm never conscious of getting them. I just become intrigued with something, and before I know it, there's a book. I figure if I'm intrigued by an idea, readers will be, too.

MIDNIGHT FANTASIES

J: I never write down an idea. Never.

S: Me either. I figure if it's good, it'll stick.

J: Exactly. When I first started writing, I would read about other writers and what they did, and I would think, *Well, if I were really a writer, this is what I should really do.* I read somewhere that somebody always kept a pen and paper by their nightstand so that when they got these great ideas in the middle of the night, they'd write them down. So I got a pad and a pencil and I put it by my nightstand, because I was always getting these great ideas all the time and never remembering them the next day. And the first time I wrote down these great ideas, the next morning I saw what I had written down and ... (*Shakes her head*)

S: Aren't they *insane*?

J: Oh! They had no ... ! They were so ... !

S: I do that, too. You think, *This is so good! I can't believe I never thought of this before!* Then you wake up and you read it and wonder, *What did I have with that hot chocolate when I went to bed?*

J: That's right. That's right.

S: They just don't hold up to the light of day.

J: Unless they're good ones and then they stick.

> *JANET: Novel writing demands so much patience. It's a long-term commitment. The novel I'm writing now won't be published until a year or more from now. I won't see the results—the public reception—until three or four months after that, and I won't have any royalty knowledge until a year later. Writing isn't a career that you get into and say, "Hey, I've got it made." It doesn't work that way. You don't receive immediate success or recognition.*

J: Ninety percent of my ideas come from curiosity. From either saying, "I didn't know that!" and "Why?"

In the case of *Heiress*, I met a woman who had a half-sister who was born on the same day, month, and year that she was. And—even though I couldn't do this in the book—they were given the same first name, the same father, different mothers. I wanted to use Abigail, then have one be Abby and the other Gail. But can you imagine? Their identity is totally stolen. And I kept thinking, *My God, what if this ... what if that?*

And the Calders ... First of all, I wanted to do a book, Western. I thought I'd like to figure out a way where the father of the hero had killed the father of the heroine. It was that loose.

S: Instant conflict.

J: Instant conflict. I mean, this was the biggest conflict

you can come up with. And he's got to be a big, mighty man, so he's got to have a big, mighty ranch. And I set it in eastern Montana, because I hadn't done Montana, and it was far removed from law and order.

I said to Bill, "Start researching. I want to know what a big ranch can be. What kind of people settled this area?" About three or four days later, he came up with the fact that most of the people who settled eastern Montana were Texans.

I said, "What? What were Texans doing in Montana?"

He had researched the Texas cattle drives to Montana, the last of the free grass, the last of the big ranches. It was the end of an era, the cowboy era.

I just went, "Wow! Wow! Wow!" Then it became an easy thing, using all this information, and then you knew exactly what I was doing.

The Great Alone, I got the idea for that when we were up in Alaska researching the Harlequin I was going to write in Alaska, about a bush pilot. I saw a Russian Orthodox church, and somebody told me, "The Russians lived here."

I thought, *Mr. Mills, you never told me that there were Russians living here when we bought Alaska.*

JANET: *It's perspiration all the way. It took me a long time to learn to be productive. I've got Hollywood to thank for that. Hollywood made me believe that every writer was moved by great creative inspirations. I've never been moved by a great inspiration in my life. I think that's a problem with a lot of beginning writers. They think they are going to be moved in some way, and when that doesn't happen they figure, "I must not be a writer." You get caught up in the Hollywood myth that there's going to be this great surge of creative energy.*

J: I think writing is more elimination than creation. Because your premises or your hooks are always going to be rather standard. If you're dealing with a mystery novel, you've got a dead body. Take *Heiress*, for example. The premise is: Two women are identical and relatives. So you have the choice of twins. Can they be twins? No. You eliminate that. That's been done.

S: So it's more like deductions?

J: You just keep taking away alternatives.

S: How would that work for a romance novel?

J: Oh, it works the same way for a romance novel. You already have your basic, just by the fact that you're doing a romance. You have: Man and woman meet, man and woman have conflict, man and woman resolve conflict. You have your bare-bones plot. So what you look for is the hook or the premise, whatever makes it unique.

And with a romance, you're automatically faced with a choice. Are they strangers? Or have they met before?

You've made a decision. You've eliminated a hook. You've eliminated a possibility.

If they've never met before, then they're strangers.

If they've met before, did they like each other? Were they married? Were they boyfriend and girlfriend? Then you have a whole new set of questions to eliminate.

S: Do you see this as simplifying, cutting away?

J: Sure, because it's exactly the way a doctor diagnoses. He diagnoses by eliminating the possibilities. The same with a sculptor; he just keeps taking away and taking away until he has what he wants. Until you get the final thing.

And there again, part of the ingredient becomes where you're setting the novel, choosing their occupations. It's rare to have her say, "I'm going to be a television reporter," and stick her on a farm or a ranch. If you're going to do that, you'd better have a reason.

Many times your setting is dictated by the characters' occupations. Unless they are visiting. Or they're there for their work. So really, it's eliminating, eliminating, eliminating . . .

Every time you can eliminate the obvious, you're getting a real hook.

S: Eliminating the obvious . . . as in, eliminating the cliche, the expected?

J: But, more the expected than the cliche. Because, either way, you end up with a cliche.

S: I tell my students, "Cliches are cliches because they're good. Otherwise, they would never have become cliches."

J: Exactly. Quite possibly one of the more popular romances is where the man and woman have been married before. You're able to have the instant tension. You start with that premise: They were married before and now they're going to meet again.

What causes them to meet? What can you do that's unusual?

That happened to me. I remember in *Wildcatter Woman*, my Silhouette, he shows up drunker than a skunk to celebrate the anniversary of their divorce.

S: What a jerk! That's great! It's certainly unexpected.

J: When you come up with the unexpected, it sort of sets the character in a way. He turns out to be a wild-catter in oil. You get a sense of both of them. You have the surface conflict: He lost everything they had. He blew it. He lost their home, everything, on a well, and he just did it without asking her for her input. And she's had it. Which wasn't really the reason she left him. She left him because he never needed her.

S: We always have the, "He squeezes the toothpaste" reason and then we have the "real" reason.

J: Right. So it's eliminating the obvious, eliminating the cliche, and eliminating the expected.

If you have children involved, you can have a child run away from home. Or maybe the child doesn't really run away from home. Maybe it's a way of getting attention.

Maybe he's a teenager who's trying to get Mommy and Daddy back.

You can play with thousands of things as long as you don't say, "Well, I've done that before, and that's been done."

If they've been done before, chances are you don't want to do them. You'll want to come up with something unique, or something that hasn't been handled before.

S: That's difficult for most of us. It seems easy for you. Is it?

J: See, I *love* playing that game of "What if?"

What if—you have a hero, and in the opening of your story he gets three kids unexpectedly. His sister has died and she's given him custody and . . . what in the world?

That's the hook. Maybe he never liked kids. Maybe

he's getting ready to lose his place, whatever it is. He's got nothing. Maybe he hated his sister. Maybe they had a feud of long standing. Now, why on earth does he have to get saddled with her kids? You can come up with eighty thousand things that aren't expected.

S (*silence*): Well . . . *you* can. That's what Richard told me about you. He said, "Janet comes up with the most *incredible* ideas."

JANET: Some authors take as long as five years to complete a book. I couldn't live with a book that long. I couldn't live with a book for even a year. I'd get bored with it. But I'm not the kind of person who can do two or three books at the same time, either. I have a one-track mind. I like to work on a book, finish it, then sift through my ideas to see which one has the best chance of maturing into a book.

J: If you have two strangers it's more difficult than to have people with a past relationship. Coming up with strangers, then something has to be different to create a hook. In the case of *For the Love of God*, he's a minister, and how can you have lusting thoughts when you're a minister?

S: Well, they *can* . . . as long as they feel bad about it.

J (*laughs*): Exactly! Or in *Leftover Love*, where the hero is ugly and assumes nobody will love him. He's always been this hulking "thing." Of course, the woman finds redeeming qualities in him. But she's actually there to find her natural mother, and he's been betrayed all the way down the line. She didn't present herself realistically, so how can he believe?

So you create things. Coming up with ideas is simply a matter of sitting down and saying, "Okay, I'm going to have a man and a woman in a romance novel." Then make the decision: Strangers or not? If they are strangers, then what unexpected thing can bring two strangers together?

S: And that unexpected thing, that's your hook?

J: Yes. Like in *Sentimental Journey*. Yes, they have a past relationship because he dated her sister, and he was the bad boy from the wrong side of the tracks. And now he's after her, but is he really? Or is it just that she looks like her sister?

You come up with things that are *not* expected. In a way, it might be easier to say, "Okay, they meet on a street." Well, that's pretty boring. What can we do to make this not boring?

Did she get mugged? Then we make it a city . . . I don't know. . . . Did a dog bite her in the rear? What can we do . . . ? Was it his dog? *Should* it have been his dog?

S: We could have *him* bite her on the rear but . . . no, never mind.

J (*laughs*): You just keep playing with the idea of a dog and you keep asking questions. Maybe he's blind and it's a guide dog.

S: And even if it bit her, he's not going to have it put down, he *needs* that dog!

J: Right. You just keep playing with these questions.

S: So what was the hook in *Gone With the Wind*?

J: The hook in *Gone With the Wind* comes late in the

book because it starts when she meets Rhett. The hook is that she thought she was in love with another man when she was really in love with this man. So, it's chasing the wrong man.

S: Not knowing your own heart.

J: Right.

> *JANET: I've never been pigeonholed. I can write historical novels or contemporary novels, action or drama, about rich people or poor people. My fans don't expect to always get the same thing from me. And they don't have any problem with that. In fact, they're guaranteed that when they pick up one of my books it will be different from all the others.*

RESEARCHING ALL THAT FASCINATING TRIVIA

S: We talked about where you get your ideas already. Sounds to me like you get them through this process of elimination you were talking about, and it sounds like you develop them during the research.

J: Yes, I recently researched Kentucky, until I was blue in the face, and nothing came. I thought I had this whole story of a thoroughbred dynasty, and I just couldn't find that hook to make it different.

But I love horses. And I thought, Why can't you do this?

I get the idea when the time's right, but you can't force it. You have to take the idea where it comes and put it where it belongs.

The research and details are Bill's responsibilities:

the layout of the area, and streets, locations of public buildings, even the decor of hotels and restaurants. If we describe a real restaurant, and the table at which the hero and heroine dine has a blue tablecloth, you can be certain that the tablecloth is blue. He's my right arm.

But even though Bill obtains the research, I still have to read it. I probably use only thirty percent of the material he brings me, but until I've read it, I don't know what I'll need. Although I don't physically go out and gather the information, I always visit the place where my book is set.

But all the questions that arise—the kind of crops in the field or the names of an area's trees—are up to Bill to answer. He also researches all my characters' occupations. Then I establish their personalities and come up with the plotline. And sometimes I bounce my logic and ideas around, asking Bill, "Could this have happened this way?"

JANET: I don't put great beauties in my books. I like down-to-earth, straightforward, plain-spoken women. Of course, I've had some fun with other types, manipulative flirts and such, but my favorite heroines are more like Jessie in Calder Born, Calder Bred.

JANET DAILEY CHARACTERS— LARGER THAN LIFE!

S: How do you create a character who is true to his times, but sympathetic?

J: Nobody is ever all bad. There's good in everybody,

and you can't have a character who's all evil. A hero/
heroine can't be all good.

S: How do you make them true to their time, but not
committing acts that are politically incorrect now, or
blatantly morally wrong? Perhaps their times were
extreme, and those actions were totally acceptable in
their day.

J: You make them ahead of their time. I think the closest I came to doing that—'cause I try not to handle
that—was in *The Pride of Hannah Wade*. My main
guy, Cutter, was the hero, the protagonist of the
book. In the opening scene he's a white officer in
charge of black soldiers and they are at a trading post
where the man will allow their horses to drink, but
he won't allow the soldiers to drink his water. And
Cutter gets angry and wipes his hand across the
black man's face and says, "Look, it doesn't rub off."
Which was very insulting to the guy, to the black
soldier. Cutter realizes that when he sees the man's
face.

His reason and his excuse is, "I'm tired of hate. I'm
tired of whites hating blacks. I'm tired of whites hating Indians. I'm tired of hate."

As an officer in the Civil War, he had seen so
much hate and its results.

The same with the female protagonist who is kidnapped by the Apaches. Her initial reaction to the
Apaches is: they smell bad, they aren't noble savages
by any stretch of the imagination. Until she is forced
to live with them, sees the love within the family
unit, sees beyond the surface. I think that's the best
way to handle it. Your character may think, *This is
the way it is, but I don't think it's right*. He does it
because that is what's expected of him, or he *doesn't*
do it, which causes him conflict.

S: Do you ever have characters that you don't feel as strongly about?

J: There are some I would say in the Harlequins that never leaped. But then there are others—Mitch Braden, the Indy man—I know they existed.

S: You say they're like old friends that you haven't seen in a long time. Do you ever want to write a sequel so that you can hang out with them again for a while?

J: No, I don't. Their story's done. I don't have anything more to say. And somebody else is over here, calling to me.

JANET: Obviously, the success has been achieved and the financial gains have been made. But there are two ingredients that keep me writing—a natural love for my work and an ongoing challenge. And there's a compulsion to tell the story in a way that entertains, yet makes my readers feel, care, and empathize with my characters. The core is my need to communicate what I know, feel, or see. And the one way, for me, is to write down the story word by word.

S: How do you create your characters?

J: Hm. There again, part of it comes from research. In the case of *Tangled Vines*, you start reading.

Once I thought, *television journalist*, I grabbed virtually every biography and/or autobiography that I could lay my hands on about television personalities, male or female. I read about Dan Rather, John Chancellor, and Barbara Walters, finding where the common threads were. If they studied, what they studied or where they studied in school. What they did. Whether they worked at radio stations or television stations. Whatever. Then finding the common threads, surprisingly, in their childhood. It's always there. It's always something stressful in the childhood. Whether it was Dan Rather's father rarely being at home, working far away so that Dan was basically raised in a single-parent environment. Or Barbara Walters with a sister who was retarded.

I found in each case there was something else that pushed them for approval on a grander scale.

After I found the common thing, it became easy to say, "alcohol abuse." When I mentioned that I was working on a book that dealt with an adult child of an alcoholic, people I thought I knew well came forward and said, "My father was an alcoholic."

I realized at that point, sure, sexual abuse is more sensational, but it's much more common to deal with the shame of straight alcoholism. The occasional slap that was unwarranted. The occasional hit that was unwarranted.

S: Alcoholism is a breeding ground for all types of abuse: verbal, emotional, physical, sexual, whatever . . .

J: Exactly. Yes. But I really felt that once you got into sexual abuse, you overshadowed everything else in the story. Because of the sensationalism of it, I felt it was better to deal with alcoholism.

S: Have you written any books where there was sexual abuse?

J: No.

S: Is that why you haven't? Because you felt it was the easy sensational road or what?

J: Well, I don't like sensationalism for the sake of sensationalism.

S: Right.

J: The only reason I would use something sensational like sex abuse or molestation would be to make a point. It's going to be the definite plotline if I ever use it. It will be the major thing, it won't be a minor point.

JANET: Characters have qualities that real people relate to and feel empathy for. Regardless of the story, you have to have good characters.

S: What if your heroine had a zit between her eyes and your hero was a bit on the homely side?

J: I've used it. I did it in the last Silhouette romance that I wrote, called *Leftover Love*, the hero was ugly. But he was larger than life in his bearing; he was a big man . . . tall but ugly. I always give them this larger-than-life quality.

S: Why do you think we want that?

J: Oh, for the same reason that we like John Wayne. The same reason we were drawn to Clark Gable.

There's a certain thing to be said for role models, for seeing someone—even a fictional character—in a certain situation and seeing them acting to correct, not react. I think that gives us that little incentive, I'd like to be like that. Obviously, this is a fictional character and maybe they will never reach that level, but they can strive. And that's what life is. Striving.

S: I think that some authors write closer to their life experiences than others. How much of you and the people around you are in your books?

J: I find it hard to see . . . but there are always a few exceptions. I think I always put a piece of me in the heroine. I probably always put a piece of Bill in the hero. Just so that I can breathe that life into them.

But I have their framework all set. I create characters that will do the story I want them to do, and I have the traits already molded into them, so that they will behave the way I want them to behave. Or, in the case of a historical setting, if I'm laying it against history, then they have to play the roles that will fit into the framework. Sometimes history dictates the characters. Whether it's The Blade or Temple in *The Proud and the Free*. Whether it's *Silver Wings, Santiago Blue,* the whole cast of women in that book. All of them had to be written to fill those roles. So, again . . . sure, maybe my love of flying went into that, but I never experienced the prejudice that they experienced.

Their personalities were so different from mine. Maybe I *wished* I was a little freer like Martie. Maybe I admired Martie's feisty, independent, thumb-your-nose attitude.

S: But I don't believe you would admire those qualities if you didn't have the seed of those within you.

J: Possibly. But I don't think I have a very big seed, if it's there.

S: Can you think of any character that you pulled directly from another person? You just wrote somebody in your life into a book?

J: No. People I meet always ask whether I'll write them into a book or a movie. But no, I don't. Now what I might do—if somebody has an unusual mannerism, whether it's shrugging their shoulder in a nervous reaction, that I've never thought of using before to illustrate a character—and I'll pick that up.

S: That's just observing the world around you.

J: The closest I ever came was in one book that I set in Iowa, called *The Homeplace*. The female characters' memories of the farm were all my memories.

S: That's the closest, really?

J: That's the closest.

JANET: I have to admit, I have a very exciting life. Not everyone gets to go to Alaska and go flying with bush pilots.

CHOOSING THOSE EXCITING LOCALES

J: I believe very much that the setting of a book and the plot have to be married. You can't just arbitrarily say, I'm going to find a place and set a book there. You have to find a plot that fits that area, because I think the background of your book sets much of its mood. I was always trying to do that marriage of plot and background. Some backgrounds make their own plot.

JANET: If someone would have told me I was going to write eighty-two books in eleven years, I

*would have said they were an outright liar; I
wasn't even sure I could write one. But it was like
a dam bursting. Eighty-two books is such a stag-
gering figure, but I wrote them all one at a time.*

OUTLINING

J: I can't outline.

S: You can't?

J: I can't. I tried to, because I read somewhere that a good
writer outlines. I can't. I tried it with either the third
or fourth book, and the minute I wrote it, even in sentence form, I had communicated the idea to paper
and there was no more need to write it. All the compulsion to write was gone, because it was on paper.

S: But what about all the good stuff that's going to come
out while you're writing it?

J: It doesn't matter. I just can't. And I learned very early
that what works for one writer doesn't necessarily
work for another writer.

S: That *is* true.

J: You must find your own way that works for you. And
any person's way—no matter how successful they are,
or no matter how unsuccessful they are—it doesn't
mean their way is wrong.

S: That's true. And I find that people like you—who say,
"I don't ever outline," but they can successfully construct a book—you're outlining it, you've just got it
all up there in your head.

J: Yes, I do.

S: You know where you're going and you know the basic route you're going to take.

J: I know the beginning, the middle, and the end.

> **JANET:** *I have often said I do a lot of my editing in my head before I put it on paper. I really know how a scene is going to affect future scenes in the book as well as how it works with the previous scene. If I see it altering things at that point, before I ever get it down, I stop and say, "Do I want it to change? Is it better if it does?" When I say I don't do revisions, I mean I don't do revisions on paper. But mentally I do revisions all the time.*

S: You know what the conflict is before you start and basically how it's going to resolve.

J: Yes, it may not turn out to be the primary conflict, but I have to keep it in my head. And I do know, with some exceptions, every scene. But I can't physically outline.

S: I have to because my brain isn't that efficient. Maybe it will be someday. I find it difficult to work with students who absolutely refuse to have any kind of outline. They want to write just whatever is their whimsy that day. And they produce reams of boring, self-indulgent material that is unpublishable.

J: There are a few who have no idea when they sit down what they're going to write. And they have to do this meandering sixty or seventy pages before they can get their brain to thinking what the story actually is. Then they need to throw it out.

S: That's fine if they have the self-control to throw it out. But so many of them don't. "Oh, that page has that *wonderful* metaphor; we have to keep it."

J: One thing that I did read a long time ago, that I do with every book, is that you can usually throw away the first three to five pages without ever missing them. And mentally, I make sure . . . do I need to throw away the first three pages. And yep . . . okay, then start on page four.

S: Then you're editing before you put it to paper.

J: That's right. I edit before. But once the page comes out of the typewriter, I will not read it again until the book's done.

S: Seriously?

J: Yes, because one of two things happens. Either I love it or hate it. And if I love it, I want to read it again. I think, "Oh . . . this is so good!"

S (*laughs*): Well, there's nothing wrong with that!

J: But if I hate it, I'll think, "What's the point of going on, it's so bad."
　　So I never read it. I mentally say, "Okay, this scene didn't work. When I get done with the book, I need to go back and look at it." And then I usually can't find it.

S: Because it *does* work?

J: Yes.

S: It was just your self-doubts.

J: It's just my self-doubts. So I wait until the end of the book before I go back.

JANET: I keep a cartoon on my desk of a woman leaning over her typewriter, looking slightly crazed, with papers everywhere, and it reads, "God, I love writing." I think that sums it up— even when it tears your heart out, you love it.

WRITING—THE NUTS AND BOLTS

S: When you began writing your first book, *No Quarter Asked*, did you have more fear then, or more now when you start a book? (This is assuming you have any fear at all.)

J: Oh! Easily the most fear was with the first book, because I didn't even know if I could finish it.

S: Let alone if anyone would buy it, actually give you money for it?

J: Yeah. But Bill had told me a long time ago that it's the things you *don't* do in life that you regret. And I didn't want to be eighty years old, wishing, "Oh, if I'd only written a book. I could have written a book!"

I didn't want that happening. I was going to write it, and I was going to finish it. That was all I wanted. Start it and, come heck or high water, I *was* going to finish it. About halfway through, I made the startling discovery: Hey, I can write!

S: Goody!

J: Yeah, oh golly, this might be good! So I never have fear sitting down to the typewriter. Fear is never part of it.

S: When did that disappear . . . halfway through the first one?

J: Yeah, easily. The fear with the first one was: I'm afraid I might not be able to do this. But after I'd done it, I thought, *I can do this*. And the fear was gone. It's a go.

JANET: I believe that you can do anything you want to do. Nothing can hold you back. No matter what, you can do what you choose.

J: The wonderful, wonderful part about writing is: There are all kinds of stories, for all kinds of people, even in romance or in mainstream. Within the romance genre, you have stories that are sexual, erotica if you will, stories that are extremely sensual, stories that have suspense, stories with that epic feeling. With mysteries, there are all kinds, because there are all kinds of readers. Or humor. You can't say there can be only one kind of comedy. You can't say, "Everyone must laugh at Bob Hope's type of humor, nobody can laugh at Eddie Murphy." See how many different types and styles of comedy and laughter can be done. You can't say, "It can only be slapstick and it can only be Charlie Chaplin." No. We are allowed to listen to and laugh at all of them. The same with reading. There's all kinds. Sure, you may like Eddie Murphy's humor more than you like Johnny Carson, or Jay Leno, or David Letterman. It doesn't matter. We can have them all, and each can have their following, and it doesn't make one comedian better than another. It doesn't make them more skilled. It's just variety, and it's marvelous! It's marvelous that you can find whatever kind of story you want out there.

JANET: *I have a lot of respect for the romance market. The Harlequins, the Pocket Books, Silhouettes—they taught me how to write. After sixty-nine books, I was finding I couldn't generate the same enthusiasm to write them. I knew that I was one step away from writing them for the "wrong reason." Not writing because I liked them, but writing them because they would sell. And I knew the minute I started doing that, I'd start writing bad books.*

S: Do you prefer writing mainstream fiction or romantic fiction?

J: I prefer writing stories.

S: How did I know you were going to say that?

J: Yeah. I never have objected—and never will object—to the romance label, and I can't ever imagine writing a "mainstream" story, where there isn't a love story within it.

I don't eliminate anything. It's never wise. I'll write whatever story intrigues me. That's the way I've always done it, because I get excited about a story idea, I want to go with it. Whether it happens to fall in mainstream, historical, Western, or contemporary, I don't care.

S: You honestly have no preference among those things you just mentioned?

J: Uh-uh . . . Now I know me. I'll always love the West.

I'll *always* love the West. It goes back to one of my attempts at writing song lyrics.

I love the West,
Where the men grow tall,
And rugged and lean,
Wear Stetson hats, and old blue jeans,
I love them out West.
Where the snakes you find are the crawling kind,

and I can't remember it . . . I'm losing it.

S: What do you enjoy the most about writing?

J: Finishing! (*Laughs.*)

S: Amen!

J: Honestly, I think, uh, that's a tough one.

S: I know it is. It's really general.

J: I think that . . . if I'm honest . . . the thing I like the best about writing is coming up with the ideas. Researching it, and seeing it all coming together in my head. And saying all those, "Oooo. I can use that!" and "Oh, gosh, this is going to be so neat!" "Oh, look at how it ties together!" "Oh, is this a miracle, or what!" I love that moment where you see all the disconnected thoughts you had just flowing together.

S: Yeah. Those are the magic moments . . . *rare*, magic moments.

J: Then, of course, getting them on paper is something totally different! (*Laughs.*)

S: That brings us to the next question. What do you hate about writing?

J: Coming up with those words. Sometimes you struggle so, searching for those right words, searching for that right emotion. Grabbing that source. Just seeking some inspiration to give you the urge to write. It's not that you're really looking for the word, you're just looking for that emotion. One of the biggest faults and traps that the writer can fall into is not being secure about the fact that you got your point across, telling something two times when you got it across the first time. It is an easy trap to have a character say something, and then have it appear again in their thoughts to reinforce the idea. It's a terrible trap to fall into.

NOVELS OR SCREENPLAYS?

J: One nice thing about being a writer, a novelist rather than a screenwriter—it's yours.

S: You get to decorate the sets, design the costumes, everything.

J: That's right.

S: I've talked to a number of screenwriters who envy us for that very reason.

J: Of course, because a screenwriter is one with absolutely no control. In my writing I tend to use what they call the filmstrip method. Which is where the scene is played out in my mind, and I can view it from different angles and decide where the focus is, where the close-ups are. And as a result, I can see the whole thing.

S: That's an excellent technique for writing good, commercial, solid, enjoyable fiction . . . don't you think?

J: Uh-huh . . . yeah.

S: I believe we are good at that . . . our generation, that
is . . . because we're the television generation. I really
do. I think it makes us better writers, at least in some
ways.

J: I do, too. Although I'm surprised when I talk to other
writers who say, "Yeah, but don't you put yourself *in*
the character?"
    I say, "No, I don't. I'm always the director."

S: I watch my characters and I listen, and I hear what
they say and get a kick out of it. I think, *Oh, that's
cool. I think I'll write that down.* I feel more like an
observer.

J: Yeah, I do, too.

S: Except for maybe a sex scene. I might kinda slip in
there for a minute or two if it's a particularly good
hero!

---

*JANET: I always wanted to be a writer. But until
you become one, you really have no idea what it
entails.*

S: What is the most difficult aspect of having a writing
career, from the business end?

J: Really, the most difficult thing to learn is the discipline and commitment that's required.

S: Was that difficult for you, or did you just always have it?

J: No. I mean, you can always make excuses for why you're not going to write today. It's endless. You can fritter your time away, instead of making use of it.

S: Are you speaking from personal experience or observation? Do you fritter if you don't look out?

J: Oh sure. Sure. It's both. I've always called it the PCDs of writing. You need persistence. You need patience. Patience is probably about the most valuable thing around, because it's going to require *patience* to finish the book, and persistence.

Once you are done you have to have patience waiting for someone to read it. Then you have to have *patience* while you wait for a contract. Then you have to have *patience* to get it published and *patience* to see the cover art and *patience* to see any money out of it, from all these things. It's just patience.

"C" is courage and commitment. It takes a ton of guts to write a book, because you never know if you are right. You always have to battle self-doubts, your own self-confidence. So you need tons of courage, and commitment. Once you start, by George, you're going to do it. You commit yourself to writing. You commit yourself as you would to a job. "Yes, I've taken on this job, and yes, I'm going to work on it every day." And you've got to have that commitment.

It almost coincides with dedication and discipline. There's a fine line. You dedicate yourself to writing. You don't allow outside things to come in. You don't allow the distraction. And the discipline to keep at it.

You can't get into writing to make money. Not in the real sense. You have to recognize that when you start out, the chances are you're not going to be one of those that makes five million dollars on your first contract. Chances are, you're not going to write *Gone With the Wind*. The odds are against it.

You have to recognize that to write a manuscript, and to make a lot of money on that manuscript— even if it turns out to be a bestseller—it's probably going to be three years down the road. You can't expect to sit down and make money at it the first year. That's where the dedication comes in. If you're choosing a writing career, you have to be willing to put in the time to become established. Get that financial momentum going to where you have this many books coming out this often. This way you're going to have a steady income, royalty-wise, to carry you.

S: Do you have any words of encouragement for the struggling romance writers out there?

J: Oh. There are struggling writers everywhere. It's hard, too, because they all want the magic. They always want to know what the magic secret is. And there isn't any magic secret. The magic secret is writing. Writing . . .

S: That's the hard part.

J: Yeah. It's the hard work, and everyone wants to find out if it's easy. You know, for years I thought writing was hard for me. Every time I'd have to do a descriptive paragraph, I'd just have to tear it out of my brain, one silly word at a time, and everybody said, "Oh, your descriptions were so wonderful." God! I just labored over these things.

JANET: Writing description is the hardest for me. I never seem to have a great deal of problem

with dialogue and working out speech manner-
isms, but I have a great deal of difficulty with
description. A lot of people have said they love
the description in my books. Maybe it's because I
work harder at it.

J: Then I figured if writing is so hard, I can't be any good. If I was *really* good, it would be really easy. Well, no, honey. That's not the way it works. And so there isn't any magic.

S: Do you feel that you have gotten better over the years?

J: Ignorance is bliss. Yeah.

S: Does it become more difficult as you become better?

J: It gets harder. With the number of books I have behind me, when a scene is going really easy and the dialogue seems to be flowing, I always stop and look. Am I repeating a scene that I've used before?

S: How on earth do you remember if you've used that joke, or that metaphor . . .

J: You'd be surprised. Once you've stopped and you look back, you say, "Have I said this?" There's usually a little alarm bell going off, saying, "Yeah. You have, honey. You've put them in the same situation that led up to it, the same way. Back off. Come at it another way."

S: I find that really difficult, too. I forget, especially when I'm writing one book right after another. "Did I just put that in the last one?" Worse yet, if I'm writing two at once.

J: Oh. See, I can't.

S: You don't write two at once, ever?

J: No. No, because if I did I'd never finish any book. I always get a better idea that I would much rather be doing. I know I'd be in the middle of one and get another idea. I'd just as soon not have all these unfinished books. I would never finish a thing. So I have to make myself start and finish this book, and that's the reward. That when I'm done, I get to think about the next one.

> *JANET: Between books I get away from it as far as the book writing is concerned, but I might do other writing in relation to some of our other businesses—things of that nature. But I pretty well try not to worry about the writing until it's time to write another book.*

S: This can really be a tough industry. What words of warning do you have for writers? How they can guard their hearts?

J: Well, it's difficult because editors serve a purpose, but you have to be true to your creative soul. If it makes you totally unhappy to write a book, and if you hate writing romances, then write something else that feeds your creative soul.

If you're dying to write mysteries, instead of whatever it is you're writing, write a mystery. Follow your heart in writing. All the money in the world will never make up for feeding that soul, for doing what the heart tells you to. Follow the heart. And I think that's true in writing or painting, or . . . Doesn't matter if bowls of fruit sell more than abstract art, if that's where your heart is. Get a part-time job. Don't paint apples, just because it sells, if your heart's not in it. If you can put your heart in it, and it works, go for it. Don't say, "Well, I only want to write Westerns" if you have never tried something else. Try that other thing, and then find out if it works for you. Don't ever be afraid to stretch. Don't say, "I can't do that," just because you've never done it.

S: This is a ludicrous question, considering the last few days. If you had it to do all over again, would you have become a professional writer?

J: Oh, yeah. I can't imagine not writing. It's like, you'd have to tear out part of me. I wouldn't be Janet Dailey anymore. I wouldn't be me.

S: What about when you're ninety-seven and those fingers won't work anymore, what are you going to do?

J: Oh, probably by then I would have moved on to some other challenge. You know, you always say, "I can't imagine life without writing," but that's simply because I don't see down the road. I just might find something that excites me so much more. I don't know what. I can't imagine life any other way. That doesn't mean that God doesn't have plans up there that I don't know about.

My grandfather came from Germany, and I remember shortly after my first book was published, and I'd gone home, a reunion. One of our usual reunions where it's just whoever's around, and it turns out to be a hundred and fifty people. And I'd had maybe one, or two, or three books published. My Aunt Genny was so excited and saying so much about how wonderful it was that I was published. And she said, "You have a God-given talent." And my Grandpa said, "Yeah, but her gift to God was—she used it." And I think about that. Maybe that's the real sin. That we have a talent and that we don't use it. When God gives you an ability, and you turn your back on it, I think that's the real sin. It's not how you use it, it's that you didn't.

S: Do you feel pretty good about your use of that?

J: I do. I do. There's a lot of Midwestern values in the books I write and the people I write. That feeling that if you do right, if your heart's right, and you work hard . . . in the long run everything will turn out okay.

The worst advice I ever got was, "Write what you know."

S: Really? Why?

J: Write what I know? I know about Iowa. Does that mean I have to write about farmers and cornfields? That's not what I want to write about. What do you mean, "Write what I know"?

But that's what my teachers told me. What I didn't realize, what I didn't look beyond, is research-ing.

S: Don't you think you write what you know emotion-ally, relationship-wise, which doesn't matter if you're in Iowa or Paris?

J: Yes, but they would always look at Mark Twain . . . he did the rivers, and he knew this. Well, Iowa may be what I know, but I didn't want to write that.

I keep thinking, what if somebody gave that advice to Stephen King? Write what you know? Poor man.

Also, I was told by my guidance counselor and teachers that I should go to college, to university, because I could get a scholarship. But then I'd have to be a newspaper reporter, a journalist, or write travel articles, or teach. But I didn't want to do that! I wanted to write *novels*! I mean, I *zeroed* in . . . *novels*! And it was really clear to me that if I couldn't do that, why spend the money?

S: What, to you, is the difference between a good, mediocre, or lousy book? Is it the characterization, plotting, pacing?

J: It has to be all three. Because if you don't have believable characters, you're already in trouble from the start. If you can't believe that they live next door, maybe they could live down the street. You have to have that ability to identify or say, "Yeah, I know them."

S: What keeps them from being believable?

J: Stupidity. No, I shouldn't say that. It's one of those things that you know it when you see it, but unless you've got an example . . . you can't generalize. So if you have flawed characters, even the best plot in the world will not save characters that you don't care about.

S: And flawed characters are . . . illogical?

J: If the reader is told that this particular character, be it a man or a woman, is strong and independent. And the first scene you see them in, they're Willy Nilly, that they are falling apart over some little thing, they aren't strong. You're trying to tell us that they're strong, but you're showing us they're fools. It's a contradiction that you can't support. You've put them into a situation that shows a different character entirely. And we can't believe the character that you told us they were.

At the same time, the best characters in the world can't save a poorly plotted book.

S: What makes a bad plot?

J: Oh, there are many things that can make a bad plot. One thing is allowing that outside, magical cure that comes in at the last minute to bring them together. Instead of the two people working to get to the point where they resolve their problems. To have somebody come in and say, "It's all okay. Everything is forgiven. You really do belong together." And it's over. No personal growth, no personal commitment.

It's sort of like if you read a mystery and you're trying to figure out who did it and then all of a sudden a guy you never met is the one who did it, you're ripped off. You're cheated.

Then there's timing. In a novel, timing keeps the action moving forward, or keeps you discovering something in every scene. That's everything. What's the scene there for? If you can't find a reason for that scene being there, why are you writing it?

It isn't sufficient to say, "I must have a love scene. That's why they're together." But that isn't true. It may be what happens in the scene, but it isn't why they're together. They're either together because you're going to lead to the point of conflict or you'll write something into the scene that foretells that they're going to have a problem in the next scene. You have to have a reason for every scene. And they need to know what that reason is, because that's the pacing that leads you to the next scene.

S: Is there any book that when you look back, you say, "That's the best I've ever written"?

J: Oh, no. I haven't written the best I can.

S: I mean, to this point, the best you've written.

J: No, I can't. I can't say best or even favorite. It's like saying which is your favorite child. I'm sure I could look back and find some books that I don't look at with as much pride, but then there's something special about each one. I look at the Calders and part of me will say, "That's it." But then I say, "No, no, no . . . *Hannah Wade. Hannah Wade* was so good!" But then I'll look at what I did with *The Great Alone*, and what I did with *Silver Wings*. No . . . I can't, because my interests are this big. (*Holds her hands wide.*) My loves are this big, and the things that fascinate me are that big.

S: You look like a little kid saying, "I love you thi-i-is much!"

J: I guess that's why I have to write. And that's why I resent—and I won't allow, and occasionally I suffer for not being what everybody expects me to be every time.

S: Well, how can you?

J: I can't. Not every book I write can be a Western.

S: Are you saying there are people who are going to be disappointed if it isn't a Western?

J: Of course.

S: But you would also be criticized if every book you wrote was a Western.

J: Exactly. And I know the publishers would like me to

be either historical or contemporary, make up my mind. But I'm going to be both. I can't live in the past, and I can't live in the present. I have to be able to live in both.

S: Which book has been the most successful for you, just on a simple monetary scale?

J: Which book? I don't know.

S: No, I mean contemporary or historical?

J: I really can't say. Each book sells more than the last, but then the backlist comes up and . . .

S: Is that true? Each of your books sells more than the last on its initial run?

J: Yes, it does.

S: Janet, that must be wonderful for you.

J: It is. They're all contemporary books, but that's all I've had out recently. But then, I can't really say that, because you've got the Calders, and they're just coming back out and they're selling again.

S: And asking which you enjoyed writing most is probably going to get me the same answer . . .

J: If you really want the truth, my favorite book will always be the next book.

S: You really mean this, don't you? It's not just the politically correct thing to say.

J: I don't think any book, even the book I'm working on, the Cherokee book—even though I'm making that communication link that I want to make, and I'm telling a story that needs to be told, and it's working— I also know that there's another story over here, and if I can just get done with this one, I can get to that one.

JANET: I've always contended that romance must be reality. It's a rose-tinted reality, but it must be reality. If you don't deal with reality, you're writing fantasies.

REALITY OR FANTASY?

S: Do you feel that your books reflect reality or fantasy?

J: I think they reflect a "rose-tinted" reality. Fantasy to me is true fantasy, that it can never be. My books realistically show commitment between people. They realistically show genuine problems that have to be solved. And they *can* be solved. The novels I write always have to reflect reality, but it's a rose-tinted mirror.

S: You just told me what is real about them; what is the rose tint?

J: The rose tint is the absolutely stunning hero, the absolutely beautiful heroine. The setting, whether it's Aspen, Colorado, whether it's Montana and the big scope of the plains, there's always that larger-than-life aspect.

S: Do you think that's necessary?

J: I like it.

HAPPY ENDINGS

S: Not all of your characters live happily ever after, but overall, they usually do.

J: Well, let me put it this way, I have the tendency that my endings are happy; they just aren't necessarily tied up neatly with all the bows. And I think that goes back to my belief: I believe in happy endings. I believe that life is a series of happy endings. That's why one area, whether it's your relationship with your husband or your boyfriend, although it resolves, there's still something here dangling that's unfinished. And when I'm writing the books, I do admit that I tend to leave a little piece of unfinished business. I believe that my main characters are going to get together and everything is going to be fine. There's going to be more trouble for them, but I believe that they're going to be able to handle it because I believe in happy endings.

One of the best compliments I think I've ever gotten—and I get a lot of good compliments—was when I was writing my book set in Vermont, *Green Mountain Man*. And my niece, Laurie, loved to read and she read my book in manuscript.

My female character had a child by a man, and the man didn't know it was his child. They met, and all through the relationship, up to the point where they got together, he still didn't know that the daughter is his daughter.

Laurie said to me when she finished the book, "But he *is* going to tell the girl that he's the father, isn't he?" And I thought, *She believed. She believed.* She wanted me to tell her that they would work it out, but she knew they were going to work it out. I believe life goes on, and if the characters live for you, when you're reading a book, you wonder what happens to them next.

S: I know what you mean. I've actually had arguments with my ex-husband about whether or not Scarlett or Rhett got together again after *Gone With the Wind* —

J: AHH! You believe they didn't, too! I don't think they did either!

S: Rhett was too burned. She just took it too far. He really *did* get over her.

J: At one point I was asked if I would write a sequel to *Gone With the Wind*, and if I would have Scarlett and Rhett get together, and I said, "Absolutely not!" I wouldn't have them get together. However, if I ever wrote a sequel, *his* child might get together with *her* child.

S: That would be interesting.

J: But no, Rhett and Scarlett would never . . . Actually, that was the highest praise, when my editor read my Cherokee saga, she said that Temple, my female character in the book, is every bit as memorable as Scarlett O'Hara, except that she grew up, and The Blade is as strong as Rhett, but he has more depth.

S: Now *that* is a compliment!

J: Yeah, I thought, *If you're just blowing smoke, honey, that's okay.*

S: What is your favorite thing, the very best part of being an author?

J: Finishing a book.

S: What happens when you finish a book?

J: I don't know. Are you this way? The hardest part for me is the last two chapters, definitely the last chapter, because I already know everything I'm going to do and it's boring. I've already got another idea that's pulling me.

PART III

Women, Men, and Sex

WOMEN

JANET: I write about women's lives, and women are involved in more things now than ever before. I can't stand writing about weak women. In the first Harlequin novel I wrote, the heroine didn't have a career. It wasn't even considered that she *might* have a career. And the hero was very dominating. In the last romance I wrote for Silhouette, the hero was ugly. And the woman was a reporter, searching for her natural parents.

My heroines say no to men; they have careers.

Women read my books and see an unhappy character become better off because she is willing to change.

MEN

JANET: Most people would say, "Women want security, and they fantasize about having a lot of money and pretty clothes—high living." But what a woman really wants is access to her man—she doesn't want to compete with his boss for his attention or for his time. She wants him to be the boss and to give his time to her.

So in a romance, if a man isn't rich, he's always in some way independent. He can be a dashing scoundrel or a hunting guide or an oil wildcatter, but he's always in control of his fate.

In a romance novel, you must remember, the man is the sex object. The heroine spends a lot of time thinking about him, so he's observed in a lot of detail, described much more carefully than the woman is. He tends to run to type, but it's a very attractive type.

Women want a man who is gentle, who has a sense of humor; a man who seems arrogant but is strong enough to be vulnerable, strong enough to change—like Rhett Butler.

SEX

JANET: When Bill and I were first married, I was a typical woman of the time. I was Bill's wife. I had no identity. I was passive. We made love when Bill wanted to, even if I didn't feel like it. I was a prisoner of my inhibitions.

My first Harlequin and Silhouette heroines were as passive as I was. Sexually, they always waited for the man to make the first move. I would have found it extremely awkward to write anything else.

But the more I wrote, the more my self-esteem grew, and so did my sexual imagination.

About ten years ago, I wanted to write a novel, *Touch the Wind*, that was too risqué for my publisher. It was eventually picked up by another publisher and became my most successful novel to that date. In it, the heroine discovered her own sexuality and freedom.

About that time, I began to allow myself more freedom in the bedroom. The wonderful thing that comes with maturity is the attitude: Nothing ventured, nothing gained. Rather than wait for Bill to initiate, I became the aggressor.

One evening in particular; it was Bill's birthday. He was out all day, and I was home, writing. At five P.M., I closed all the curtains, lit candles—the whole romantic number. Then I set the air conditioner on high and put on a fur coat with nothing underneath. When Bill got home, I opened the coat and let it slip slowly to the ground. He was shocked at first, but he loved it!

Maybe you tried something new, and it didn't work out. It's perfectly okay to laugh about it.

It's wrong to take lovemaking too seriously. If you expect bells to go off every time, you're in for disappointment. Just because you don't have an orgasm doesn't mean your man's not a great lover. Making love means caring and trying to please, and as long as that feeling is present on both sides, why not simply enjoy it? You can even have a good laugh together sometimes. Realizing I didn't have to be the perfect lover had its payoffs. My anxiety and doubts disappeared, and our lovemaking improved tremendously. The frequency hasn't changed, but it's much more intimate and spontaneous now.

At this point in our lives, Bill and I are well aware of each other's preferences. Better yet, we're able to fulfill them. I really love to be kissed on the neck. Years ago, I'd just wait and hope he'd do it. But now I'll say, "Um, hon, get my neck." And Bill? He loves it when I nibble on his ear. It really turns him on.

ROMANCE

JANET: As you grow older, your notions about romance stay pretty much the same, but your ideas about love change. Romance still means walking through the woods on a clear autumn day or sharing a glass of wine in front of the fireplace. You always think of it in those strong courtship terms. But love is stronger than that. Love comes from shared situations, shared feelings. The link of friendship holds you together. As time goes on, you learn to value this even more, because you discover the rarity of it. There's a point in a book where romance begins to turn into love. That's what we hope will happen in our own lives.

The erotic element is fun, but the relationship is really more what it's about. Courtship is exciting, and it's wonderful to be able to experience that in the context of love.

JANET: Romance is a mood, a state of mind. That's why we say, "I'm in the mood," or sometimes, "Wait until I'm in the mood." When I write, I try to create that state of mind, that feeling. It's a nice feeling, and it's one of the reasons romance novels are so popular.

JANET: On the whole, I think romance is thoughtfulness. That may not sound very sexy, but it is. In courtship, a man can't do enough for a woman. He tells her she looks nice, gives her flowers, kisses her hand, is attentive to everything she does and says.

Disillusionment with marriage sets in at a point when he stops acting that way, and the woman feels a tremendous loss. She has lost that wonderful part of the courtship when he treated her as if she were the most important person in the world.

You have to work at romance. You can get a man to be romantic by doing something for him. You can bring him his coffee and orange juice in bed, and the minute he feels like the pampered king of the kingdom, he wants to do something benevolent. It's just the way courtship worked with you, but turned around. In a real relationship you have a two-way situation.

I remember that once when Bill and I were on the road, we ended up walking on the coast of Cape Cod on a dreary, blustery, cold, miserable day. We had to go down a long stretch of beach to get to the car. It was so cold that we could hardly walk, and at one point we had to huddle behind some rocks to get away from the wind. We cuddled up to each other to get warm and we watched the waves, which looked pretty threatening. We felt especially close at that moment, and it has become a memory we both cherish.

MARRIAGE

S: A lot of this, we've already talked about, but we'll go over them anyway. What do you think constitutes a good romance relationship or a good marriage?

J: Commitment and trust. If there isn't the emotional commitment and the physical commitment—then the wedding rings, the vows, throw it all out the window. It doesn't exist. There is no relationship, because you haven't committed to it. And if you don't have the trust, you'll never have the respect. If you don't have that, you can't love. So you've got to have commitment in a relationship.

S: Is it something that one person has to earn or that one person has to give?

J: It's all going to be dependent on the individuals and their experience. With some maybe it's as automatic as breathing. With others, it may come hard.

S: Probably based on past experiences. If someone has betrayed your trust once, does that ruin the trust in a relationship forever?

J: No. It goes back to that old saying, "Fool me once, shame on you. Fool me twice, shame on me." Everybody gets a second chance.

S: Is that how you see that? I always interpreted that phrase to mean, if I am stupid enough to give you a second chance to betray me, then that's my own fault. That's what I thought it meant.

J: No. I grant you, the second time is my fault . . . but at the same time, I think everybody deserves a second chance.

S: How many?

J: God gives you as many as you want. I don't think in the human world you do, and I don't think you should. You should recognize that when you give the second chance, that you are open. And if you have put your heart and soul back into it, blindly, without recognizing it, chances are it could happen again.

S: Sounds like almost a qualified trust.

J: Uh-hm. It's qualified at that point. You have to earn it, or the other person has to earn it, but you still get the second chance.

MEN'S AND WOMEN'S ROLES

S: Do you think that men's and women's roles have changed in the past twenty years?

J: Ha-ha!

S: I know, stupid question . . .

J: We are in such a state of flux, this whole world. I was lucky. I was brought up in a home with a liberated woman, and I married a man who was liberated and I felt I could do anything I wanted to do.

And so I never felt limited by anyone I was

around. But that isn't true of the world as a whole and of society as a whole.

We are, right now, in a society without tradition, and when you rip what has been a role out of lives, and don't have something to put back in, there's a hole. Everything starts falling apart until we reestablish a tradition.

I keep thinking how it must have been for the pioneers, those first ones who were on the wagon train west. They had traditions that they had observed back home: Christmas, family get-togethers ... Then certain catastrophes occurred and *ripped* it, *ripped it out*! They were stuck out on the prairie with no other human being for miles around.

Tradition got ripped to pieces and it had to be reestablished.

It can be done. We just haven't got to the point where we understand equality and how to handle it between men and women, between races. We still don't know how to handle it.

OBSERVING "DAILEY" TRADITIONS

J: I remember once, when Bill and I first got together, I thought to myself, *I am not going to do anything that I am not prepared to do for the rest of my life.* Now, he gets coffee and orange juice in bed every morning. Every morning I bring him his coffee and orange juice. And I asked myself the first time I did it, "Are you ready to do this for the rest of your life? If you're not, stop right now. Bring it to a halt."

Making coffee has become, in our own private lives, a way of saying, "Yeah, honey, I love you."

S: Do you think he knows that?

J: Oh yes. Oh yes.

S: So that's what making the coffee is about. I noticed that it's a real ritual around here.

J: Uh-huh. And every once in a while, he'll get up and get me a cup of coffee. And that's his way of saying the same thing.

S: Does he have a ritual that he does?

J: He never leaves without telling me goodbye. Never goes anywhere, never walks out of the house without saying he's going to be outside. (*Laughs.*) We can be mad. Just have been in the biggest, dirtiest fight, and Bill'll stick his head in, "I'M GOING OUTSIDE! NOT THAT YOU CARE!"

S: Do you feel that the changes in society have also changed your relationship?

J: Naw. Bill's . . . They broke the mold when they made him.

S: Do you think your writing reflects the changes that are going on in society?

J: Yes. To a certain extent, because you read my first Harlequins, they reflected the society of their times, and they started reflecting the more liberal relationships. I'm not going to say "free love" because they don't reflect "free love." I don't believe there is such a thing as "free love," and now you see the pendulum swinging back to a more conservative side, more moral values.

PERSONAL CONVICTIONS

S: Moral values . . . Ah, yes . . . Let's talk about your personal convictions.

J: Oh-oh. Personal convictions. I don't know what that means.

   I have found that when things go wrong, they go wrong because it's the best thing for you. And if you aren't getting something that you wanted, it's because there's something better.

   Two things that apply: For every door that closes, there's another one that opens. And, things fall apart so that things can fall together.

   Every time something doesn't go right, whether it's business plans, personal plans, or whatever, I know that it's going to work out for the best. I don't know why. It's just something that my character needs to go through—my *personal* character—for some other reason. But it's always worked.

S: Is that even the really tough stuff? Most of us, when we look back over our lives there are four or five things that really, really hurt, even years later. Those too?

J: Yes. Even those. My senior year of high school was the time of the Hong Kong flu, and I came down with it. I had a fever of 104 degrees, and the doctor came to the house—doctors still came to your house —

S: Back in the o-o-o-ld days.

J: That's right, back in the *old* days. And he gave me a heavy dose of penicillin, which is the only thing that ever cured me all my life. And I developed an allergic reaction to penicillin.

   Eventually, I got better. And, of course, my senior year I didn't know what I was doing with my life. It was that whole, "What do I do now? School's over. I'm glad school's over, but do I go on to college? What do I do with my life? I don't know what I want to do."

   So you have all this nervous anguish. And I lost all

my hair. They never knew if it was because of the fever, the allergic reaction, the stress, or a combination.

But it was astonishing. We don't call it a crown of glory for nothing—but at the time I learned that the people who were my friends were still my friends.

S: Even if you had a scarf on your head.

J: Even if I had a scarf on my head. I did end up getting a wig, but it looked like a wig.

S: How long did that last? Did it just fall out and immediately grow back?

J: Uh-huh. Well, they put me on cortisone to try to force it to grow back, and every time it would get about an inch and a half it would fall out.

S: Oh no. How awful for you.

J: It was about two and a half, three years.

S: Boy, that is tough. Especially at that age.

J: And that was when I met Bill.

S: Well, apparently you didn't need hair to get Bill.

J: At the time I was going to confess to him, he said, "I already knew it."

And I thought, *Oh, okay, I guess I don't have anything to confess. I worked all this up for nothing.*

But at times it was difficult, some times more than others. Some times it was, "Okay, so what?" But it did make me look at other things, like, if I had got caught up in vanity or if I was working toward vanity . . . there's just no chance to do that. (*Laughs.*) Just no chance when you have no hair. It just eliminates all that.

S: Now, Janet, you can't tell me that you don't enjoy being a beautiful woman . . . come on. . . .

J: Bill keeps me square and on the ground. There's such truth in what he said, it makes you realize the real truth of it. He's told me this for years, "Honey, you're beautiful . . . on the inside." And I've realized how much more important it is to be beautiful on the inside.

S: I guess, but I have to admit, I'd like to be both.

J: That's true. We all like to know we look good.

S: At least in someone's eyes.

J: I guess so, but again, I look at Evie and I look at Marilyn and I look at others, and I see the beauty on the inside that so shines through that they appear beautiful.

S: Oh, absolutely. And vice versa, too. Someone can appear very pretty, then you get to know them and you say, "Wait a minute . . ." But that *is* true. My eighty-two-year-old grandmother is beautiful.

J: Also, when you're really "beautiful," there's tremendous responsibility that goes with it. Someone asked me, "How can you stand being fifty years old and having all these mirrors around? Doesn't that bother you?"

It probably would if I went around worrying, saying, "How many more new lines have I got here? How many more lines have I got?" But if you start doing that, I think you get caught up in feeling that you must be perpetually young and svelte. I don't want to put on weight, simply because it makes me so uncomfortable with my medical condition, and because of health. But I don't ever want to spend so much time taking care of, and making sure of, my appearance. My identity is not in my outward appearance. And if you want to identify me by my appearance, then you aren't meeting *me*. You aren't even seeing me.

S: I'm working on that. I'm not to that point yet. I envy you having arrived there.

J: I just don't want to spend that much time. There are too many other things to do than sit there, day after day . . . (*applies imaginary makeup*). On a book tour, I can get out of bed twenty minutes before I have to leave the hotel room—assuming I've showered the night before—I can get out of bed, be fully dressed, makeup on, and my bags packed.

S: We're talking full makeup, your "show" face?

J: Yep, yep.

S: That's phenomenal!

J: I just don't want to spend the time. I've been with women who are forty-five minutes to an hour in the bathroom, getting ready to go somewhere.

S: I got over that as soon as I had my first child.

J: I'm talking about women who didn't have any kids. And I just thought, *This is not worth it.* I guess it doesn't feed whatever's necessary in here. (*Points to her heart.*) It doesn't feed the real soul. The other thing about being married to Bill, the fifteen years difference in our ages, I have learned that age is so relative. He was already in his thirties, so thirty wasn't old. Then he was already in his forties, and forty wasn't old. The same with fifties.

There's a line in a John Denver song, "It really turns me on to think of growing old." The first time I heard it, I thought, *Yeah! Yeah!* It does! It turns me on!

S: It does? Why?

J: The freedom!

S: You can just be cranky and tell it like it is . . . that type of thing?

J: That, and the freedom from other people's expectations.

S: Do you really think when you are older you'll feel differently?

J: You do! You worry far less what people think of you now than when you were younger, and it will grow even more.

PART IV

Success and Satisfaction

> **Janet:** Bill asked me, *"Do you want to be the number-one bestselling novelist in the world?"* I said, *"Sure."*

Certainly, success means different things to those who search for it and those who attain it. To most, success can be defined by society's obvious symbols: generous bank accounts, executive properties, profitable investments, fame, public acclaim and adoration.

But while Janet has reached all these pinnacles and more, she doesn't use these enviable prizes as a measure of her success.

To Janet, success equals personal satisfaction. And she finds her satisfaction in many of the simplest things in life.

S: In the sense of being a writer, what is success?

J: Communication. Success to me is taking that idea and getting it down on paper. Watching the tear in the eye. It's getting that thought across. It's entertaining people with a story that also maybe makes them think. Whether it's thinking about a relationship, history, thinking about something they didn't know. It's communicating. It comes right down to that.

S: Did you have a moment when you knew you were successful?

J: Boy. I don't know. I'm sure there must have been, but as a defining moment ... ? It probably occurred one of those times like when my niece Laurie would say, "But are they going to get together? Is he going to tell her that he is her father?" Those moments when you know the story is continual. That the people are alive. I have touched the reader.

S: The characters are so real that the reader knows they have a future?

J: Yes. Yes. I guess those are those moments.

In my mind, unless I say otherwise—and I can't think of a single book where I've said otherwise—the hero and heroine are together. Whether it's Sheila and Rafaga in *Touch the Wind*, Sam and Kelly in *Tangled Vines*, they are together. I don't mean it was easy for them, but they are together.

S: I think that readers want that.

J: Definitely.

> *JANET: Once you are successful, you have to prove to yourself that you're worth it. It's lonely and it's hard, but when you're finished, you've done something no one else could do.*

LIVING UP TO THE IMAGE

JANET: I'm not any different than I was before, but I constantly run into people I knew who are awed, who act like I sprouted wings or something, which is, of course, ridiculous. Bill told me, "Success doesn't change you as much as it changes the way other people look at you."

The first time I met really avid readers, I wanted to talk about other authors I had read and enjoyed, and I knew we would have in common.

They wanted to talk about my books, and that threw me. I didn't understand for a long time why they would look at me as being different from them, because I don't feel any different from anybody else in the whole world.

They do have images built up in their minds, but you only have to live up to the image that you build of yourself, and not let their attitudes change you.

JANET: I couldn't have dreamed this big. The numbers really are too big to comprehend.

THE DREAM . . . AND BEYOND

JANET: Sometimes it's like I have to pinch myself. I always dreamed that I would be a writer, but I didn't dream this big. You only dream that the first book will be accepted. You don't dare dream beyond it.

If I had been told before I started writing what was going to happen, I would have said it was virtually impossible. I never dreamed it would be like this. I never dreamed past the first book. I was just hoping I could sell that. I swear that no writer dreams past the first book.

JANET: I always thought success meant you had some free time. I didn't realize you are only as good as your next book.

JANET: Maybe you have to keep proving to yourself that you are worth it. Each new challenge gives you the opportunity to prove yourself once more. But you always start doubting again.

MONEY

During childhood, Janet's weekly allowance was twenty-five cents, and a portion of that sum was saved for the Sunday school collection plate.

Today, Janet's income is more than $1 million per year. Every day an average of 43,000 copies of her books are sold worldwide.

J: I grew up basically without television. We didn't have television until I was about eleven or twelve years old. Number one: It wasn't that prevalent. Number two: We couldn't afford it.

    I remember our first television was a used one that Mom saved money for by saving all our dimes. We never spent a dime. All of our dimes went into that bank.

S: How long did it take to save that much?

J: I don't know, but she paid ten dollars for that first television.

S: That's a *lot* of dimes!

J: It *is* a lot of dimes.

S: Where did she save them?

J: In a little bank that would count them as you put them in. That's how we got most anything we wanted . . . at Christmas, too.

TELEVISION APPEARANCES

If fame and recognition are any measures of success, Janet has received far more than her "fifteen minutes" worth of fame.

During a guest appearance on NBC's popular daytime show, Days of Our Lives, *Janet played the role of a famous investigative reporter, who had been summoned to Salem, where* Days of Our Lives *takes place. Her character probed the death of Roman Brady, a favorite character on the show.*

Two home videos were based on Janet Dailey books— Foxfire *with Leslie Nielson and Tippi Hedren and* When a Spider Bites, *which is based on* Ride the Thunder.

Janet has appeared on hundreds of television programs, including Nightline, 20/20, Today, Donahue, Hour Magazine, Lifestyles of the Rich and Famous, *the Playboy Channel,* Good Morning America, *and all of the other morning network programs.*

Television interviewers seldom choose to host novelists, because they feel they have no pertinent issues to discuss on the air.

But Janet uses this prejudice to her advantage. She says, "They always talk to romance writers, because it gives them a chance to ask, 'Why do people read this stuff?'" She puts them in their place by replying, "Why do people watch television?"

BILL: *I've built a massive swimming pool at our house, and I'm having tiles made to go around the edge which will be ceramic reproductions of all of Janet's book covers. With her writing speed, I may have acres of tiles around my pool before I'm finished.*

BELLE RIVE

In 1992, the Daileys built a plantation-style mansion on the shore of Lake Taneycomo in Branson, Missouri. The twenty-acre site encompasses formal and informal gardens, broadleaf woods, lush pastures, tennis courts, a twenty-five-by-fifty-foot pool, and verdant lawns that sweep from the house down to the fog-misted lake traveled by paddlewheel riverboats.

The 11,250-square-foot house is called Belle Rive, which means "beautiful river."

The house was inspired by Rosedown, an antebellum plantation in St. Francisville, Louisiana, visited by the Daileys in 1989 as part of their research for Heiress.

Belle Rive's entrance has ornate wrought-iron gates and a circular driveway that curves around a fountain. The spectacular twenty-five-room house is graced by massive white columns, a marble entry, oak staircases, crystal chandeliers, five bedrooms, eight bathrooms, and a 300-square-foot living room with a grand piano. The amenities also include a fireproof room in which are stored the manuscripts and first copies of each of her books, a well-equipped gym, and most importantly, Janet's office.

Architect Bob Killingsworth, AIA, of Dallas designed Belle Rive. The decorator was Gay Freeman of Freeman & Associates, Dallas. Janet and daughter-in-law, Mary Dailey, bought many of the items in St. Louis.

The property includes a house occupied by Janet's mother and stepfather, a large house that is the office of Dailey Enterprises, and a carriage house in which is stored the Silver Streak trailer.

JANET: I'm glad we did all the traveling when we did. I'm becoming quite a homebody. I love being here on the lake. It's very quiet. I have the horses, my son has horses, and I can go riding anytime I want. It's become very nice just to be at home.

THE JANET DAILEY APPEAL

S: Why do you think you have been so successful? What's the key?

JANET DAILEY'S PHOTO SCRAPBOOK

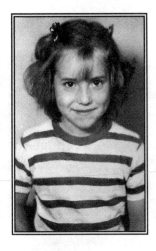

Me in second grade: Mom's harum-scarum tomboy bookworm.

Me with my cousin David Freeman (ages four and five), my raft-building, tree house–building buddy and cohort in crime when we innocently moved a gravestone in old Early cemetery to build a fort. We only confessed to it a few years ago!

Age eighteen, my high school graduation picture. I was voted "Most likely to get married and have five kids.". . . Well, I did get married, but instead of five kids, I gave birth to ninety books, with more on the way.

LMJ Armicia was one of the Arabian mares Bill bought me to commemorate my novel *Heiress*.

Heiress was a yearling. By the time she was four years old she was almost totally white and a real beauty.

Bill snapped my "Daisy Mae" pinup shot late one afternoon while I was actually hoeing in the garden. We used it in a newsletter and had a couple of DJ's on tour request a poster. . . . We complied.

Bill and I outside our travel trailer that served as our home for six years while I wrote the Americana series.

I am one of Louis L'Amour's biggest fans and the proud owner of all his books. This private luncheon at the Beverly Hills Hotel will always be one of the high points of my life. He was every bit as wonderful and warm as I hoped he would be.

Belle Rive, our new home, was another one of Bill's more extravagant gifts to me for my novel *Masquerade*. We had a housewarming party in the spring of 1992 with over 400 guests (can you believe it?).

For three years I coanchored the local Southwest Missouri telecast of the Easter Seal Telethon.

On three different occasions I was a guest cohost with Gary Collins on "Hour Magazine." In our infamous cooking segment, I explained that when they passed out cooking talents I thought they said "book" and went back for a second helping.

LaVyrle Spencer, Sidney Sheldon, and me at a gala book party. Sidney very kindly gave me writing tips—I don't think he had any idea I had already written nearly ninety books at the time!

Boxcar Willie and Ralph Emery, easily two of my favorite people in the entertainment world. Both have written books, too.

This was a publicity photo that I now use as my business card. A photo is worth a thousand words (at least!).

A quiet moment alone for me and Bill.

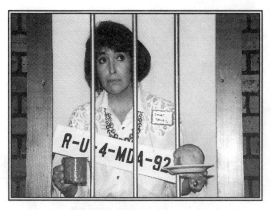

No, I wasn't doing real time—this is the Muscular Distrophy Association Jail-a-thon, where they told me to look sad and pitiful.

During our Kenya safari Bill and I, along with Boxcar Willie and his wife, visited a Masai village. We met the village chief's wives (all five of them) and daughters and "toured" their houses made of cow dung.

To be recognized by your peers and given a Lifetime Achievement Award is truly a great honor and a proud and humble moment. I will always be grateful for it.

Signing books and enjoying my fans.

All my ninety-some books were prepared on a trusty typewriter. However, I am finally joining the modern world and the next book I write will be done on a computer!

J: I don't know. I really don't. I've thought about it a lot, because I'm asked this question all the time. And I've tried and tried to understand what singles my books out. There is the recurring theme of the land, the recurring theme of commitment.

The characters are always very real to me. They're like friends that I haven't seen in a long time. Even now, I don't think of them as characters in a book, I never refer to, "that character I wrote in *Calder Sky*," I always say "Chase Calder, Maggie Calder, Todd Calder." I always say, "Hannah Wade."

JANET: I think all my stories have a common tie to the land. They're about tradition and have a hard core of decency. Sure, readers want to fantasize, but they also want an emotional connection to truth and old family values.

JANET: The first thing is story. The second thing is traditional values. And by that I'm talking about loyalty, fidelity, honesty in relationships. It's also the touching of feelings.

A writer must write it so the reader will feel it, to the point where he hurts and cries and laughs, and he feels the warmth of it.

PART V

Fans

JANET: There isn't any one kind of fan. You almost feel that each book brings out different ones that it appeals to. Of course with *Silver Wings, Santiago Blue*, my first hardcover, I heard from many people who were either women pilots, WASPs, or knew one or flew with one. I had a lot of male readers on that book, and a lot of them said something like, "I was stationed at such-and-such a place, and they had WASPs flying out of the base." I heard from a lot of people who were relating to the material in the book directly.

Usually we hear from people who have suddenly made a change in their own lives. Whether they've gone back to college or they've started writing or they've set up their own business, it seems the books have motivated them in some way to change their lives. They weren't happy before and now they're going to try something that they've always wanted to do. They've been encouraged in some way by the books.

I suppose I remember most clearly the number of letters I received after *Heiress,* saying, "I want you to know after I read your book, I called my sister."

I get letters stating, "I recently went through a prolonged illness with a family member, and I don't know how I would have gotten through it without your books." This tells me many people who have to deal with hard and difficult situations find in my stories an escape avenue that's so necessary in our world today.

But the really fun part is when I get letters from men. After *The Great Alone*, I received numbers of letters from men saying they were stationed in Alaska during World War II and that's exactly the way it was. They seemed to relive the moments through my fictional characters. That told me the feel of Alaska in a particular time period was there.

FAN LETTERS AND BOOK SIGNINGS

Janet has a mailing list of 55,000 fans who receive a newsletter which the publisher issues about her. She actually receives some fan mail that is simply addressed to "Janet Dailey, U.S.A."

JANET: We still answer some of the mail individually, when it's related to some specific book. When it's something general, then we usually acknowledge it through the newsletter. But we read everything that comes in; we don't just let the secretary read it and forget it. We read it personally.

S: Do you remember your first fan letter?

J: Yes, we were in San Antonio, Texas. Bill had gone down to Maldanado's jewelry store, because he had a setting come out of one of his rings. He was getting it remounted. And he was talking to Phil, the owner, who talked us into going to an estate showing. We were staying at the local campground. Lo and behold, this letter came to the campground.

It was from Elaine Donaldson. She and her husband had a used bookstore there, and she knew where I was. That was the very first stamped fan letter I'd ever received. I think I called to thank her, and she said, "Why don't you come down to the bookstore?"

So I went down to see her, and I met the lady who had sent my first fan letter.

Curiously — and I don't know if readers would like to know this — Harlequin never forwarded the letters that were sent to me through them.

S: Is that still Harlequin's policy?

J: I don't know. It was then. They say it's usually addressed to Harlequin, so it's theirs. I never received the letters from readers. When Harlequin used to do their little magazine, there were little things in there that said, "Hey, I like so-and-so's book." Excerpts from fan letters.

S: That's sad, because a lot of readers may think the authors don't care enough to write back.

J: I've written one fan letter in my life. That was to Roy Rogers and Dale Evans after I read Dale Evans's book, *The Littlest Angel*. I was so moved by that book that I wrote to them, and I received a letter back. I was so stunned and awed that they would write me.

I remember how it felt to get a response; I know how it feels when something affects you enough to want an autograph. It's hard to ask for an autograph. If someone cares enough to ask for one, then an autograph is the least you can do for them. I wouldn't be here if not for them.

Several times I've gone to autograph sessions and had fans ask me to sign each one of my eighty books. Do you have any idea how hard it is to lug in eighty books? If they can carry them, I can sign them.

MAINTAINING THAT "GLAMOROUS" J. D. IMAGE

JANET: When people first meet me, they always say, "I thought you would be taller." I tell them, "Well, I think tall."

J: I do recall most vividly the most embarrassing time,

and the one time I wish I could have pretended I wasn't Janet Dailey.

We have our horses and our son Jim's up on the hill. One of his mares and a foal had gotten out of the fence and taken off. Jim came and asked me if I would help get them back in.

I put on my grubbiest jeans and sweatshirt and old boots. It was hot, in June or July, and I pushed my long hair up under a baseball cap. We took off through the woods to find the horses. Finally, we caught them in this godawful place. We were gone about two or three hours, and you can imagine the sweat and dirt and grime. I mean, it was all streaking. . . .

Now, I'll never know why I decided to walk back into the office through the public entrance rather than through the private one. But I did, and I heard my assistant, Sandy, say, "Here's Janet. She'll sign your books for you."

The lady just stared at me. She was *scared*, and I just knew that this was not who she wanted to sign her books. She probably didn't even want me to touch them.

Of course, I laughed and explained the whole thing, how I was out chasing horses. And I said, "Well, you've just met the real Janet Dailey, and if you still want an autograph, I'll give you one." She didn't say a whole lot, and I knew I had just totally destroyed her image of me. I just demolished it.

But I don't think she wanted me to chase horses, either.

I suppose if I'd been wearing some nice little riding outfit, the boots, the red jacket, that would have been okay. But the cap, the sweat . . .

It was a real eye-opener, and I learned that if I leave the house, I'd better be prepared.

S: Which books have your fans loved most?

J: I've written so *many* books that, depending on which reader you're talking to, they will determine which was their favorite.

S: I've really enjoyed your little romances.

J: And I'm proud of them!

S: As you should be!

J: Some of them are wonderful little books and I am proud of them. And there are readers who love them, and that's good.

S: Obviously, they fill a certain need. Maybe a reader doesn't have the time to invest in a larger book.

J: My mother would dearly love me to write them again. Because it's an evening or two a read.

J: *Santiago Blue* . . . I got quite a number of letters from men that said, "I flew with those women. I was stationed here. I know exactly what you're talking about."

S: Would your average fan be surprised at how many male fans you have?

J: Yes, absolutely. Many times I get a letter that says, "My husband and I read your books. And he liked this."

S: I believe you. I heard an elderly gentleman say that someday he wants to look you up and thank you. He said, "I just love her books to death, because she just writes about real people." Isn't that a recommendation . . .

JANET: You know at the point when people are buying the book strictly by your name, without even reading the blurb to see what it's about, that they're buying out of loyalty and you'd better give them the best you can. I find I'm a very competitive person with myself. I always want to do better than the last time and I always want to try new things. So it's a combination of the two. They both sort of push you on to jump a higher fence.

S: Any special words for your fans?

J: There is nothing more intimate, no relationship more intimate, than between an author and a reader, even if we never meet face to face. Because we are sharing the same experience, and I guess that's why when a reader comes up and says, "Janet, I understand perfectly." Because there has been a link. There has been something that we shared in common. And we know we shared it. And so it's natural to be on a first-name basis. It's absolutely natural and right. It's a bonding experience that feels right and feels good. And I guess if there is anything I want the readers to know, it is that I suspect that I am going to be writing as long as they are going to be reading.

S: I think that they would love to hear that.

J: And the best compliment and the highest compliment anybody can give me, and I've had some and they probably are the most precious compliments of all, is when I have received letters from readers who say, "I used to think reading was boring, until I picked up one of your books." 'Cause I figure, if I can turn any-body on to the joy of reading, I have given them the greatest gift in the world.

I can't imagine life without books. They just open worlds for everybody. Anything you ever want to know is in a book somewhere. Any adventure, any trip, any mystery, any challenge. And it's wonderful, and there're always stories waiting to be told.

JANET: There are a lot of people out there who couldn't care less what I write next. I recall once in an airport I saw a lady reading one of my books, and foolishly, I asked her what she thought of it. She said, "Well, I've read better." (Laughs.)

CRITICS

JANET: Obviously I've been accepted by the people who count. Readers have no ax to grind.

J: I've always been amazed at the easy psychological leap that critics of romance novels make when they say that the readers don't have enough romance in their lives. What does that mean? That Stephen King's readers don't have enough horror in their lives?

S: I think it's because they don't read romance. It's easy to be a snob if you haven't read it.

J: Oh, isn't it! It's not like I've ever written the Great American Novel. I don't know that I would want to.

S: Is there really such a thing?

J: If you look at *Gone With the Wind*, or *The Thorn Birds*.

S: Those are the great American novels?

J: Well, they're the big ones . . . they're the big boogers.

S: But even they aren't perfect books; they're just wonderful books.

J: But in their time, they were hugely successful.

S: So are you, my dear.

J: But I haven't written that equivalent. I haven't written *Bridges of Madison County*.

S: No one can know, until years from now, if you're writing literature today. People who tell me they write literary fiction—and they always pronounce it *lit*-errarrry—I have little patience with them.

J: Every time I hear the word "literature" I sort of have this image of a Cecil B. DeMille epic, where the letters are in gold stone and they leap out at you to trumpet fanfare. LI-TER-A-TURE!

S: Just in case you would have missed the fact and thought it was simply a boring piece of self-indulgent writing, we must tell you in advance, *"This* is *literature!"* I thought the definition of literature is writing that endures over the ages. How do they know that what they wrote yesterday afternoon is going to be literature?

J: And does it really matter?

S: To them, apparently.

J: Obviously.

S: Let it.

J: Yes, let it.
   I have to tell you, because it's one of my favorite stories. As I've said, I don't think well off the top of my head. And usually, in an interview situation, when I'm thrown a question that I don't expect, I usually try the old politician's thing of stalling, or whatever. You know, "What a *great* question!"

S: Right, and any minute now I'm going to come up with an answer!

J: I was asked by an interviewer for whom I had high regard. I won't say the person's name, but he was of the ilk of, say, a John Chancellor, what I regard as a real high journalist, a man I respect. And I was asked what book most influenced me as I was growing up. At that point, I'm wanting *desperately* to impress them by coming up with some book that was still true, but impressive.

S: At the age of seven, you read *A Tale of Two Cities*, right?

J: Right. I was going through the list, *Count of Monte Cristo* . . . anything by Dumas. I was running all these titles through my head, *Rebecca* . . . and I wanted to do *My Friend Flicka*. But my mouth opened and out came . . . *The Pokey Little Puppy*.

S: No . . . oh, Janet.

J: It did.

S: No wonder Bill coached you about interviews.

J: And as that came out, I realized the absolute truth, *Pokey Little Puppy* was the first book I ever read. And fortunately, I kept talking. I said, "That was the first book that I *personally* read. I learned how to read sufficiently so that I could read it alone. And it opened up the world of books to me." I saved it!

S: You landed on your feet!

J: I did! But I couldn't believe that I had done it!

S: It worked because it was an honest answer.

J: And even while I was straining to come up with an impressive one, the truth came out.

S: *The Pokey Little Puppy* just plopped out!

J: I did an author luncheon in New York with . . . the *All the President's Men* guy . . .

S: Robert Redford?!

J: No, the real one. Bob Woodward. Anyway, he was there, and I think John Chancellor was there, and another gal who's written some Broadway stuff, and I related that story, which everybody got a real hoot out of. But the truth, the truth will win out.

S: Yes, it will. And the truthful answer is always the gracious one, even if it isn't what you had intended to say.

People's Margot Dougherty called Janet's writing "escapist literature, smooth and shallow."

JANET'S RESPONSE: It's true that they're called escape novels, but they won't work unless there's an element of reality, too. I show a genuine conflict between the hero and heroine. Real or imagined, the conflict exists and they can't wish it away. The characters cope with it, find a way to resolve it, and that resolution involves change—it brings them closer together. We can all recognize that kind of pattern from our own relationships, even if the setting is idealistic and escape-oriented.

BILL: We've talked to critics before, and they can't see any value in this [type of literature]. And, of course, our answer is, "We're not trying to write the Great American Novel. We're pleasing ourselves. We got twenty-two million readers in this country and fifty-three million around the world. We couldn't care less, really." It's nice to be on the *New York Times* [bestseller list], and we are. But if you've got 22 million readers who love the books and they can associate with Janet, that beats hell out of a dozen critics.

THE FANS WANT TO KNOW . . .

S: What are the most common questions your fans ask?

J: Where do you get your ideas? When did you start writing? How did you start writing? How many hours a day do you write? Or, what is your writing schedule like?

S: Do they ask you how much money you get for books?

J: They ask. My pat answer, which you've probably read somewhere, is, "Money is our yardstick for success, but is not the yardstick of satisfaction." I would write whether they would pay me or not, but I'm just not so stupid that I'd give it back.

Bill has said that a thousand times over the years . . . you can't begin with the intention of making money; you begin with the intention of doing the job, and doing it well. And if you do it the money will come, and you won't be able to stop it. It's absolutely true.

You do it because, in your heart, it's the right thing to do. It's what you want to do. You know you can do it the best you can. And when you do it time after time, honestly from the heart, you cannot stop.

You can apply this to every walk of life, if you're a waitress and you enjoy waiting on people and serving them, and you're doing it because you get genuine pleasure from making their evening pleasant, making sure their food's good. You're going to get a sizable tip. You can't stop it.

S: Mary Kay Ash, who formed Mary Kay Cosmetics, said, "Find something that you love to do so much that you would do it for free, and someone will pay you well to do it."

J: Exactly, yes.

PART VI

All Those Books!

HARLEQUIN "AMERICANA" SERIES

S: Of the fifty states romances, do you have a favorite?

J: Again, it's like asking which child you love most.

S: That's what I thought you were going to say.

J: Now, if you were to ask me if I had a favorite *state* . . . boy. . . . Texas is just my idea of *the* state! There are story ideas in Texas that just won't quit!

There's something that happens when you say "Texas" that immediately sets a tone.

S: The men get bigger and the women get feistier and—

J: Exactly! There's something about the word "Texas." There are some words that just have that panache, that BOOM, that feeling that you don't get when you say, "Iowa." It's my home state and I love it dearly. I think it's rich in ideas, too. But there's something about Texas. It's a romantic place.

S: I'm not going to ask you if you have a least favorite book, because I know you well enough now to know that you aren't going to say anything bad about any of your children. But do you have one that . . . say . . . was the most difficult to write?

J: Delaware. Finding a book to set in Delaware was my most difficult. I believe totally in the marriage between a setting and a story. You can't just arbitrarily say,

"Well, this book has to have a city background so I'll just set it in *this* city." No, you have to have a particular reason to choose that particular city because it will work into the story. Trying to find that marriage of a story idea and a setting in Delaware just drove me up a wall. However, I think I wrote one of my best books about Delaware. It was *The Matchmakers*. It was one of my fun books. I love it when I can inject humor, but humor is hard.

MASQUERADE

S: *Masquerade*.

J: *Masquerade*. Bill was born and raised in New Orleans. We spent three weeks there, scouting the location. Not arduous duty, believe me.

S: You have a thing for New Orleans, don't you? You get a little glimmer in your eye when you talk about New Orleans.

J: Yeah. New Orleans is a hard city not to get that glimmer in your eyes. You know, we have four unique cities in the United States. Four *totally* unique cities. One is New Orleans, for obvious reasons. The French Quarter and this whole "mask behind the mask." We call it the French Quarter, and it's all Spanish. This duality ... (As a sidebar, the other cities are Boston, San Antonio, and San Francisco.)

Picking up on that mystery, the "lake of the river," the Irish being hired to dig their canals because "who cared if the Irish died" ... It was great, great fun to go in and use New Orleans today and mirror the New Orleans of years ago. Writing that scene, where he's walking down the street, finding out that he has a son, knowing that he'll never ever be able to know him, but looking up and the rain coming down, and the tears mingling with the rain. Those scenes . . .

S: After you write a scene like that you go, "Oooo, ahhhh. What did that come from?"

J: Those are the ones.

THE CALDER SERIES

S: You love the Calders. Let's talk about them.

J: Well, *the people* love the Calders. The endless, endless, endless letters I get on the Calders just startle me. As a matter of fact, I had a man come to Branson about two years ago, while this house was under construction. He kept coming back, day after day. I was working on a book here, and the office kept saying he wanted to ask me questions about the Calders. They said, "Please do something about this man . . ." Finally, I went out.

Well, he and his wife were traveling. They were headed to Montana, and he wanted to see the Calder ranch. He had read the books endless times and was trying to figure out where they were set, where the town of Blue Moon was, and he wanted to visit all the places. He said, "I recognize the places are fictional, but you based them on something, and I just wanted to see them, really."

He wanted to see, and he wanted to know. And this is what has happened with the Calders. The endless letters saying that, "I named my son Chase." Or "I named my son Webb." Or "I named my son Benteen." They live. The Calders live, and I think they live for everybody who has read them.

S: Yeah. They stand out. If you were to ask me which Janet Dailey books stand out, those are the ones.

J: And the crossover Louis L'Amour readers, the Western readers, they came by leaps and bounds. The men readers who read those books and then went ahead and picked up *The Great Alone* . . .

S: Really.

J: Yes. Then *Silver Wings* . . .

S: How did you "discover" the Calders?

J: Originally I had an idea for a story about a large ranching family, but I wanted it to be in the north, where you would still have the big acreage. I had decided on Montana because it was wide-open country and there was a degree of isolation because of the low population level. It was going to be a contemporary story, but I still had to know how the ranch got into the family and what the family's background would be, so I had asked Bill to research it. As he was working on it, he said that most of Montana was settled by Texans. The XIT ranch, which was one of the biggest in Texas—it covered ten counties there—had a ranch in Montana, and many other famous Texas ranches were also in Montana.

Well, this was something I hadn't heard of, and I thought, This is fascinating. Then he told me of the Dust Bowl years and the homesteaders that had come to Montana. I saw then that I didn't have just a single story, I really had a generation story. When I decided to do the Calders, I knew that I had a lot more to work with.

NO QUARTER ASKED

S: What was it like when you first found out that they wanted your first book, *No Quarter Asked*?

J: *Oh!* It seemed like we had been waiting forever since I had sent the manuscript off. Forever! Months! And I hadn't heard anything. So Bill said, "Call." We figured out the time change between here and London, England, made the phone call, said who I was, and was put through to Katherine . . . Katherine . . . I've lost her last name . . . but she said, [*strong, aristocratic British accent*] "Ooo . . . Mrs. Dailey, I was just typing your contract." That was the last thing I remember. I have no memory at all of anything else she said. No memory whatsoever. Just that absolute, unbelievable, "Oh, my God!" I'm sure she thought I was a dribbling fool.

S: When did you first hold *No Quarter Asked* in your hand?

J: I have no memory of that.

S: Do you remember seeing it for the first time?

J: I remember seeing it on the shelves. We were down in Rockport, Texas, and we went into the little T.G.&Y. store. It was the only place that sold Harlequins. I walked in and there it was. It was so pretty! And I waited around just in case someone would come by, just hung around the rack to see if somebody would buy it. And, of course, they didn't. So I took all the copies and bought them. As I was going through the checkout with all eight of them, the woman at the counter said, "Do you realize these are all the same book?" And I said, "Yeah. I hear she's pretty good."

SILVER WINGS,
SANTIAGO BLUE

JANET: I always wanted to write about women in World War II. But I was worried about whether my readers would accept that kind of book. But I went ahead and wrote it anyway.

BAMBE LEVINE[*]: When she tried to tap the mainstream market in 1984, her faithful audience held its breath to see if she could succeed. Her sweet reward came when *Silver Wings, Santiago Blue*, a compelling story about the creation of the Women's Air Force Service Pilots during World War II, reached the *New York Times* bestseller list for nine weeks and was a main selection of the Doubleday Book Club.

JANET: While I was writing the book, I didn't even think about it. It wasn't my concern. Obviously once it was a finished product, I knew that it would be scrutinized very heavily by the critics. So I was very curious and apprehensive, shall we say, to find out what their reactions would be. I remember the most critical review I received just tickled me to death. They criticized me for not doing a better job of the four characters in the book and making the book more of a story about the Women Air Force Service Pilots. I was sitting, laughing my head off, because they criticized me for doing what I tried to do.

---

[*] Bambe Levine was Janet's former public relations person.

THE GREAT ALONE

J: Where would you like me to start with *The Great Alone*? The storyline on *The Great Alone* began when we were in Alaska doing the research for my Harlequin, *More Than Magic*, and I saw my first Russian Orthodox church. I couldn't figure out how the Russian Orthodox Church had gotten there. Then I found out that there were Russians living there, something that my history teacher never told me. And then when we went back to Alaska a second time to do research, we flew out of Seattle to Ketchikan and hopped up the coast to Sitka. And I *love* Sitka. Then we went up to Juneau and up to Skagway, and over on into the Yukon and then came back, flew to Anchorage and made a base in Anchorage, then flew from there to the Aleutian Island chain and up to Prudhoe Bay. Actually, we *wanted* to fly to Prudhoe Bay, and we had gone to Nome, and I don't have to tell you, I thought I had been such a world traveler. We were going in May, and somewhere I had gotten the idea that you didn't have to take parkas and boots and stuff, because you could rent them when you got there. Now, I'm sure that was probably in a tour package, but . . .

S: They neglected to mention that detail?

J: Yeah. So I go up there in my Nikes. And I didn't take a heavy coat. I took things that you could layer. I'm into layering a lot. It's a lot more practical. So we get to Nome and I decide that I want to go play around in one of the little Eskimo villages. The streets of Nome, at that time, were not paved. They were dirt. And this was spring thaw.

S: So they were mud.

J: They were mud. So much so that when you watched a vehicle going down the street, it was up past the hubcaps. So that kind of gives you an idea of what it was like to go across the street in Nome.

S: You probably didn't go very quickly.

J: And I loved it because we stayed at the Nome Nugget Inn and just down the street there was the Polar Bar! It was hilarious! Anyway, we went to the airport and made arrangements with this bush pilot to get out there and he saw that we didn't have jackets. We didn't have anything. So they loaned us jackets. These sweaty, smelly . . . warm . . . jackets. And it was just like you read about. We had the weirdest things flying in the airplane with us: somebody's stove or parts for a refrigerator or . . . I mean everything!

S: No Teamsters up there, huh?

J: Yep, and we'd fly to one little village and then the other. He's doing a little sightseeing for us. "Oh, look, there's a moose" and he'd (*makes a hand motion of the plane banking and diving*), which I love! And he had been trying for a week to land at Little Diomede in the Bering Sea. And Little Diomede is American and Big Diomede is Russian. And as we're flying in—somewhere in my pictures I have a photo of the Chukotskiy Peninsula—and there's Russia! Then we land, and he hadn't been able to make it because of the cloud cover. It had been so low that he couldn't make an approach to the landing strip on the ice. He knew that any time now the ice would be going out.

S: Going *out*?

J: Yeah, it was spring thaw. Then all of sudden we see

these great big orange oil drums that had been painted and placed to mark the section of ice that was our runway. We buzzed the island so that they would know the plane was coming in.

S: That's how you "radioed" the "tower," huh?

J: Right. And we landed and taxied back and the little snowmobiles came shooting across the ice. We landed closer to Big Diomede because that was the only smooth ice there was. The rest is all . . . crinched. So I have a picture of me and the bush pilot and the Eskimo gal . . . one of the other passengers, beside the plane, on the frozen Bering Sea. It was the thrill of my life! And then we come back and we go back to Point Barrow, 'cause I wanted to see Point Barrow, and I have a picture of the midnight sun at noon. So, at the hotel we're still in our Nikes, and it's still spring thaw, so we ask if there's a close place to eat. And they say, "Oh, yes, there's an absolutely *great* Mexican restaurant right next door to us." And we say, "A *Mexican* restaurant next door?" It was called Pepe's North of the Border.

S: No kidding! A little understatement there.

J: Just a little. And, of course, the first thing I wanted to know was: What was this Mexican restaurant doing in Alaska? And they quickly informed us, where there's oil, there's guacamole. There are so many people from Texas and Oklahoma working in the oil fields, and of course, Barrow is where you fly out of.

One thing I discovered about Alaska, from the moment we landed in Ketchikan, is that if you're a woman—it was myself and my secretary on this trip, Bill didn't go with me—you are obviously going to handle your own luggage. And with the exception of

when we got to the hotel in Anchorage and the door-
man helped us with our baggage, we put our bags
into the taxis and we took them out of the taxis, to
our rooms and everywhere else. There wasn't any
such thing as someone to help us with them. We had
tried to hire some taxi guys to take us around and
show us Point Barrow, 'cause I didn't want to traipse
around the whole thing. We're sitting in the taxi
stand, having no luck. Absolutely no one wanted to
help us. They didn't care how much we were willing to
pay. They didn't want to and that was all. Nobody
wanted to take us around. So we went to the manager
there at Pepe's and he said, "I'll bet Joe, the water
man, will take you around." Because at Point Barrow,
the water is brought into the house, and their septic is
taken out. There are no pipes in the ground because
pipes would freeze. So they don't have utilities.

Joe, the waterman, was more than happy to take
us around. He drove us all over and told us more
about everything than we could possibly imagine we
would ever want to know. They had last summer's
geese in underground cellars, caches where they keep
the things they've killed. He told us who had killed
polar bears and who hadn't, and who had skins
hanging out and who had carpeted their houses with
polar bear skins.

S: Isn't that illegal?

J: It's legal for them, for Eskimos.

So he's out there driving us around and showed us
where Will Rogers and Wily Post, where their plane
crash was. And we're driving back and all of a sudden, we're in this little alleyway—we had to go wherever Joe the water man went—and we're coming out
of the alley and there's a gun barrel pointed right at
the window of the car. And I look out the other side
and there's another one there on the other side. We

had gotten right in the middle of a shootout between the police and some man who was intoxicated and holding hostages.

S: Janet!

J (*laughs*): They forgot to block off the alley!

S: You have nine lives!

J: Yep, Joe had taken us down this alley into the middle of this . . . but obviously, we got out of the car unscathed.

S: That must have taken a few years off your life!

J: So then we decided we were going to head back to Fairbanks and I decided I wanted to see Prudhoe Bay. We found out that we could fly from Point Barrow to Prudhoe Bay early in the morning, and then we can spend the day in Prudhoe Bay and there's a flight from Prudhoe to Fairbanks late that evening. Perfect! Perfect timing! Let's do that! We landed at Prudhoe and got off the plane. We walked in and this was how big the lobby area was (*indicating her office*) and in another section was our baggage. We picked up our bags and walked over to the counter. They were trying to get another flight out, so I said, "Well, let's just wait." Because we didn't see any taxis out there. We thought we'd just wait until they got their other flight out and then we'd ask what we should do. As soon as that flight finally left and things settled down at the ticket counter, we walked over and said, "How do we go about getting a taxi?" And we get this sort of . . .

S: That "Y'all ain't from around here" look?

J: Yeah! And he says, "There aren't any taxis in Prudhoe Bay." So I say, "Is there any place where we can rent a car?" And his smile just got bigger.

S: No Hertz in Prudhoe Bay.

J: He says, "You can't rent a car in Prudhoe Bay." So, I say, "How far is the town? Can we walk?" He says, "Town? There ain't no town in Prudhoe Bay."

S: No taxi, no hotel, no town!

J: This was just one royal compound on top of another royal compound.

S: He must have gotten a big kick out of you.

J: We wanted to see Prudhoe Bay!

S: That was it, honey! You done saw it!

J: We got to laughing, and this one man came up and he said, "You know, maybe the guy down at the little commissary building, sometimes he rents out his pickup truck." He gave us the phone number, and we called and arranged to rent this truck. You know, negotiate the price, stuff like that. All of a sudden, the guy from Wein Airlines came over and he said, "We got to thinking about that, and we can't let you rent that truck. You don't know this area, and it's nothing but ice roads. There are no roads, as such. These are just ice roads that we plow out. You're here, and you flew in with Wein Airlines; we're responsible for you. You're our passengers and we do that. But one of our men is going off duty on the incoming flight and he'll drive you to wherever you want to go." And he did. He drove us all through the various oil companies. Each oil company had their own little compound. He drove us all through the compounds and showed us the first well and showed us where the pipeline came. He drove us everywhere. And when he brought us back, he took us to a little commissary place where you can buy your woollies and all your other cold-weather gear. And because there's no town, there's no restaurant, there's no nothing, he invited us back to eat with their crew. They had a little eating area there for the crew.

S: How nice.

J: It was. But I'll never forget him saying, "There's no town in Prudhoe Bay!" It was the greatest . . . *the greatest* trip of my life. Awesome, awesome trip.

We spent two months in Alaska researching. I probably had fifteen to thirty books that I bought for the research, plus I went to the library. So there was tons of research that I did before I ever started. But once I started the book, every day was research. Every day was a panic.

S: You probably couldn't write a single scene without research.

J: Oh, no, not at all! It didn't matter how many times you thought you had everything covered and you had all the information you needed. I remember the Aleutian Indians used to wear birdskin parkas. Birdskin was so much warmer, and it was also reversible. And I had learned this somewhere and it just fascinated me, because the birdskin feathers would repel the moisture but would also insulate.

S: They left the feathers on?

J: The feathers, the down, everything. And I learned so

much about birdskin parkas, I think I could have made one.

S: You probably could have.

J: And I got into the very first scene where they go into their home, which is sort of an earth house situation, and they take their birdskin off. And I said, "Wait, what did they wear *under* the birdskin?" I called Bill, who promptly began calling libraries and had his secretary call libraries. I mean, they were calling everywhere and nobody could tell us what the Aleutians wore under those birdskins. *Finally*, they located an anthropologist at the University of Alaska in Juneau, I believe, and he said, "Honey, they wore the same thing under those birdskins as a Scotsman wears under his kilt. Nothing." Which really presented a *whole new scene* for me. A-a-all this, that I hadn't counted on at all!

S: And with this information . . . ?

J: Ah-ha, it changed the whole texture of the situation. Then later, about two chapters into the book, it hit me that I was writing much of the book from the point of view of the Aleutian Indians, the natives. And I was making comparisons to things they would never have seen. Tree trunks—there are no trees. The chance of them seeing a tree or understanding what a tree was . . .

S: I see what you mean. Grass would be out.

J: It was just endless what I found I had to throw out. Hair had to become white as an eagle, the head of a bald eagle. You suddenly had to make your descriptions compare to their lives and what they knew. I had to run through the book and start tearing things out. There was no chestnut-colored hair. Believe me, they wouldn't have known what a chestnut was. I had to make all those changes. And then when I wanted them to move to Kodiak, and it was the point where the Russians had brought the first sheep and cattle, the first sheep and cattle that the Aleuts had ever seen. In 1700, what did a Russian cow look like?

S: Probably not a Jersey.

J: Was it like a Holstein or what? So then began all this frantic research again, what would a Russian cow look like, what would their sheep look like? You just race around, gathering this information that amounts to one sentence. Yet you know it was significant in their lives, so you can't just wave it away.

THE GLORY GAME

S: *The Glory Game.*

J: Polo. I remember becoming fascinated by polo. I remember researching and I saw a polo match. And we had gone—I can't even remember the name of the club—but at the time it wasn't important. I wasn't going to use that setting of California, so I only wanted to see the match. And who do you think is playing? Tommy Lee Jones. I thought, *Wow, this is something!* The actor Tommy Lee Jones playing polo. And I thought, *Now this is really Hollywood.* I couldn't believe it, you could see actors play!

And I had a friend who had just been divorced after umpteen years of marriage. Her husband had left her for a younger woman. And I thought, *Why don't I have a heroine compete with her own daughter for another man?*

HEIRESS

S: *Heiress?*

J: *Heiress*, interestingly enough, combined my absolute love of horses with a story that was most enjoyable to tell, because it was always, "Who did Daddy love?" And it was "Love is never divided."

S: Children have such a hard time with that, don't they?

J: Yes, they do. And truthfully—I don't even know if I want to admit it—part of me still wishes . . . I wanted Abby to die. Originally, I had worked it out so that she was the one who died. Abby was so much stronger, I don't know. I don't think Rachel could have made peace through the children.

S: This is so strange, hearing you go over your own ending. Your readers will be fascinated to know that it could have so easily gone the other way.

J: When I wrote Rachel's death, I just bawled.

S: Do you often cry when you kill somebody you love?

J: Oh, yes. I do.

RIVALS

S: *Rivals?*

J: Researching the Oklahoma Land Rush and that whole era was fascinating for me. Going out into the Cherokee Strip, where the big land rush was, was so awesome. As soon as I heard someone say that in a sense that area was settled by losers because everybody who hadn't been able to get a farm elsewhere after the war, or their homes had been destroyed, this was their last chance. They were determined people. But the idea fascinated me.

ASPEN GOLD

S: *Aspen Gold*?

J: *Aspen Gold* is the one time that I have a character that is totally Oedipal. You can try to make excuses for what you wrote . . . But it's really a story about choice between fame and family and to decide which you are going to do.

TANGLED VINES

S: *Tangled Vines*.

J: *Tangled Vines* is probably the pinnacle of blending your background and marrying your research to your characters, so that all the information comes from the characters that they are. They are the land, almost. They are the business. That they think in terms of the wine-making business. I really think it is the best use of research I have ever done.

S: Do you appreciate the sacred art of wine-making? Do you love wine?

J: I *love*, absolutely *adore*, a good wine. I can never remember, from one time to the next. If I up and get it, I don't remember what that bottle was. I just enjoy the wine, a glass, maybe two.

THE PRIDE OF HANNAH WADE

J: *Pride of Hannah Wade*, the whole premise started out as the "typical heroine gets carried away by the noble savage and falls in love with an Indian." And as I'm researching the setting, making my mind up where it will be, what tribe it will be: Sioux, Cheyenne, Comanche . . . Anyway, I'm reading about abductions of white hostages and I start reading accounts of women who had been captured by Indians, and survive and the ostracism, the absolute repugnance of the public for them, that they had survived. That they had not killed themselves.

And the more I read this, it's like today's rape victims, that they were at fault. That they should have done something. It's their fault. And all they did was survive!

S: And they are permanently sullied, right?

J: Yes. And I realized, doing the research, *this* is the story. I originally titled the book *The Rape of Hannah Wade*, because in my mind the true rape happened when she returned to the white culture, but of course the publishers felt that was too strong, so we changed it to *The Pride of Hannah Wade*.

S: That's nice too though, don't you think? Are you okay with that?

J: I am okay with that, but it's one of those books that reads so deceptively simple.

S: Those are the best kinds, though.

J: Yes. They are.

PART VII

The Future

S: How about future projects?

J: Future projects. Well, I have a contemporary western that I really like, set in Nevada. I'm still playing with the title. It will either be called *Notorious* or *The Queen of Diamonds*, the "diamond" being the ranch. Sounds a bit corny to me, so I'll probably kill that one.

S: Ten years from now, will you be sitting in that chair? In this house?

J: I assume, yeah, I assume. I always say that I'll be here as long as God doesn't have plans for me somewhere else. Who knows? I always figure whatever happens, happens because it's supposed to happen, and it's the right thing to happen. Right now, I think this is the right place, and this is where I belong, so that's where I'll be.

S: Doesn't sound like it would frighten you a lot, though, if you weren't here.

J: No. Uh-uh.

S: Or make you terribly sad.

J: Uh-uh. No. I learned something when Bill and I retired back in '74. We sold everything. What didn't go into our trailer, we didn't own. I mean, we got rid of *everything*.

At the time he suggested we do this, I thought, *Oh, I can't sell everything. I can't! All these wonderful, precious things. They mean everything to me. I can't . . . Aw, they're just things.*

It was the greatest lesson I ever learned and I still feel that way.

If a tornado came along and wiped us out tomorrow, yes, it would be a shame. There are a lot of beautiful things in here that are somebody's heart and soul. Whether you talk about the carpenters who did all this marvelous woodworking here, or the leaded glass windows, there's a lot of pride and joy of the workmanship that would be destroyed. That would be the shame of it. And . . . but . . . naw, aw, we'd just build it somewhere else. It's just a house and those are just things. And that's a valuable thing to know.

S: Do you think that means you enjoy it any less?

J: No, I don't think you enjoy it any less.

S: Perhaps you might enjoy it more?

J: Yeah, yeah, I think so. I think so because the things that will really hurt are like the family pictures, the things you can never replace, the sentimental things. Those are the irreplaceable things.

S: Ten years from now, mentally, spiritually, emotionally, do you think you'll be different?

J: I know I'll be different. I don't know in what way I'll be different.

S: What's the trend?

J: The trend is: Enjoy life and the living of it.
   And I don't expect that to change. I still expect to enjoy the sunsets and to enjoy the beauty of a flower, and the fun and the laughter of a dog, and the freedom of horses. I can't imagine ever changing the love of family.

S:Sounds like a good trend. And how about the career? Speculation, of course.

J: Speculation. I expect I'll still be writing. I expect I'll have my Texas trilogy, quatrology, septology, whatever it turns out to be, and a bunch of other work. I don't see the writing stop.

I hope by the end of ten years, I'll have the Iowa book done that I've been talking about for at least ten years already.

That's the problem. It's not a lack of ideas, it's a lack of time. I just can't seem to get 'em all together, get 'em all done. Of course every time I get an idea written, five more have taken its place. So I guess you just keep going.

S: And other goals?

J: I want to be fluent in another language, learn to play the piano, celebrate my sixty-fifth birthday with Bill . . .

SONJA: We'll have to stop for a minute, because I have to turn the tape over.

JANET: Good, 'cause it's about time for a potty break. (Starts to leave the room, stops at door.) That's not on the tape, is it?

SONJA: Yes, but we'll take it out. We don't want your fans to know that you do things like that. Rose-tinted reality, right?

JANET: Right!

PART VIII

Interviews

BILL DAILEY

*JANET: Bill is the other half of each Janet
Dailey novel. If there's a secret ingredient
enabling me to have this romantic life, it's Bill.
Most writers have to hire an agent, a business
manager, and a publicist. I have all those in my
husband. He not only gave me the moral support
to try for my dreams, but he handles all the
aspects I don't have the time or the experience to
manage. Yet he doesn't like the limelight and
doesn't want his name anywhere on the books.
But when a novel with my name on it is published, I know how much work he's put in to
bring it to completion.*

S: First, I'd like to ask you if there are any subjects you
would like to talk about?

B: Naw, I'll just answer your questions to start with and
that might jog my memory of something I might not
have thought of. Otherwise I might try and outguess
what you're doing.

S: Okay. If I ask anything that you don't think is important or you'd rather not discuss, we'll just go on to
something else, all right?

B: Okay.

S: I have all the statistics on where Janet was born, et cetera, but how about you? Where were you born and raised?

B: I was born in New Orleans, and I was raised all over the country. My folks were in show business. Carnivals, circuses, the Grand Ole Opry, you name it.

S: As a child you went along with them, with the carnivals and circuses?

B: Yeah. Yeah. That's what I said. I was raised in the business.

S: Do you think that's where you learned what you're using now?

B: Oh yeah.

S: What did they do, more specifically?

B: They had all kinds of joints, carnival rides, circus equipment, and everything. My dad used to own his own carnival. He and Tex Ritter were partners for a while.

S: In what type of enterprise?

B: A lot of clubs on Bourbon Street in New Orleans. Plus, carnival rides and stuff. So, I was just raised that way.

S: What does the son of a carnival owner do? Take tickets and —

B: Everything there is in the carny. Whatever there is, I've done.

S: Were you a barker?

B: Yeah. I did bark. I did it all.

S: Traveling with carnivals and circuses . . . seems like a kid's dream. But I'll bet it was hard work.

B: Oh sure, yeah. Everything's hard work.

S: Did you enjoy it?

B: Oh yeah, I wouldn't change my life for nothing.

S: What was the best part?

B: I don't know. There's traveling around, meeting all kinds of people. Learning life the hard way.

S: That's the only way to learn it, huh?

B: Yeah. School can't teach you that. I only went to the fifth grade of school. That's the furthest I've ever gotten in school.

S: It was probably difficult for you to be in school, if you were always moving —

B: Oh, yeah. I never went to the same school twice.

S: Education comes in all forms, doesn't it?

B: Yeah.

JANET: He's a typical Harlequin hero. He's a self-made man (who only had a fifth grade education), and he thinks so fast he's always five steps ahead of everyone else. He knows exactly where he's going, and he says what he thinks. He doesn't pull any punches. It's impossible to keep

*up with him sometimes. He's the most intelligent
and dynamic man I've ever met.*

S: Did you have brothers and sisters?

B: Two sisters.

S: The only boy with two sisters . . . m-m-m-mm. Were
you the oldest, youngest, middle?

B: The oldest.

S: Did they travel with your parents and you?

B: Uh-huh. We were all raised in the carny.

S: Your mom and dad, are they still living?

B: No.

S: And your sisters, do you see them?

B: Yeah. As a matter of fact, one of them was just here a
week ago.

S: Do you consider yourself close to them?

B: Yeah. Same as anybody else, you know. Sure.

S: When I was a kid, we moved about every four months
and it was hard for me to develop relationships. Was
that hard for you? Did you have a best friend?

B: No, not really, but you have your friends within your
realm of the people you work with. You know what I
mean. You meet new people on the road all the time.

S: So you were with a consistent group as you traveled?

B: The whole carnival.

S: How many people were in your carnival?

B: About 150. It's just like anything else. Some of them you like, some of them you don't. What the hell, you know.

S: Do you remember Tex Ritter?

B: Oh yeah. My God, yes!

S: What do you remember about him?

B: Everything.

S: Everything . . . could you be more specific?

B: Well, I got some memories of him, but I sure as hell wouldn't want you to put it in the book.

S: Oh, okay. We'll keep those to ourselves.

B: Right.

S: So, you were in the carnival, the Grand Ole Opry and all these different areas of show business through your childhood, adolescence, all the way to adulthood?

B: Yeah, all the way. I was raised in it all the way up.

S: When did you branch off from your parents and start your own enterprises?

B: Oh . . . God . . .

S: I mean in your twenties, thirties or —

B: On and off all the time. When I was fourteen I went into the Merchant Marine.

S: Really? Where did you go?

B: Ended up in the Philippines. I spent five years in the Merchant Marine and came back and went back on the carnival again and was dimwit and dumb nothing. Got tired of the road and ended up in Omaha, Nebraska. A painting company, then a construction company, an oil company . . .

S: Painting, like painting houses?

B: Houses, commercial buildings, that sort of thing. And I just started one business on top of the other.

S: Do you prefer to start a business and then turn it over to someone else by selling it or putting someone else in charge of it? Or do you like to keep it going yourself?

B: Once I get a project started, the excitement for me is to take a project and make it happen. Once it's happened, then I go on.

S: It appears to me that you have about fifteen projects, at least, going on right now.

B: I always have projects going on.

S: It's like you're doing business with everybody in town on some level.

B: On some level or another. Always.

S: Are they friends/business —

B: Business.

> **JANET:** *We like to keep busy. Bill has a good eye*
> *for business opportunities.*

S: You work very hard to get these projects going. Why
do you do it?

B: Well, if I don't do that, I'll be doing something else. I
don't know how to answer that. Why do you do
what you do?

S: People ask me all the time if I like to write, and I said,
"No, I hate writing. Writing is very hard work and it's ex-
hausting. Why would I like it? But I *love* having written!"

B: Yeah.

S: And I'm wondering if you enjoy the actual work or if
the payoff is looking at something and knowing that
you helped to bring it into the world.

B: Oh sure, I like that. Sure.

S: Whether it's a beautiful building or a career . . .

B: Sure, I like making things happen.

S: I get the feeling that the money is secondary to you.

B: Always has been. You can't work for money. If you
work for money, then the money rules you. Then
you're working for the love of money. I work for the
love of doing it, and that's what I do.

S: Of all the things that you've brought into the world what are some of the things you're proudest of?

B: Well, needless to say, I'm very proud of Janet, because I've worked my butt off on my side of her career, to give . . . for her to have the recognition that she's had, and that hasn't been an easy job to do. And I'm very proud of Jennifer[*] because when she came to me, she had talents, but she had no . . . nobody was doing anything. And I'm very proud of what I've achieved with her.

S: How about Belle Rive? It's beautiful, but how do you feel about it?

B: I'm very proud of it. We've taken an idea, a thought, from Louisiana and designed it and put it on the property.

S: Every day, do you have at least one moment when you take pleasure in knowing that you did that?

B: Oh, every day.

S: The other night, when I was driving by, the lights were on—the front of the house, the fountain, the tennis courts—it was a fairyland.

B: Yeah.

S: Janet said it was a wonderful moment, seeing the crane lifting those big, beautiful columns into place when the house was under construction. What was that like for you?

---

[*] Jennifer Wilson is a singer/dancer/entertainer being promoted by JanBill Limited. She is the star of her own show at the Americana in Branson.

B: I've been in construction, so I don't enjoy . . . I mean, it was neat to see those big columns, 'cause we ordered them from South Carolina or some damn thing and had them trucked in.

S: Down that small, winding road?

B: Sure. No big deal.

S: I guess not, if you're in the business, but it sounds like a big deal to me.

B: Anyway, you'd enjoy seeing those big things go up, but to me that was a construction job.

S: Really? Until you were done?

B: Until I was all done. And then, of course, when it's all done, then you can go, "Oh, my God, that's ours!"

S: That must have felt good.

B: Oh yeah. I have the unique ability, and Janet doesn't. She can't even see what five minutes is going to look like. But I have the ability to see things done, in living color. And that's why I'm able to do what I can do, in construction and other things. 'Cause I can see it already, in the plans. So it was easier for me to design that, lay it out, and build it.

S: I see. Tell me about your children.

B: Well, let's see. I've got two children, just like everybody else has children. They grew up.

S: I understood that you had five.

B: Well, I've got five, but they're by a former marriage.

S: Five overall?

B: Right, but way back when they were adopted ... I should never have done it, but it's a done deal now. But nevertheless, yeah, I have five. But I only count the two, because those are the two that we helped raise.

S: And that's a son and a daughter?

B: Uh-huh. And that son works for us. My daughter's in Omaha.

S: Could you give me their names and ages? Unless they won't want everyone to know how old they are.

B: I don't know how old they are.

S: In their mid-thirties?

B: Right.

S: Do they have children?

B: Yeah. Jimmy's got Maloy, and Linda's got three.

S: What was it like for you, being a father? Was it easy or did you have to work at it?

B: Oh, I had to work at it because I grew up ... different than a lot of kids.

S: Do you think you raised your kids differently than a lot of people raise their kids?

B: I don't know. All those things you ask me ... is like what you might have gone through. I didn't go through a family atmo-sphere.

S: I understand that.

B: And so I can't answer your questions.

S: You didn't have the "Beaver Cleaver" family, huh?

B: Yeah, yeah, shit, no.

S: But it was still a family, just different than maybe some other people's idea of a family?

B: Right. They never ever wanted for anything. I've made them work for what they've got. We help them out constantly, but they didn't get a free ride. But, well, they got born, and they're in their mid-thirties, and they're happy.

S: What more can one ask?

B: I don't know.

S: You must have done something right.

B: Well, somebody did. We didn't raise them by ourselves. My ex-wife, we got divorced, because we weren't compatible. It wasn't because of any other reason. And then, of course, Janet came along in my life, and we *were* compatible.

S: How long were you married to the children's mother?

B: Oh, 'bout three years . . . thereabouts. I mean, we just weren't compatible.

S: I understand.

B: So when we split, we split with the agreement that we'll always stay friends, and we'll never have a problem, and whatever the court says I have to give, I'll give, no matter what. The point being is we're still friends today. She comes down here all the time. She stays with us sometimes, and whatever, and, and Janet and she are real good friends, and it works good.

S: Do you find that people don't understand that?

B: People, lot of people, don't understand. They think I've got the best of both worlds, and I'm laying both of them.

S: Just because you get along with your ex?

B: Yeah. You know, that's not true.

S: People will think whatever they want to, huh?

B: Yeah. Personally, I don't care. Don't make no damn difference to me what they're thinking.

S: How about your grandchildren?

B: I don't know.

S: What's it like, being a grandpa?

B: I don't know.

S: You don't?

B: No.

S: Okay, well —

B: I don't think about those things.

S: I think sometimes we feel like we have to play the role of "parent" or "grandparent." Whatever that means. But I don't think our kids need somebody who's trying to play a role. They just need *us*, whoever we are. That's all we can be, and we just hope that's enough.

B: That's right. That's all I am. All right. They either like me or they don't. That's it.

S: How many grandchildren do you have?

B: Four. Maloy—he's Jimmy's—and then three with Linda, my daughter in Omaha.

S: I love the painting that Janet did of Maloy. Isn't that good?

B: Yeah.

S: I know men hate answering questions like this; it's "romantic stuff." But the readers are going to want to know . . . Do you remember the first moment you saw Janet?

B: Yeah.

S: Can you tell me about it?

B: Yeah. I seen her on the street corner, on a Sunday, coming back from church.

S: She was, or you were?

B: Oh, she was!

S: She was.

B: Oh yeah.

S: All right. And what did you think?

B: I don't know. I was just flirting with her.

S: What did you say to her?

B: Well, I don't even know what I said, I was just flirting with her. Few days later, I saw her again at this hotel, or restaurant, or something. I was remodeling it, the whole building, and she came in and sat at the little counter right there. I sat down, and we just got talking again. She told me she was going to secretarial school, learning to be a secretary, and I told her, "Why in the hell don't you quit school and go to work, and learn it that way?" I gave her my card, and I left town. I was gone for thirty days. I covered a nine-state area, so I was busy in construction. I told her, "Go over to the office, and apply for a job." And she did, and she got the job. When I came back, there she was again . . .

S: I bet that didn't ruin your day, eh? Did you already like her by then?

B: Oh, I liked her, yeah.

S: Did you like her right away?

B: Yeah.

S: What did you like about her, Bill?

B: Personality, I guess.

S: She seems like a very positive, upbeat person. Has she always been that way?

B: Yep. Oh yeah. She hasn't changed.

S: You don't think she's changed much over the years?

B: Oh no. No. Hell no. Gotten older . . .

S: Well, don't we all?

B: Yeah. Well, no, she hasn't changed at all. So that's how we met, and we started to date, and one thing or another, from time to time. Three or four years later, whatever it was, we ended up getting married.

S: Do you remember a particular moment when you decided you wanted her to be your wife, not just somebody that you loved?

B: Naw. I don't think about that.

S: It just sort of evolved . . . ?

B: Yeah.

S: Is that one of those things that women think about more than men?

B: Yeah. Yeah. Yeah.

S: You said that she helped you out with your business —

B: She is my right arm.

S: Looking back, can you tell me the types of things that she did for you?

B: She ended up being my head secretary, handling everything in the office. Everything.

S: What did she bring to your life?

B: Peace of mind.

S: Peace of mind?

B: I didn't have to worry about somebody ripping me off, or orders getting done, or anything else. Uh, it just happened. And I was able to do what I can do best, and that's promote.

S: Did you find that she was a strong person, a good fighter when she needs to be?

B: Oh yeah.

S: She was pretty young at that time, to have that much going for her.

B: Eighteen.

S: She's a gutsy, smart woman. I've noticed that when I've been working with her.

B: Yeah.

> **BILL:** *I went to Jan and laid out a plan for doing these stories. She would do the writing, and I would manage her career and take care of all the research and the business. We would be a team. And that's the way we've done it.*

S: Of all the things you've done for Janet, is there anything in particular that you're the proudest of, that you feel really good about?

B: Any *one* thing?

S: Or half a dozen. Whatever stands out in your mind.

B: Hell, I don't know. Everything . . . everything. I'm pleased with everything.

S: Janet says that you do—or did—all of the research for her —

B: I still do.

S: What is that like?

B: I personally don't do some of that now 'cause I have my office to do some of it. But I follow through and make sure. That's why I've got secretaries. I give them directions and they get back to me. My secretaries make the calls. I don't personally make the calls anymore. That's why I got help. They find it, and they'll go and pick it up, and Janet will go through and get what she wants out of it. I don't have time to do that. And then once she does this she gets it back to the girls, and the girls take it back to the library. Done deal.

S: A lot of time and energy saved.

B: Oh yeah.

S: Time that Janet can devote to what she does best. Right?

B: Sure. Anyone can run it back to the library.

S: When you didn't have the secretaries to do this for you, how —

B: Then I did it all myself.

S: A lot of writers are going to read this book. What advice can you give them about researching? Where did you start?

B: I started by talking to Janet and seeing what she was going to need. If she was going to write about Sioux Falls, South Dakota, I got to have weather, I got to . . . Of course I don't know, nor does she, when she's going to start a book, she doesn't know if it's going to be in the wintertime, or the fall, or the spring, or something. I got to have weather charts. I've got to have the history of the area, the demographics of the area . . .

S: Where did, where would you go for all that?

B: Libraries.

S: Just the library, huh?

B: Oh yeah. Libraries will give you a lot of stuff. Well, a lot of times, they help you, and get it for you. You go there and tell them what all you want, and everything like that, and then go and have a cup of coffee or something like that, and then come back, and you got it. You give them ten or fifteen dollars, and that's the end of it, and it's over.

S: You don't do windows, right?

B: No. Tired of it . . .

S: That's the key, huh? Hire everything done that you can?

B: I do. I don't like to work.

S: For somebody who doesn't like work, it appears that you do a lot of it. What part *do* you like?

B: The promoting.

S: Do you get a charge of getting on the phone and setting something up?

B: I don't know if it's a *charge* or not.

S: What would you call it?

B: It's something I like to do.

BILL: I keep her schedule, make sure she's not disturbed, check that eyes that start out blue, stay blue, through the whole book. I do everything for her but the final typing.

S: Okay, back to researching. What percentage of your material would you say you found in the local library in an area?

B: Oh, I don't know. You go to libraries, you go to the Chamber of Commerce. You go to the weather bureau. You go to the forest service.

S: The forest service?

B: Yeah. Sure. They can tell you what kind of trees you got there. They can tell you all kinds of things. They tell you what animals are there, in that particular area. They'll tell you everything. So it's not just all libraries . . .

S: Can I have that tip?

B: Yeah. You can . . .

S: I've done the library and the Chamber of Commerce, but I'd never thought of the forest service or the weather bureau. Who else?

B: Government offices all over the whole country. Just go in and get anything you want. It's free.

S: What other type of information can you get from government offices?

B: You can get anything you want. Anything. You name it, you can get it.

S: When you're doing the research, do you find that certain stories or ideas pop out at you, and you read it and you go . . . Wow!

B: No. I never ever look for ideas or anything. Never. I don't want to know any. I don't care anything about the ideas. She's the author. It's her idea. All I do is assist her with the material she needs for the idea. Sometimes when she reads that research, it might spark something for her, but that's hers. I don't recall doing anything like that.

JANET: I rely on Bill for the veracity of my male characters. He tells me if they're behaving in a true way.

B: The only time I have anything to do with Janet's writing is when she's said, "Would a man do this?"

S: The male point of view, right?

B: Right. The male point of view, and I can only answer yes or no, in my lifestyle.

S: Right.

B: And my lifestyle, it's a little different than some sonofabitch growing up going to church every Sunday, and all that kind of thing. My lifestyle's a little different.

S: So you can't speak for all men, but you can speak for you, right?

B: Yes. And then she takes that from there.

S: Janet could have been about anything she wanted to be. There are people who are that talented. But she chose to be a writer, and your lives have gone one particular direction, instead of another. How do you —

B: She chose to write a book, because she had free time . . . because we were retired. So she chose to write a book, which is what she'd always wanted to do. But working for me, and working with me, you can't write a book and work twelve, fourteen hours a day in your own business. You can't do that.

S: That's true.

B: So when we did retire and hit the road, then she did what she wanted to do, which was to write her book. Then she wrote another one . . . and another one . . .

S: So you see them more as a series of decisions, rather than the big decision?

B: Oh yeah. It was my idea on the third book, where I said, "Hey, I'll make you the number one author in

Amer . . . in the world." And it was my bright idea, and I laid out a whole game plan how I could do this. And that's when I started the research, and the editing, and doing all these things, and the promotion. That's how that happened. There's no author in the world that can write a book every week.

S: Not even Janet?

B: No. Hell no! You've got to have that teamwork. You've got to have that. You've got to have that or you can't do it. Every month we had a new book that came out. You can't do that on a consistent basis without help. You know. So I ended up being her helper. To do that.

JANET: He's the other half of this writing career. He's not involved in the plot creations, but he supervises the research and the editing, and all the dealings with the publisher. He knows me so well, he even tells me when I'm going to begin another book. I will have an idea in mind, and about a week in advance, he'll tell me the actual day I'll start.

S: Have you noticed that in this business a lot of husbands tell their wives, "You can't do that. Why are you wasting time? Why don't you get a real job?"

B: Oh yeah. Yeah. . . . We had an advantage, though. If you want to look at it this way, our advantage was that we didn't have to do a damn thing when we retired. We wouldn't have had to do anything if we'd lived for ten lifetimes.

S: Uh-hum.

B: We were very well off, from all of our businesses.

S: Right.

B: We did what we did because it was fun and challenging.

S: Whose idea was it to go on the trip?

B: Mine. To sell out and don't do nothing. Just play. Live our life and just grow old, just out on the road. Just something new. Travel all over the world and live with it.

S: Just for the adventure of it?

B: Yeah.

S: Get to know people and locales . . . ?

B: Oh, we didn't care about that. If we got to know people, fine. We didn't set out to meet people.

S: Do you ever want to go out on the road again . . . now?

B: What? No. It's not what it's cracked up to be. You can't work your butt off all your life, and just all of a sudden sit in a rocking chair.

S: What happened? Did you get bored?

B: You go crazy.

S: Is that what happened?

B: Yes.

S: Did that surprise you? Did you think you were going to enjoy it, and then got bored?

B: Oh, I thought I was going to enjoy it, sure, or I wouldn't have done it. It was fun for me to lay out this game plan for her and then it became fun for her, too. Then we ended up having fun doing it.

S: You had a goal to work on together.

B: And we did it together. Just like I had when she worked for me. I was doing very, very well before I met her, but I did extremely well when I didn't have to watch my backside. Extremely.

S: And you feel that's exactly what you did for her—?

B: Oh I do that for her now. All she has to do is write the book. I'll handle every goddamn thing else that comes up in this business . . .

S: Is that right?

B: And do.

S: Yeah.

B: And do. And do.

S: Is that right?

B: And do. And do. Nothing happens that I don't approve.

S: Um-hum.

B: Not even you.

S: I realize that.

B: Yep.

S: I understand that.

B: Well, she needs that.

S: She needs that?

B: Yes, she does. There's still a partnership, and there always will be.

S: I know you approved me for this project, and I want you to know I appreciate that. It's a great opportunity for me and it came at a time to really help my family. Thank you.

B: Oh . . . well . . . that's okay. I mean, you're welcome.

JANET: Our biggest thrill is creating things, whether it's a book or developing a piece of land.

S: You were saying, it's the end result that you find fulfilling.

B: The end result's what I care about.

S: I think you care about helping the people involved, too.

B: Oh yeah! I mean, they're the ones. Without them I'm nothing.

S: I think that some of your pleasure, whether you'll admit it or not, is in giving something good to somebody. Like, if you get Jennifer going, she's going to have a lot better life than she would have had you not helped her get started.

B: Oh, yeah, I enjoy that. And Janet, she'll—if anything happens to me—she'll never have to worry for the rest of her life. And, uh, that's important to me.

S: People seem to want power, lots of it. And I suppose that having it enables you to open doors for yourself and others that you care about.

B: That's correct.

S: It feels really good to make a simple phone call and open the way for someone who deserves a break.

B: Right. I know that I'm in a position where, if I call up the president of a country, company, I'm not going to be put on hold. But I've paid my dues to earn that. Nobody's given me a damn thing.

S: Then why are you giving it to other people?

B: I don't see it as "giving" it to them.

S: Do you choose people who are hard workers in their own right?

B: Yeah. I don't set out deliberately to choose.

S: You don't?

B: It just happens.

S: Really?

B: Sure. It just happens. It just happens. Everything happens by itself. I've helped other authors to get started. That they would never have been published or maybe I would have said that they would have never have been published, but they had an easier time. Melodie

Adams; I got her in there immediately. Uh, who are some of the other authors? Patricia Maxwell . . . and who else? Uh, there . . . Janet can tell you, uh, I . . .

S: Really?

B: I don't pay attention to that. In many cases I don't even get anything out of it.

S: Yes, you do.

B: Huh?

S: You get satisfaction.

B: Oh, yeah, I get the satisfaction. I don't get an agent's fee or anything like that for it. I have no idea what I get out of it. I just pick up the phone and make things happen. You take this right here . . . her. (*Indicating Jennifer.*) Hell, I know what I'm doing. She's a number one show, morning show. She beats all the nighttime shows.

S: Does she really?

B: We got more crowds than the nighttime shows have.

S: And you can get people out of bed at ten o'clock in the morning to come down and —

B: Yeah. Everyone can tell you that. And it's not me that's saying that, ask anybody in town. And that's a good high. It's a good feeling to know that you've taken somebody that just waltzed into town, and you've molded it and twisted it, molded it and set it all into place, and done all these various things, and sit back and say, "Well, here it is." And she will be a superstar. There's no question about it. I've done made up my mind. And when I make up my mind, that's the way it is. So . . .

S: Okay, so you don't get a charge out of it.

B: I get satisfaction.

S: You get satisfaction. Is that what it is?

B: I don't know what it is. You keep asking me and I don't know.

S: I'm trying to figure you out.

B: Yeah. Well, you ain't going to figure me out.

S: Here's what I see . . . a man who works really, really hard, putting out a lot of effort to help a lot of people . . .

B: Hmm.

S: . . . and people do that for a lot of different reasons. Some of them more . . . uh . . . virtuous than others. Okay . . .

B: Uh-hum.

S: And I noticed something downstairs when we were interviewing. You weren't comfortable with a lot of the questions that I asked you.

B: Now, I wouldn't say I was uncomfortable with them.

S: But —

B: I don't know how to answer your damn questions.

S: Okay. Okay. It's all right. Maybe I'm just asking them the wrong way.

B: Well, I don't know. I've never been able to answer them.

S: But, as I was saying, when we were downstairs, when I stopped and thanked you for what you had done for me, you were fine with that.

B: Oh.

S: That's when you got to be you.

B: Uh-hum.

S: And I thought, *That's interesting*. We had talked about all the success, your personal history, and basically, all I got was, "Okay, fine. Next subject." But when I stopped and said, "Thank you for what you did for me . . ."

B: Uh-hum.

S: And suddenly, we're talking. Really talking.

B: Yeah. Well . . .

S: I just thought it was interesting.

B: Uh-hum.

S: There's a lot of husbands out there, mine included . . .

B: Yeah.

S: . . . who have wives who are either trying to get published, newly published, or have published quite a

few but are still struggling. They might appreciate
some advice. I know it isn't always easy to live with a
writer. Sometimes we're brain dead from working too
hard, or we're nervous about deadlines, or we get
down when we have a problem with an editor.

BILL: *We sold millions, because we told the people not to buy it.*

B: Long time ago, we were writing all these Harlequins.
Janet said to me, "I got this idea for this book in
Mexico and Texas, and the *Touch the Wind* character,
and all that, everything." And I said, "Well, let's go
do research." Well, Harlequin won't accept it. They're
selling Harlequin.

S: You want that in the book?

B: Yeah. You can put that in there.

S: Okay.

B: Yeah. Because I told them that.

S: Don't mince words, huh?

B: Aw, no. I told Janet, "If you want to write it, you
write it. Let's go research it, get it written, and I'll
handle it." So, under contract, we had to send it to
Harlequin. Now, we knew they weren't going
to accept it, 'cause it wasn't their format. But we had
to submit it to them. So what happened was, they
turned us down. They said, "No. We can't accept
that. Go ahead and give it to another publisher." I
said, "Fine." So we went to another publisher. Then I
went back to Harlequin, and I convinced Harlequin,

when this book comes out, that—it's racy and it's got some nudity in it. . . . I mean it's not like a Harlequin.

S: Spicier?

B: By far . . . and she was known as a Harlequin author. So I told Harlequin, I said, "Why don't you do this, so that you're not embarrassed. Let me put a page in the back of your book, your Harlequin books, and tell all Janet's fans not to buy the book, because it might be offensive to them." And they said, "Yeah, that's a good idea." The dumb sonofabitches did it. They put the disclaimer, not only in the back of Janet's books but all copies of Harlequin books.

S: Did they really?

B: We sold millions, because we told the people not to buy it, and that dumb sonofabitch . . .

S: Whatever you do, don't read this book! Right?

B: Yeah. And they did, and I could not believe that they did that. And they couldn't believe after the fact of what my scheme was. And then, of course, that kicked her off into the bigger books. We finished our Harlequin contract, and we went on and graduated into the bigger books.

S: On one of the lists, I saw that *Touch the Wind* sold an incredible amount —

B: Aw man . . .

S: It was on the bestseller list for weeks. On the *New York Times* bestseller list for —

B: For months. Yeah. It was unreal. All over the world. So the moral of the story is: Write what you want to write. Somebody will publish it.

•

> *JANET: I never suspected I would be anywhere near that successful, but Bill believed all the time that I was better than I thought I was. And it wasn't just, "Honey, I know you can do it." He got involved and organized the business side of things and did things for me so I could really concentrate on writing.*

S: And what's the moral for husbands who have wives who are trying to make it in this business?

B: Well, the real thing, right here, is give the wives the freedom to do what they have to do. And I think the wife should come down out of the clouds and remember that she has a husband and a family. But when she goes to write, she's in her own world, and I think that the family should give her that time. But when a wife leaves her typewriter she ought to go back to being a wife . . .

S: Uh-huh.

B: . . . and not carry on, and bitch and gripe, and all that other stuff.

S: You think writers tend to do that?

B: Oh yeah.

S: More than, say . . . secretaries or grocery clerks?

B: Because they . . . I don't know. I guess it's because they are a "writer," you know.

S: You've met a lot of bitchy women writers?

B: Oh yeah. Oh yeah. They think they're . . . they're above it all, or something, some of them. I mean, it's unreal.

S: It's hard for the husbands, huh?

B: Oh yeah. Oh yeah. Sure it is.

S: I see.

B: Uh, you've got to give them the time. That's why when Janet works, she types X number of pages a day. I'm well aware of the pages she has to do. I'm well aware she needs that free time. She needs to do it, but when it's over, it's over. That day's over, it's over.

S: And then she can be with you . . . ?

B: She can be with me, or pick her flowers, or sit in a sauna, or do whatever in the hell she wants to do. But in the meantime, I have to let her sit back there and work.

S: My husband used to play football, so he calls it "running interference" for me. When I'm writing—unless the house is on fire, and the fire extinguisher won't put it out, or unless a tourniquet won't stop the bleeding—he won't let anybody bother me about it. He's wonderful about that. He screens all the calls, deals with the emergencies . . .

B: That's right. I do the same thing.

S: He tells my kids, everybody, that I'm on a deadline and no one is allowed to have a crisis for a week.

B: I do the same thing.

S: Do you?

B: Yeah. When she's into a real tight scene or something . . . no calls.

S: Unless it's earth-shattering.

B: That's right. And we handle it. That's the way I do it. I've always done it that way . . .

S: Don't you find when she works at home, people tend to feel she's available to them?

B: Oh yeah. Oh yeah.

S: I have that problem and I think a lot of writers do.

B: And the more successful you get the more people think they can just walk in on you any damn time they want. They know you so well.

S: Is that right? You found that there are more demands on her time, now that she's even more successful?

B: Oh yeah. There's a lot of people who are in awe about it. But Janet's no different today than she was years and years ago. She hasn't changed. The public has changed her. They perceive her differently. She's still the same person.

S: How do you think they perceive her? I asked her this yesterday.

B: As a superstar.

S: Which would mean?

B: Superstar in the writing business, untouchable.

S: Do you think they see her life as very different than the way it really is?

B: Yeah. They seem to forget that it's a job. No different than their job.

S: Right.

B: Whatever they do for a living, the only thing is, they're not publicized. Janet is publicized.

S: Which is just part of the business.

B: That's the only difference. But they perceive her almost bigger than life . . . and she's no different than anybody else.

S: I'm sure they see her as a woman who never sweats, who never gets her hands dirty, who has servants do everything for her, and who wears silk and satin all day.

B: That's right. But she washes her own clothes. People drive by the house, or they see it in a magazine, and they'll say, "Oh, she's got maids," and all this shit. Well, we've got a housekeeper that comes in once a week. We got a gal who comes in and takes care of the flowers in the house once a week. We have six people who work the yard all the time to keep it nice.

S: But you've still got Janet's mom coming over and sharing recipes and saying, "Where's my pan?"

B: That's right. That's right.

S: I spent some time in Rye, New York, one summer and some of the mansions there are astonishing. I drove by one that looked like an enormous stone castle, and I saw somebody getting out of a Jaguar. Bill, they had a bucket of Kentucky Fried Chicken with them.

B: Right.

S: And I thought, *They eat Kentucky Fried Chicken just like me, in that mansion!*

B: Oh yeah.

S: And then I thought, *Well of course they do. They're just people.* But we want to believe the fantasy, the fairyland existence. We want to believe in princes and princesses. But it also feels good to know that they eat the colonel's fried chicken, too.

B: Yeah, right . . .

S: Because if they can accomplish their dreams, and they're just people like us, then maybe we can reach ours, too.

B: That is true. People change you . . . in their images. Jennifer, for instance. When she came here, she was just another girl singer and dancer. Nobody ever knew her name, or nothing, but I took her, and I made her a star. I put her name out in lights, and I did all these various things, but now she's a star. Everybody knows who Jennifer is. They don't say, "Jennifer Wilson." I want her to be known as "Jennifer," not "Jennifer Wilson," okay? Madonna is known as "Madonna." Elvis is known as "Elvis." There's logic behind it, what I'm doing.

Everybody looks at her, two years older, and says, "Oh, oh, can I have your autograph? Can I have my picture taken with you?"

S: Everyone wants a little piece of the dream.

B: That's right. Success breeds hopeful successors.

S: It does, doesn't it?

B: It sure does. Every time.

S: Anything else for husbands?

B: Support them.

S: How do you support Janet, say if she gets a bad review?

B: Aw, we love them.

S: You like bad reviews?

B: Yeah. We don't care. Bad reviews sell books.

S: Okay, then maybe that isn't a good example. There has to be something that would bother Janet, dealings with an editor, whatever. How do you support her, make her feel better at the time?

B: Tell her not to worry about it.

S: You say, "Don't worry about it."

B: Yeah. I just tell her, "Don't worry about it."

S: And that works?

B: Yeah, you know, why worry about it? You laugh all
the way to the bank. What happened yesterday's
gone. You can never ever bring it back.

S: Don't you think a lot of writers lose track of the fact
that this may be art, but it is also a business?

B: They do. They do. It is strictly a business. It's a love of
business. When they get away from the love of business, that's when they're in trouble. It's the love of
writing for the business. It's the love of writing. You
cannot work for the almighty dollar. Can't do it. It's
impossible.

S: Right.

B: If you forget the dollars and write a book because
you love to tell that story, then the dollars will
come. You can't stop it. Janet can stop writing
tomorrow. She can die tomorrow, and money will
come in in spite of her. Once it's in motion, you
can't stop it. But where writers make a mistake is,
you've got to dedicate so many hours, or pages, or
something, every day to work. There's no excuse.
What would you do if you had a nine-to-five job?
Would you go in to your boss and say, "I'm sorry, I
can't work today. I've got laundry to do." And,
unfortunately, a lot of writers don't have a husband
or boyfriend who would go out and do those other
things for them.

S: No. They don't. You're right.

B: They don't have the knowledge, they think it's
stupid.

S: For all those women out there who are working, trying to be a success, and they're with some man who's

saying, "That's stupid! Why don't you get a real job?" What would you say to those men?

B: I think they're an ass! And you can quote me.

S: Thank you. I will. I appreciate you saying that, and so will a lot of other women. Why are they an ass? Why is that a stupid thing to say?

B: Because you work together as a partnership, and if you're doing it together as a partnership, and you've approved your partner to write this book, then help her to write the damn book. She needs someone to help her.

S: Will it pay off for them in the long run?

B: Eventually. Eventually.

S: You really do believe that?

B: Yeah.

S: You don't believe it's wasted time and energy if a woman writes and a man helps her write?

B: No. Because if they're truly together when the book comes out, and it's all published and everything, and you see it in the store, you know—without your own name being on there—you know, hey, it's there!

S: And that's your payback, along with the check, huh?

B: Aw, that's your payback, and you also got a happy wife. You've given her a lollipop that . . . I mean, she's in awe. She's in glory. She's jumping up and down. She's celebrating, then get back to the next one.

S: Then she can even buy the dinner when you celebrate.

B: Yeah, well. That's right. Whatever.

S: And that makes it worth it too, huh?

B: Sure!

S: That's really good advice. Thank you.

B: Sure. Absolutely.

S: For those guys who worry that it's not going to pay off, would you please tell them for us, women, that there is money to be made in this business.

B: There is money in this business and lots of it. On the other hand, when you first start out, you can't lose what you haven't got. Nothing ventured, nothing gained.

S: Pack of paper and a typewriter ribbon, huh?

B: That's right . . . That's all there is.

S: As businesses go, it's really a cheap one to go into.

B: It sure is. Low investment. Low overhead.

S: On the other hand, a lot of women don't make much money writing.

B: A lot of women do not.

S: Why do you think that is true?

B: Well, everybody can't be in the top ten.

S: True.

B: Everybody can't be a superstar.

S: What do you think separates those writers from a superstar? Is it just the hours, putting in the time?

B: No! The hours ain't got nothing to do with it. It's the promotion. If Janet had just written two or three books, she wouldn't have been any different than anybody else.

S: You wouldn't have been sitting in Belle Rive?

B: No. Well, we could have had that anyway, even if Janet had never even wrote.

S: But she wouldn't be as happy as she is, because she wouldn't feel that she had contributed to it, that you two had built your lives together. If you had just given it to her —

B: Well, no. Not really, because I could not have done what I did without her help.

S: Oh, I see what you're saying. Either way, you two would have done it as a team, whether through the writing or other businesses.

B: Once you're married, it's fifty-fifty. The law says that. Try to go to court and have it any other way.

S: That's true.

B: Yeah. You're damn right.

S: Back to what you were saying before about women getting up there in the clouds. I'm not going to ask you if Janet has ever done that because —

B: Janet has never. Never. Never, ever, ever, ever, ever. She's gotten a little cocky once in a while, when she sees her stuff, but I mean, that's soon brought under control.

S: Don't you think there's a fine line between cockiness and self-satisfaction, too . . .

B: Right.

S: I think it only becomes conceit when you delude yourself into thinking that your success has made you better than someone else, or different in some way.

B: Uh-hum. There are women, and I know of one, that was married. I got her very first book started, she would have never, ever had gotten it if I hadn't've pushed her though. And, uh . . . God, I wish I could remember her . . . Janet could tell you who she is. She was from St. Louis at the time. She won't even give us the time of day, half the time. She's a big shot. So much so that her husband couldn't stand her anymore, and he left her . . . And that's wrong.

S: What would you say to a husband who finds himself faced with that situation?

B: Well, if he can't bring it under control . . . You know, there's too many, too many other women you can have a life with, without putting up with a bunch of bullshit. Yeah. Tell her not to let the bull hit her in the back when she leaves. Kick her out. I told you, I come from a different school. But there are authors that way. They get cocky and smart, and they say, "You're not working now and I'm bringing in the money." No matter how much a man will even help his wife. I know of one author . . . can't remember what her name was ... wouldn't want you to use it anyway ... but her husband even helped her, and she went off the deep end. She got too big for her pants. She forgot how she got where she got.

JANET: Bill and I are a team. You can't be Rodgers and Hammerstein when you are only Rodgers.

S: This has worked very well for you, this teamwork that you're talking about?

B: Oh yeah.

S: You doing all these things so that she can have the time to sit down and write, I can see in my own life, how wonderful that would be.

B: You also got to remember, as far as Janet and I are concerned, she still oversees the office. She is not divorced from our business by no means. She always has been my right arm and always will be my right arm. She just happens to write. And when she's done writing, then she'll do whatever else I need to have done. Sure. She watches that office. She makes sure that things are done correctly in addition to me. She's still right there. I mean, after all, that's ours, too. Jennifer is ours, too. And she's owner of all of this shit. I mean, we're selling this to us (*indicating the theater/hotel*).*

S: Are you?

---

* The Americana Theater and The Lodge of the Ozarks.

B: Yeah. And it just all happens that we're . . . you know, we're the bankers.

S: Right.

B: It just so happens she still loves to write. Whenever she does not have fun in writing anymore, she's done. Just like I told her. "Whenever you don't like writing anymore . . . You're not having fun . . ." When she gets burnt out, and she don't want to write anymore . . .

S: Do you think she ever will?

B: Never.

S: She enjoys it too much.

B: Aw, she does.

S: Can you think of any more advice to the husbands?

B: I've known Janet so well, and I know when she's struggling with a scene, and there's times I come up to her and I say, "Let's get out of here for a while."

S: Do you just kidnap her?

B: Oh yeah. "Let's go have a cup of coffee some-place . . ." Now we could have coffee right there.

S: Sure you could, but she needs to get away.

B: Yeah.

S: When you go out, do you talk about the scene?

B: Sometimes. Sometimes we don't. Sometimes it's not

important. I really don't have anything to do with her writing. I stay the hell out of it . . .

S: I think that's when the trouble starts, when husbands start telling their wives how to write.

B: Janet cannot—in any way, shape, nor form—promote. She can't even promote herself . . . out of, ah, out of the office. I don't mean that badly. She has a talent, and I have my talent. She never interferes with my promotion . . . at all . . . in any manner whatsoever.

S: You two seem to have everything compartmentalized.

B: Right. If I knew how to write a book, I'd write the sonofabitch myself and make a million. I don't.

S: So you help her to write the book and make a million.

B: That's right. That's right. I'm not a storyteller. She is.

S: A lot of husbands think they are, though.

B: Yeah. And they're full of shit. And you can quote that, too.

S: Okay. I will.

B: If they are a creative writer, then go sit and write, and do their own book. If they're not, then stay the hell out of the business. Just help her to be a creative . . . help her with what she needs.

S: So you've never changed a scene in a Janet Dailey book?

B: No. Ever.

S: You've never shaped a character?

B: Nope, never done that.

S: Got to go? Okay. Thank you, Bill.

B: Okay.

S: You gave me good stuff.

B: Okay.

JANET: Bill is a restless person and always has these proj-ects going, and it's wonderful for me because I'm exposed to so many things that can stimulate both my mind and my imagination. Bill is the greatest thing going for me as a writer.

LOUISE—JANET'S MOTHER

J: My mother was eighty-two years old when she bought her first swimming suit. When I'm eighty-two, I want to do something equivalent.

S: What mother?

J: My mom.

S: No. Not Louise!

J: Yeah.

S: How old is Louise?

J: She was born in 1911; she had to have turned eighty-three this year.[*]

S (*gasp*): You're kidding!

J: See, I want to be like her.

S: Yeah, I can see why. She looks like she's about sixty-five, maybe seventy tops.

J: I know.

S: I can't get over that.

J: She's a go-getter. She wears me out. Every time I talk to her, I hear, "I just washed the floors and the ceilings, and the basement." And I go, "Geez, Mom, give me a break." Shortly before they moved into the cottage, I was going to have someone go over and clean it for her. But Mom just decided that was ridiculous to have somebody clean for her. But I said, "Come on, Mom, they can at least wash the blinds." She said, "Why? I can do that, one room at a time." So I said, "Okay."

LOUISE—INTERVIEW

S: How do you feel about Janet's success?

L: Well, I think it's wonderful. Why wouldn't I?

S: What is it that you're the most happy for her about?

---

[*] Interview conducted in the summer of 1994.

L: She's tried to write and monkey around with little stories over the years, and we never discouraged her. And when she used to write her stories, we always liked them. We always played games with her, she had three older sisters, and she was constantly having us read stories to her.

S: Did you begin reading to her early?

L: By five she knew every book there was by heart.

S: Do you think that had a lot to do with it?

L: I don't know.

S: How about you, Janet?

J: Yeah, I think you have to fall in love with books.

L: She had a Jack and Jill book that she just loved and she wanted to keep it and when she was twelve, I told her that she was too old for it. And she always liked these "Who did it?" and "How did they do it?," you know, all these books that you could buy at the dime stores umpteen years back . . .

J: Rainy-day fun books. They had all sorts of things: pages to color, connect the dots, find the hidden animals, crosswords, jokes, everything.

L: We could only give her one at a time.

S: Why?

L: Because she'd never stop until she had it done. So if I'd have to go out of town—and I had to go out of town to get them because the stores in our town never had anything like that—I'd get one for her.

And then when she was older there were the preschool books. Well, she had all those done and knew all those things before she got into kindergarten. Which I didn't realize is not right. 'Cause then she was bored.

I think that's what's wrong with our school system today, if a child is far behind and the others are far ahead, the teacher won't take this little one who's behind and help her. If you didn't get it, that's just too bad.

S: So I guess you were Janet's first fan, weren't you?

L: Well, I think she had a lot of fans.

S: Then who were her first fans?

L: Well, all the family encouraged her in her writing. I can't say that I was her first fan because she had a couple of sisters, Marilyn and Evelyn. The family was behind her all the way.

S: Do you remember anything in particular that she wrote when she was young?

J: Whoops . . . (laughter.)

L: She had to write a poem. So she wrote the poem, "Is My Mother a Hypochondriac?"

J: I won first prize. Poor Mom, I made it all up.

S: Then it was fiction?

J: Oh, yeah, it was all fiction.

L: Parts of it were fiction but she drew it all from me, you know.

And I gave her a real shock once. When she came back from Japan, when she was real sick that time. She was in Kansas City. And we had her little Mandy. I sat down and had her little Mandy write her a letter.

J: Yep, Mandy wrote me a letter to tell me how she was doing, my little Yorkie.

L: She was so lonesome for her little dog and she didn't have her in the hospital. So after we'd seen her I came home and said, I have to have Mandy write her a letter. 'Course, Mandy didn't like to be brushed and I said, Grandma brushes me every day. I'll be so glad when you get home. I might think things, but I never had the ability to put them together.

S: Where do you think she got it from then?

L: I don't know. 'Cause there's nobody in the family who does that type of thing. She had a great-aunt who was a cousin of her grandfather who might have had the ability to write. She wrote more biographies, stories about the family. And I don't think that Janet ever knew her well enough to grasp anything from her. It's all in your head. I don't care what anybody says, if you don't have the ability, you're not going to write it.

S: What do people ask you about Janet?

L: Most of them ask me, where does she get her ideas? I tell them I don't know. How could I? I'm her number one agent. I'm always telling everyone she's got a book coming out, she's got a book coming out. It's one of those things that we all live for and she's got it and she's good.

S: If there is a downside to having a daughter who's a bestselling author, what would it be?

L: None for me, but maybe for her, because so many times, maybe she would like to just go do something, and not have to think that people will come back and say, "Did you see her? Did you see Janet Dailey there?"

And then there's my other girls who come out and people will say, "What did Janet do while you were there? What did she do for you?"

The girls tell them, "We go there to see *her*, and we're not going anyplace but just to be with her."

Her stepfather, Dad to her, says, "She's just a down-to-earth, barefoot and blue jeans girl."

RICHARD CURTIS—JANET'S AGENT

R: Personal information . . . ah . . . born this century, but very early in it, 1937, so I was brought up during World War II. I have very vivid impressions of the war. I was born in the Bronx, a borough of New York, raised in Queens, another borough of New York. Then when I was thirteen, we moved to Long Island and that's where I went to high school. I consider myself a Long Island boy.

S: Where on Long Island?

R: The South Shore in what they call the Five Towns or also known as the Gilded Ghetto. It was the place where a lot of Jewish people from the city, after they became nouveau riche, they moved out there.

I went to Syracuse University, which was then a mediocre school, because I was a mediocre student. I became serious at Syracuse University and made up for all the reading I had never done as a child. I went from kind of "zero" to being the editor-in-chief of the *Syracuse Review*, the campus magazine. And I believe I published Joyce Carol Oates's first story. She walked into the office one day and handed me this, and I didn't understand it, but it was so brilliant that I published it.

S: So, you had a good eye even back then.

R: Yes, but I *still* don't understand Joyce Carol Oates.

S: Well, at least you know good stuff when you see it, even if you don't understand it.

R: Right. I got my B.A. at Syracuse and decided to extend my education to avoid the army. So I went to the University of Wyoming on a fellowship and got my master's degree there. When I graduated I joined the Scott Meredith Literary Agency and worked for Scott for seven or eight years. That's how I was trained as an agent.

During that time I wrote some "dirty" books, which were a lot milder than even mildly erotic women's fiction today. And after seven or eight years, I decided that I would like to try full-time writing.

So I left his agency in the late sixties and became a freelance writer. But in due time, I didn't like freelance writing.

S: What type of thing were you writing then?

R: I was writing paperback originals, and I was beginning to collaborate with a number of principals on nonfiction books. I collaborated with an ex-criminal on a book about his life of crime. I collaborated with Warren Avis, who created Avis Rent A Car. I collaborated with a woman on a very important book about the dangers of the peaceful nuclear industry. And several other pieces. I wrote juveniles, adult, nonfiction, fiction . . .

S: Did you write one about Malcolm X?

R: Yes, I wrote a book about Malcolm X.

S: I saw that in my local library, and I wondered if it was you.

R: Yep, that was me. My son now goes to private school and I was talking to his teacher the other day. She said he had told her, "*My* father wrote a book about science, and it's in the school library!" The teacher was very impressed.

S: As she should be!

R: I've had over fifty books published.

S: That's great.

R: And I can't name one of them, and neither can you. Just about all of them are out of print.

   So I did that for several years, then kind of drifted back into the life of the literary agent. And in 1969 or 1970, some of my old Scott Meredith clients asked me to take them back. For a few years I was a writer in the morning and an agent in the afternoon. In 1972 or 1973, I made a commitment to developing my agency full time and stopped writing, except for a column that I started writing in 1980. But the agency grew and grew. I specialized in genre fiction, which was what I had learned at Scott Meredith, and went from strength to strength. Over the period of the eighties I became the mighty . . . ah . . . mighty "emperor" of —

S: Don't worry; I'll put emperor in quotes.

R:—of pop literature that I am now. (*Laughs.*) That's a

very rough thumbnail sketch of what I did. I think I incorporated my agency in 1979. But in 1980, after discovering the appalling ignorance of authors about their profession and giving a number of lectures about it, I decided to start writing a column for authors about the aspects of the business that I didn't think they understood. That column was published in *Locus Science Fiction Monthly* from 1980 until 1992.

S: When you went from being an author to an agent, I understand that it wasn't one moment, but back and forth. You still do. To this day you still write. I know this sounds simplistic, but which do you prefer?

R: I have a right lobe of the brain and a left lobe, and I try to be creative as an agent and as a writer, and more lately, as an artist. (I paint in my spare time, whatever *that* is!) And I try to bring some intelligence to what I do with both lobes of the brain, to sort of cross-fertilize what I do. I don't think I'm a hard, methodical, scientific businessman who cares about the money solely. I try to put some creativity to my work as an agent and the creative side of me is very important. So I kind of gravitate from one to another over long periods of time.

S: Having been a writer and an author yourself, don't you think that gives you a certain empathy for your clients?

R: Yes. Most agents that I know, I must say, didn't start as agents. Most of them were editors. I've always half-jokingly said, "In order to qualify as a literary agent, you should have to write at least one book. That should be your test. Whether you write it well or not, the mere act of writing a book will give you an enormous understanding and a compassion for writers and an understanding of the process that goes into it." And having written as many books as I did, I know all the tricks of the trade. I know if a writer is cheating on her margins (making her margins large so the manuscript will appear longer). I can hold a book in my hands and tell if the book is 10,000 words less than the contract calls for and say, "Get back to work." I know, because I did that in 1981.

S: So we can't fool you, huh?

R: No! But I try to bring to the editorial side of agenting the feeling that I'm more collaborator than editor. You and I are working on this book together. That's my involvement. But I try also to be creative as an agent. I guess that's why I was talking about left brain and right brain. I think agenting really is an art form as well as a profession and a business. And I think it's very important to create. Because what you're really doing as an agent is synthesizing an author, a publisher, and a work of art. And if you synthesize them well, there is harmony. And if you don't, there is disharmony, bad karma, bad "wa," and bad vibes coming out of it.

S: That's true.

R: I'm talking about my column, because it was as a result of the column that I attracted Janet Dailey as a client. I had written a number of columns that were highly critical of publishers' royalty and accounting practices. And one day my office phone rang and Bill Dailey was calling me—Janet Dailey's husband. And he told me that Janet had read my criticisms of the publishing industry. And they felt that at that time they were being very badly dealt with by her then publisher, not naming names. She thought she was being screwed by some accounting practices. Bill said if I could really put my money where my mouth was, if I were as good an agent as I talked a good game, they would be interested in engaging me.

S (*laughs*): That sounds like Bill.

R: Well, he actually put it more bluntly, but . . .

S: I imagine he did!

R: So it was a result of my writing that Janet asked me to represent her.

S: And this was when?

R: Around 1982, I believe.

S: She's been with you quite a while.

R: Yeah.

S: What was the first deal you handled for her?

R: At that time she was published by Pocket Books, and it happened to be one of my most satisfying moments in my representation of Janet. It turned out that I was having a difficult time with Pocket Books. I had been very critical of their royalty accounting practices. And I had been informed—not formally, but kind of sotto voce—that I was not really welcome to submit to Pocket Books. That anything I sold them would be looked at extremely critically. In other words, I was being shut out of that company, one of the major ones, and still is, in the publishing industry. So when Janet Dailey, being their romance and women's fiction star, came to me and asked me to represent her, I had the *profound* satisfaction of informing them that I was now the agent of one of their biggest authors. Their luncheon invitation was really one of the most gratifying I have ever received. So that was how it all began with Janet.

S: Were you able to solve the problem that she was having at the time?

R: Well, yes . . . actually, what I solved was that I believe I helped to organize through my column other people who had had similar experiences with this particular practice. (The problem involved book clubs owned by publishing companies. They were selling books at reduced rates to their own club. And since the authors' royalties are based upon a percentage of the net sales price, they were receiving limited monies for those books, sometimes as little as one cent per book.)

The first book that came out of that was *The Great Alone,* which was Janet's novel about Alaska. She had had a long, multibook contract with Pocket Books for a variety of novels—like eighteen novels—which included the Calder quartet, *Silver Wings, Santiago Blue, The Glory Game, The Pride of Hannah Wade,* a number of those books. But this was a new, one-book contract.

In any event, when Bill contacted me, I flew out to Springfield and drove to Branson. They lived in far humbler circumstances then than now. Basically, they lived in what is now the office. But even that was far humbler than what they have now. Believe it or not, Janet baked a cherry pie for me.

S: You're kidding!

R: Yep.

S: She swears she can't cook.

R: It was a *delicious* cherry pie, and I remember it to this day. I recall teasing her about, "Can you bake a cherry pie, Janet girl, Janet girl?" (*Laughs*.) It was very homey, and I liked them both right off the bat. Janet was very cautious at first. And I've realized subsequently that when it comes to revealing her ideas for books, she is very guarded, because they are so precious to her.

So the first day was sort of—get acquainted and cherry pie. The next morning, because I get up very early, I wandered out of my room. They had put me up at their house. And Janet was in the living room, watching the early morning news. She turned it off and we had a cup of coffee together. She started talking to me about her ideas for her next book. It was still before daybreak. And as she talked, I saw her eyes glowing. That was a very memorable moment for me because I realized that really was what turned her on, talking about her dreams for her next book or her book after that. She loves talking about them. When she did, her voice changed, her face changed. Her eyes glowed, and her passionate personality really shone through.

S: Yes, I can relate to that, just from the time that I spent with her.

R: Sure.

S: I think she lives for that next book. It's what drives her to write the present book. She wants to write this one so that she can get on to the next one.

R: Right. So that was the story of our first contact, first impressions.

S: It sounds as though that was the moment when it clicked, when you knew you would be able to work as a team.

R: That's right. And in due time we sold *The Great Alone* to Pocket Books for a lot of money. But they still didn't get along comfortably. It wasn't that close editorial relationship that Janet could have hoped for. So, I don't know exactly when, but in the late eighties, when Fredi Friedman became an editor at Little, Brown, it was still a Boston company. They had New York offices, but it was still the hundred-and-fifty-year-old, old-line, Boston company that had begun to feel its age. And they were looking for a commercial author, just about the time that Janet began thinking she needed a classier publisher. So we really had a marriage there. And that was when she switched to Little, Brown.

S: I would have thought *that* would have been your most satisfying moment.

R: It was a *very* satisfying moment.

S: The most lucrative?

R: At that time Little, Brown didn't have its own paperback company. It wasn't part of Time Warner; it was just a hardcover company. I had brought Janet to New York and taken her around to all the hard/soft companies. Hard/soft is where the money is.* So that when Janet decided to go to Little, Brown—a company that didn't have a paperback company—it really floored a lot of people. They couldn't understand why we would take less money for a hardcover-only publisher, rather than a

---

* In a hardcover only deal, the hardcover house auctions off the paperback rights and then they and the author split the paperback royalties, whereas in a hard/soft deal, because it's all one company, the author gets a full hardcover *and* a full paperback royalty.

hard/soft. One editor at New American Library had been courting Janet. When I called him and told him that she was going with Little, Brown, he literally fell on the floor. He jumped out of his chair to his feet and as he did, the chair kicked out from behind him. So when he tried to sit back down, he landed on the floor.

S: Oh, no!

R: He did! He fell on the floor.

S: You seem to have that effect on a lot of people, Richard.

R (*laughs*): So that was how we ended up at Little, Brown. I'll tell you the funniest story that I can think of for your interview:

Because they were a hardcover house, when it came to paperback reprints, they couldn't do it in their own line. So they had to auction the book off to outside paperback companies. The first of Janet's books to come under that contract was *Heiress*. It was a *terrific* novel. Fawcett had taken a floor* for $750,000. And the auction happened to take place on the day of my son Charlie's birthday party. Maybe his third or fourth birthday.

S: An important one.

R: Yes. It was held in my apartment. We had a magician. I decided that I was going to stay home that day, and listen to the auction going on from home. As soon as the day dawned, 9:00 A.M., Warner came in with a bid of $900,000.

---

* A floor refers to a minimum bid.

S: A nice way to start the day!

R: A *great* way to start the day! And throughout the day
the bidding went up. Well, I'm at home, and the birthday party starts, and the magician arrives. We have
maybe fifteen or twenty children sitting on the floor of
our living room, watching this magician doing tricks. I
think it was Jean Griffin, who was conducting the auction for Little, Brown. She called me in the early afternoon and she said, "We're up to a million one." And,
suddenly, all the children in the living room went, "Ya-
a-a-ay!" And she said, "What the hell is going on?" So I
jokingly said, "I've organized a cheering section for this
auction." Of course, what had happened was that the
magician had pulled a bird or something out of his hat.
But it turned out that every time she called me with
another number, in the background she'd hear this,
"Ya-a-a-ay!"

S: Your little shills, eh?

R: Yeah, and we ended up with Ballantine/Fawcett getting that book for a million eight, I believe it was.

S: My goodness!

R: It was a spectacular event. But it was so funny that
every time the phone rang it just happened to be
when the children were shrieking and it sounded as
though they were all cheering for this author.

S: That *is* funny. Let's see, what else? What would you
say is the one key to Janet's success?

R: One of the things that I admire about Janet, that I feel
is so rare in an author of her stature, is her professionalism. Many authors reach a successful point in their
career where they stop growing. They say, "Okay, I

know everything there is to know. I've got it all down pat and I'm closing down shop. I'm basically going to just churn out the same formula every time." Janet has never been that way. She accepts each book not only as a challenge, but as a frightening chasm to be crossed, almost like the heroine in one of her own novels. It's a really scary adventure for her. She has incredible courage because she's never hesitated to throw out a scene, a chapter, or even a section if she felt it didn't work. I've seen her set aside work which some other author might have been satisfied with. And I felt that was an act of incredible courage and searing self-honesty. It's something that I admire, that I don't think I've ever seen an author of that stature do. It's almost unheard of these days.

And that's one of the most satisfying aspects of representing her.

S: So do you feel that's the key to her success ... she simply works very hard at it?

R: She certainly *does* work hard. I'll tell you another story which *I* think is funny, and I think Bill and Janet would, too. When Bill and Janet visited New York for me to take them around to meet various publishers, I brought both of them to Random House. We sat down in the office of Robert Bernstein, who was really one of the great figures in publishing. He left Random House after a while, but at that moment he was really one of the towering figures of the industry. We were in this magnificent library room. He was in tweed. It was every author's fantasy of what it would be like to meet your publisher. We were sitting around the table and Bill started talking about how he and Janet worked together. He said, "As a matter of fact, I even tell Janet the day on which she is going to start her book." Everybody in the room sort of leaned forward, including me, because I had never heard of that. And

Robert Bernstein, in his elegant politeness, said, "Would you mind explaining that?" So Bill said, "If it weren't for me, Janet would never start one of her books. She'd sit on her butt. She'll do anything to get out of starting a book. She never feels she's ready, because she thinks there's always more research to do, more traveling, more on-site research, and so forth. I can never get her to start her book on her own. So I turn to Janet and I say, 'Goddamnit, woman, on July 20th, you're startin' this novel!'"

Well . . . everybody was just absolutely shocked!

S: I'll bet!

R: No one had ever heard of this, and you've got to picture this room. It was like Versailles! And Bill is saying something like, "Goddamnit, woman. This is the day you're going to start your book!"

So we all looked at Janet, figuring she would say, "Aw, Bill, shut up." But she said, "Nope, he's absolutely right. If Bill didn't tell me when to start my book, I'd never start one."

S: She told me the same thing. I told her that I couldn't imagine what I would say if *my* husband were to say something like that to me. I'm sure it would be pretty earthy. But I guess it's just part of their relationship.

R: Yes. And I feel that, although Janet does the writing and is the creator, Bill plays so many roles for her that facilitate the creative process, that when I talk about Janet, I often find myself referring to her as "them."

S: So does she.

R: Yes, she does it, too. She sometimes says, "We." And I really admire that. It's very hard to judge anybody's marriage from the outside. And there is a relationship there that is central to Janet's creativity. Bill clears away all the "junk" that concerns so many authors. Everything from, "What am I going to wear for my author's picture?" to hairstyles, to being the road person on her trips. All the things that might get in an author's way of settling down and focusing on the work, he takes care of all that stuff. And to the extent that is part of every author's makeup, every author's concern, I think it's an invaluable service. You don't write in a vacuum. You write, and then there are all these other considerations—finances, publicity, travel. And to the degree that he facilitates all this stuff, she really is able to focus entirely on her work.

S: Yes, he certainly is a great boon to her in that respect. Was there anything else? Any final words?

R: There is one other thing, something they said to me recently and probably to you. They looked at me and said, "If writing stops being fun, we'll stop doing it and go do something else. We had a great life before Janet became a writer, and we'll have a great life if she ever stops writing. But it's gotta be fun. It has to be a challenge for all of us." So, to them, to her, writing is a form of risk. And I think that comment sort of reflects what it means to her, to them, to be a writer.

S: She said that to me, too. But she also said, "I'd be half a person if I didn't write."
    I realize you've contributed many things to her success since she first came to you. Could you name any one thing that you feel was the most satisfying, the most important contribution to her career?

R: I think there are two things. I wrote to her in a letter once that one of the things that my clients pay me to do is to think. Something any good agent should do . . . is think, not in terms of just a book, but in terms of a career. And you're always trying to think of how any single book or any single plan fits into their career vision, or your vision of their career. And I think that's one of the things, the satisfaction of seeing her career grow, of helping it to grow.

And how have I helped it to grow? Mainly, I think, by being able to talk about her characters as living beings. Every author needs some sort of a sounding board to articulate how they feel about a character. And one of the most valuable things I think I've done for Janet—although I don't believe she needed it—was that I reminded her to ask herself, "What was going on before your novel actually began?"

Because in Janet's work the backstory—the thing that happened maybe a century or half a century before the novel began—that story must be well understood by the author, Janet or otherwise, before you can write the real novel. So you have to ask yourself, "What was going on before the book opens?"

S: I know that you have plans for all your clients. How do you see Janet's future?

R: Janet feels that some of her work in the eighties reflected the kind of glitzy society that was going on in the eighties. The kind of society that was written about by Jackie Collins, Judith Krantz, Danielle Steel. And I think that some of the elements in her books were an attempt to reach that wider audience. And I think she succeeded. But I think she longed to return to some of the elements that "got her here." That includes the land and the American values that created the West and the Midwest.

S: And that is reflected in her new book, isn't it?

R: It *is* reflected in *The Proud and the Free*. And I think
the interesting thing is that as the glamour of the
eighties recedes and some of those values which Janet
feels are so important return to our society, she is in
the position to be a spokesperson for those values.

PART IX

Publishing
Record

NO QUARTER ASKED

Publisher:	Harlequin
Book Number:	124
Publication Date:	January 1976
Setting:	Texas
Heroine:	Stacy Adams
Hero:	Cord Harris
Occupation:	Rancher

Synopsis: After her father's death, Stacy Adams was devastated. She'd spent her entire life traveling with her father while he built a career as a freelance photographer. Exploring the world had left her with little time for making friends and even less to consider her future.

Now, alone, she was at a crossroads. Although comfortably wealthy, she needed to decide what she wanted to do with her life. What better place for contemplating her future than an isolated cabin in Texas?

Sadly, all hopes of having a tranquil vacation disintegrated the moment she met her new landlord, Cord Harris. The rugged rancher was the most arrogant, overbearing man she'd ever encountered. His accusation that she was a spoiled city girl, incapable of surviving without the luxuries in life, rankled all the way to her toes. Even worse, she found herself in his debt, forced to allow him to set the terms of payment.

Determined to take anything he dished out, Stacy began working alongside his cowhands. But as her love grew for the wild, open land, so did her love for Cord.

Once her debt was paid, how could she ever bear to leave them both behind?

BOSS MAN FROM OGALLALA

Publisher:	Harlequin
Book Number:	131
Publication Date:	March 1976
Setting:	Nebraska
Heroine:	Casey Gilmore
Occupation:	Ranch owner
Hero:	Flint McCallister
Occupation:	Ranch manager

Synopsis: When Casey's father was thrown from a horse and broke his leg, the responsibility for running the family ranch fell directly on her shoulders. Even with the accompanying headaches, Casey welcomed the opportunity.

But the bank, which held a loan on the property, decided to send a "boss man" to run the ranch and protect its interests until Mr. Gilmore was on his feet. The thought of someone other than a family member holding the reins of the Anchor Bar Ranch was more than Casey could stand.

"You're looking at one girl who isn't going to be bossed around by that know-it-all! I hate him!" she proclaimed before she had ever set eyes on Flint McCallister.

But Flint made it clear that he didn't want her in his life, either . . . a reaction she hadn't expected. And Casey decided that perhaps she did want a part of Flint's heart—if he would only allow her inside.

SAVAGE LAND

Publisher:	Harlequin
Book Number:	139
Publication Date:	May 1976
Setting:	Texas
Heroine:	Colleen McGuire
Hero:	Jason Savage

Synopsis: After their mother's death, Coley and her brother had traveled to their aunt's ranch, hoping she would welcome them, although they had never met. When a violent rainstorm separated brother and sister, Coley found herself caught in a flood, rescued by a dark, sinister man with a vicious scar across his face. "The mark of Cain," he had called it. And not without good reason. The locals believed that Jase Savage had lived up to his surname and his reputation by killing his brother. While Coley didn't want to believe that the same man who had saved her life could have taken his own sibling's, she had to admit that there was a bleak side to Jase's character. Even while she was falling in love with him, Coley realized that she wasn't exactly sure what this mysterious, brooding man might be capable of doing.

FIRE AND ICE

Publisher:	Harlequin
Book Number:	147
Publication Date:	July 1976
Setting:	California
Heroine:	Alisa Franklin
Hero:	Zachary Stuart
Occupation:	Gambler/businessman

Synopsis: Even from the grave, Alisa's mother managed to manipulate her life. Believing that no woman was complete without a man, her mother had included a particularly devastating clause in her will: Alisa would receive custody of her seven-year-old sister, Christine, *only* if she were to marry and remain so for a year.

The state of matrimony was one place where Alisa had vowed *never* to live. A traumatic attack by a lust-besotted stepfather had introduced Alisa to the darker side of mankind. And subsequent encounters while dating had convinced her that men were all too eager to force themselves on a woman if given the chance. She had formed the opinion that the opposite sex was comprised of either brutes or wimps, and she wanted nothing to do with any of them.

But how could she leave that poor child in the care of her aunt and uncle whom she loathed? Alisa's mother had been short on parenting skills, and Alisa had practically raised Christine. She couldn't deny her maternal instincts for the girl. Alisa would have to fulfill the hated clause. And what better way for an heiress to get a husband, whom she didn't want in the first place, but to buy one?

Zachary Stuart, a dashing gambler and businessman, had inherited his own set of problems when his father had died: a stack of debts and a California winery that was falling apart. He needed money; Alisa needed a "husband." It seemed like the perfect solution . . . at the time.

It was business, nothing else. Alisa was certain she could pull it off without a hitch, gain custody of her sister, and get away with her heart and her virtue intact.

But Zachary had other plans. He warned her, "I'd be careful if I were you. You already have one warm spot in your ice-encrusted heart for your sister. Someday a fire might come along and melt the rest away."

LAND OF ENCHANTMENT

Publisher:	Harlequin
Book Number:	151
Publication Date:	August 1976
Setting:	New Mexico
Heroine:	Diana Mills
Occupation:	Model
Hero:	Elijah Masters (Lije)
Occupation:	Rodeo cowboy/rancher

Synopsis: As a successful model, Diana Mills knew that it was her beauty that drew people to her. Longing to be accepted for herself alone, Diana hid her loneliness behind a mask of composure and poise.

After dating so many men who thought her a possession rather than an individual, she had nearly given up the idea of meeting Mr. Right. But that was before rodeo cowboy Elijah Masters saved her from a fall during a photo session. His granite-gray eyes looked past her superficial beauty and saw the vulnerable, loving woman beneath.

Warning her that his heritage was deeply rooted in the soil of his New Mexico ranch, Lije asked her to become his wife. When she agreed, she knew it would mean relinquishing her life in the city. But she wasn't prepared for the drastic change in her lifestyle.

How would she ever become a helpmate to Lije in this harsh, hostile land?

Mistaking her feelings of insecurity for regret at having married him, Lije demanded she return to the city and seek a divorce. But she didn't want to go anywhere. How could she convince him that for her, home was by his side?

THE HOMEPLACE

Publisher:	**Harlequin**
Book Number:	**159**
Publication Date:	**October 1976**
Setting:	**Iowa**
Heroine:	**Catherine Carlsen**
Occupation:	**Teacher**
Hero:	**Rob Douglas**
Occupation:	**Writer/farmer**

Synopsis: In the space of only two weeks, Cathie Carlsen had lost two of the dearest parts of her heart—her grandfather and the family farm. The first farmer to have broken the virgin ground with a plowshare had been Cathie's great-grandfather. And even if the passing of a family's land from generation to generation was becoming a thing of the past, Cathie had never contemplated the possibility of losing this precious property. She had fully intended to live, raise a family, and die on that land, like her ancestors before her.

But Fate seemed to have different ideas. Destiny arrived in the form of a handsome city slicker named Rob Douglas, who had other plans for this sacred ground.

Teaching Rob's son, Tad, was a breeze. It was the father who had a few things to learn. But along the way, Cathie discovered that maybe she, too, had some growing to do, and a few lessons to take to heart.

AFTER THE STORM

Publisher:	Harlequin
Book Number:	167
Publication Date:	December 1976
Setting:	Colorado
Heroine:	Lainie MacLeod
Hero:	Rad MacLeod

Synopsis: The proverbial wolf named Poverty was certainly knocking at Lainie's front door. The posh home in the exclusive Denver neighborhood was indicative of what her family lifestyle had once been, but was no more. With her father's death and her mother's constant illnesses, Lainie's world had shrunk until her life was nothing more than a struggle to keep a roof over her mother's head and pay the mounting debts.

Lainie had another option, one she was unwilling to take—her husband, Rad. After being separated for five years, he still refused to give her a divorce. And in spite of their lengthy absence from each other, the bitterness and misery were still fresh when they met under social circumstances.

In his usual condescending manner, he offered her money. She told him, "I'd sell myself in the streets before I'd ask you for anything!"

But that was before her mother's health took a turn for the worse, before the doctor told Lainie that the woman was dying, before he suggested the life-giving treatment.

Lainie knew that Rad MacLeod never gave anything without receiving something in return. She knew he would want to see her grovel. He would want to hear her beg. But she hadn't anticipated that what he really wanted was *her*.

"I want back what has always been mine," he told her. "What I already bought and paid for once. You are still legally my wife. All I'm asking is that you take up those duties once more." In return he agreed to pay all her debts and the costs for her mother's treatments.

What frightened Lainie most was that she wanted to accept his offer, and she knew it had nothing to do with her mother or her need for money. She still loved Rad. She was beginning to wonder if she had ever stopped.

DANGEROUS MASQUERADE

Publisher:	Harlequin
Book Number:	171
Publication Date:	January 1977
Setting:	Alabama
Heroine:	Laurie Evans
Occupation:	Secretary
Hero:	Rian Montgomery
Occupation:	Hotel owner/ entrepreneur

Synopsis: After the death of her parents, young Laurie Evans had been sent to live with her aunt and uncle. She soon realized that she was destined to live in her cousin LaRaine's shadow. Everyone and everything in Laurie's world revolved around her more confident, vivacious cousin. Although Laurie had gone to the same schools and had been given an equally beautiful bedroom across the hall from LaRaine, she had been frequently reminded that she was merely the "little orphan."

So Laurie shouldn't have been shocked and hurt to see the picture in the newspaper or to read the caption, "Hotel owner and entrepreneur Rian Montgomery seen escorting the rising young newcomer LaRaine Evans at a recent Hollywood party." The man was rich, handsome, famous, with all the important show business connections. Why shouldn't her cousin have the best . . . as always?

But cousin LaRaine was leading a complicated life. She

had agreed to visit Rian's aunt in Mobile while he was on a business trip to South America. At the same time, she had been offered her dream—a role in a major motion picture. If she went to Mobile, she lost the part. By doing the movie, she would risk her engagement. As always, when finding herself in a difficult situation of her own making, LaRaine asked Laurie to bail her out. And, as so many times before, Laurie found it impossible to say no.

Before she had really considered the wisdom of such a ridiculous plan, Laurie found herself in Mobile, meeting Rian Montgomery's aunt, posing as her cousin.

Everything would have gone as planned except for a couple of hitches. Laurie hadn't anticipated that she would get along so well with Rian's charming aunt, a woman so sincere, so kind, that Laurie could hardly stand to lie to her. Laurie hadn't expected Rian to cut his business trip short and appear at his aunt's home to "surprise" his beloved. And, most disturbing of all, Laurie had never intended to fall in love with her cousin's fiancé . . . a man she could never have.

NIGHT OF THE COTILLION

Publisher:	Harlequin
Book Number:	180
Publication Date:	March 1977
Setting:	Georgia
Heroine:	Amanda Bennett
Hero:	Jarod Colby

Synopsis: A cotillion celebrating Jefferson Davis's birthday . . . held in a *Yankee's* house! Unheard of! And even worse, the cotillion's official host was a Yankee carpetbagger, industrialist Jarod Colby.

The town's socialites were all atwitter with this juicy gossip, but Amanda had even more reason to be excited—

and anxious—than the others. Jarod Colby had been her first love. And after three years, the girlish, romantic fantasies he had inspired remained, trapped forever in her heart and imagination.

Six years ago, she had been tramping through the woods, dreaming about love and romance and the handsome man she would one day meet. Jarod Colby had cantered his horse across the meadow, a dark, mysterious figure dressed in black, and Amanda had fallen instantly, deeply in love, never to fully recover.

But when she had dared to approach him, she had found the real Jarod Colby to be nothing like the Jarod of her dreams. Rather than kind, solicitous, and romantic, he had coldly rejected her, and the pain and humiliation still lingered.

At the cotillion, Jarod—and every other man in attendance—noticed Amanda, the perfect Southern beauty. After apologizing for his previous offense, he determined to change her opinion of him. But Amanda soon discovered that he was still an arrogant, overbearing aristocrat, insisting that she dance with him, insisting that he take her home.

Soon Jarod made it all too clear that he wanted Amanda, was determined to have her. Amanda was no one's fool. A man like Jarod was accustomed to getting what he wanted. The only reason he was so adamant about having her was because she had denied him, and he didn't like being refused. Or perhaps it was because she had admitted to him that she was a virgin, and he found the idea of deflowering her a challenge.

He hadn't mentioned marriage, and she wasn't surprised. Jarod Colby wasn't going to marry some small-town girl, the daughter of his plant manager. Many women, far more sophisticated and worldly than herself, were available to him.

Faced with the alternative of having an affair with Jarod Colby, Amanda wondered how deeply she cared for him. Was she still wrapped up in her illusions of the past?

Was the attraction between them purely physical? Or was there a chance of deeper emotions being involved? If there was, she had the depressing feeling that it would only be on her side.

VALLEY OF THE VAPORS

Publisher:	Harlequin
Book Number:	183
Publication Date:	March 1977
Setting:	Arkansas
Heroine:	Tisha Caldwell
Hero:	Roarke Madison

Synopsis: Tisha's father wanted to control every aspect of her life: what she wore, where she went, the trust fund her mother had left her, and, most importantly, the men in her life. A reformed rogue himself, her dad knew how much trouble a rebellious spirit like hers could get into.

But Tisha didn't understand why he was so concerned. With her, he had nothing to worry about. Tisha had always thought herself immune to physical lust, too ruled by her mind to be betrayed by her senses.

Until Roarke Madison kissed her.

Tisha decided that perhaps her father had something to worry about after all. Daddy's little girl had grown up!

When Dad found out about the kiss, he demanded that Roarke make an "honest woman" of his beloved daughter. Roarke resisted, claiming that Tisha had initiated the whole encounter in a scheme to trap him.

But if he objected so strongly, why did he offer her a beautiful diamond engagement ring?

"He's one of those predatory males who charm you into letting your guard down, then rush in for the kill," she said. But Tisha had to admit . . . ladykiller or not, the man's kisses were to die for!

FIESTA SAN ANTONIO

Publisher:	Harlequin
Book Number:	192
Publication Date:	June 1977
Setting:	Texas
Heroine:	Natalie Crane
Hero:	Colter Langton

Synopsis: Raising her departed brother's son was a mixed blessing for Natalie. She loved little Ricky dearly, but it was difficult trying to make ends meet with the expense of raising a child on her young shoulders.

The night she met Colter Langton had been a low point in her life. Wrongly dismissed from the last in a string of odd jobs, she was tired, discouraged, and didn't know where to turn.

Her encounter with Colter hadn't exactly raised her spirits. Although he had offered her and Ricky a ride home, Natalie knew the generous action had been prompted by Colter's daughter, Missy. The girl seemed lost, emotionally neglected, and that didn't surprise Natalie, considering what a cold, heartless man Colter Langton appeared to be. Natalie couldn't help feeling sorry for the girl, wishing she could help.

She was given the opportunity much sooner than she had expected, in the form of a strange proposal. With all the heated passion of a December night, Colter Langton asked her to marry him. He made no claims of love or devotion, offering only the explanation that he needed a full-time housekeeper and caregiver for his daughter. She needed a job, he observed, so they must be the perfect match.

With serious misgivings, Natalie agreed. Somehow, she had to care for Ricky; maybe a marriage of convenience wouldn't be so bad after all. Within twenty-four hours, she was Mrs. Colter Langton. At least, she was wearing a heavy gold band on her finger and the minister had pronounced them husband and wife.

But Colter told her bluntly that he didn't care about anyone, including himself, that he had been fortunate enough not to be "cursed" with emotions.

If she had held any hope that this marriage of convenience might grow into one of love, or even affection, that hope died when she heard those words. Could any heart be so cold, so distant that love couldn't span the divide?

SHOW ME

Publisher:	Harlequin
Book Number:	200
Publication Date:	August 1977
Setting:	Missouri
Heroine:	Tanya Lassiter
Hero:	Jake Lassiter

Synopsis: Tanya found it difficult to explain to her seven-year-old son why his father stayed away from home year after year. Was he dead, the boy asked, or in prison? She tried to reassure him with the obvious excuses: Jake was building bridges in Africa, and the political situation was too volatile for her and John to visit him there.

Unsatisfied with her flimsy explanations, the boy needed more. To placate his curiosity, she agreed that they should write to his father, asking him to return for a visit.

Little did Tanya know that Jake would return ... and at the most inopportune moment ... just in time to find her in the arms of another man.

Jake had never been a predictable man, but Tanya couldn't help being surprised when he suggested they call a truce, try to live together in peace for two or three

months, and then, if things didn't work out, consider a
divorce.

They agreed that their attempt at reconciliation would
be based upon a new and deeper level of intimacy, and
most of all, trust. But how could trust flourish when the
past was shrouded in lies and secrecy? Tanya knew that
no matter how hard they worked to revive their dying
marriage, their efforts were pointless. Once Jake knew the
truth, which she had been hiding from him for so many
years, their marriage, their love, their lives together would
end.

BLUEGRASS KING

Publisher:	Harlequin
Book Number:	203
Publication Date:	June 1977
Setting:	Kentucky
Heroine:	Dani Williams
Occupation:	Horse rancher
Hero:	Barrett King
Occupation:	Horse rancher

Synopsis: Barrett King was used to buying what he
wanted, and his family owned the finest racing horses in
Bluegrass country. Except The Rogue. Dani Williams took
great pride in knowing that her prize horse was the very
best, and all of Barrett King's money couldn't buy him.
Some things just weren't for sale.

Most people couldn't see beyond Barrett's charm and
handsome facade, but Dani knew he could be ruthless.
Barrett saw Dani as a child, a teenager at best, and that
rankled her, too. Mostly she just hated him, felt he didn't
deserve the air he breathed. Though she wasn't sure why
he should stir such deep emotion in her.

Then tragedy struck her family, and The Rogue was

gone. Everything their family had worked for was lost. Somehow, it was Barrett King's fault; she was sure of it. She just didn't know how. Publicly, she accused him of causing the accident, her allegation supplying grist for the media mill.

With his life and career in shambles, Dani's father made her promise to leave the business of horse racing. Reluctantly, she agreed. But Dani couldn't stay away from the track any more than she could continue to nurse her grudge against Barrett King. She found that a thin line separated the passion of hate from that of desire.

A LYON'S SHARE

Publisher:	Harlequin
Book Number:	208
Publication Date:	October 1977
Setting:	Illinois
Heroine:	Joan Somers
Occupation:	Secretary
Hero:	Brandt Lyon
Occupation:	Owner of a construction company

Synopsis: When Joan Somers had been hired as a personal secretary by Brandt Lyon, she wondered if he were the type who constantly chased his female employees around the desk. She had even speculated that it might be exciting to be caught.

"I had wanted someone older, with more experience," he had told her. She had assured him that she was well qualified, and he had decided to give her a chance.

Joan readily admitted that within the first few months on the job, she had developed a major crush on her boss. She had nurtured secret fantasies that he might see her as a woman, but he had been businesslike all the way. Afraid that her fellow employees would discover her infatuation, Joan treated Brandt with nothing but the coolest formality.

Even when Joan made the effort to date other men, she found herself constantly comparing them to Brandt Lyon and finding them lacking. It was ridiculous, she told herself. Infatuations were all right for an adolescent, but she was older and supposedly wiser.

Armed with resolve to get over her crush, Joan hadn't anticipated that Fate—and a Chicago blizzard—would intervene, making her decision moot.

How was she supposed to ignore her feelings for this virile, sexy man with the two of them stranded, alone, at the office? And how could she control her passions and desires when the need to stay warm forced them to sleep together on his office sofa?

The barrier between employer and employee had been permanently breached. There was no point in denying it anymore. She loved him. Foolishly, futilely, she loved him.

THE WIDOW AND THE WASTREL

Publisher:	**Harlequin**
Book Number:	**211**
Publication Date:	**November 1977**
Setting:	**Ohio**
Heroine:	**Elizabeth Carrel**
Hero:	**Jed Carrel**

Synopsis: Nine years earlier, Jed Carrel had advised Elizabeth not to marry his brother, not to be seduced by the glamor of the Carrel name. She'd ignored his warning, but she couldn't ignore the raging fire Jed's unexpected kiss aroused. Finding him arrogant and insulting, she was relieved when he went abroad shortly before her marriage to his older brother, Jeremy.

As time passed, Elizabeth became a mature woman, a mother, and a widow. Her social duties and raising her daughter, Amy, left her with little time for a personal life.

Living in her mother-in-law's home, she was satisfied with her luxurious lifestyle and predictable routine. At least, she was until the day Jed returned unexpectedly.

Although cynical and rugged, he stirred dormant emotions, reminding Elizabeth that she was a woman. Suddenly she longed for something more in her life, something she knew only Jed could give her.

But he'd always been the irresponsible, reckless member of the family. She was a fool for falling in love with him. Should she accept his proposal of marriage when his own mother warned that he'd never be more than a penniless adventurer?

Jed had asked her to trust him. But how could she, when she had her daughter's future to consider?

THE IVORY CANE

Publisher:	Harlequin
Book Number:	219
Publication Date:	January 1978
Setting:	California
Heroine:	Sabrina Lane
Hero:	Bay Cameron

Synopsis: Sabrina Lane had once been a talented artist. Her entire life and future had been based on the ability of her eyes to see the things her hands would paint. It was only natural she should feel bitterness at the injustice of her fate. A tragic car accident had taken her sight from her, her dreams, and her joy of living.

But Sabrina was determined that she would learn to cope with her limitations. She wanted no special treatment from anyone. More than anything else, she didn't want pity.

When Bay Cameron insinuated himself into her life, she resisted, thinking he was offering sympathy, another crutch for her to lean on. She made it clear to him that she intended to stand on her own two feet. "I'm tired of your patronizing attitude!" she told him. "Go and join the Boy Scouts! I'm tired of your good deeds!"

But the moment Bay pulled her into his arms and kissed her, she knew that he had strong feelings for her . . . and those emotions had nothing to do with pity.

For Sabrina, that realization was the most frightening of all. She owed him a tremendous debt of gratitude; he had shown her that, blind or sighted, she could still live, love, even pursue her art. But Bay Cameron was a domineering man, even when he tried to be gentle. And the only thing Sabrina was willing to have dominate her life was her work.

THE INDY MAN

Publisher:	**Harlequin**
Book Number:	**223**
Publication Date:	**February 1978**
Setting:	**Indiana**
Heroine:	**Susan Mabry**
Occupation:	**Secretary at a law firm**
Hero:	**Mitch Braden**
Occupation:	**Race car driver**

Synopsis: Susan had never officially accepted Warren's proposal. In fact, he had never bothered to formally propose;

he had simply told her they were going to be married, and she hadn't objected.

With Warren, life would be calm and collected, as orderly as the man himself. But Susan had a hunger for more, a need she had never realized until the Indy Man himself, race car driver Mitch Braden, appeared.

His outlandish, brazen flirtation with her caused a stir of emotion in the otherwise staid Warren. However, the feelings Mitch aroused in Susan's jealous fiancé were nothing compared to the turmoil his presence caused in her. Whether Susan was ready or not, she found herself hurtling down the fast lane with Mitch and liking it . . . a lot!

DARLING JENNY

Publisher:	Harlequin
Book Number:	227
Publication Date:	March 1978
Setting:	Wyoming
Heroine:	Jennifer Glenn
Hero:	Logan Taylor

Synopsis: Nursing a broken heart and a wounded ego, Jennifer had boarded a plane for Wyoming. She needed to get away, needed the solace of the Wyoming wilderness and her sister's love. What better place to put the past behind her and heal her spirit?

Men! Finally Jennifer had seen them for what they really were. Beneath the charm, the good looks, the exuded masculinity and sexuality, they were selfish, egocentric creatures who were interested only in their own pleasure and gratification, no matter the cost to the women who loved them.

She had allowed a man to take advantage of her once before, but never, ever again!

When Jennifer arrived in the magnificent Tetons, she

found that she had run away from one source of conflict and directly into another. Her sister, Sheila, was involved with exactly the same kind of man who had broken Jennifer's heart . . . maybe even worse. Jennifer was determined to save Sheila from suffering the same fate she had.

But matters of the heart seldom go as planned, and before she knew what was happening, Jennifer found *herself* falling under Logan Taylor's spell. She had thought she had learned her lesson, but Logan was determined to tutor her. And his instructions were to succumb, not resist.

REILLY'S WOMAN

Publisher:	Harlequin
Book Number:	231
Publication Date:	April 1978
Setting:	Nevada
Heroine:	Leah Talbot
Occupation:	Secretary
Hero:	Reilly Smith
Occupation:	Jewelry designer

Synopsis: All Leah had hoped for was a short visit with her brother in Austin, Nevada, to celebrate his birthday, and sharing the chartered plane with the mysterious Mr. Smith had seemed like the perfect way to get there.

But a violent thunderstorm turned the simple flight into a tragedy. Leah realized that she had survived the plane crash only to face a prolonged death, exposed to the harsh elements of the desert.

Fortunately, Reilly Smith had survival skills, drawn from his Native American heritage. He showed her how to find food, water, and shelter, the basics to keep them alive until they could find a way out of the wilderness.

The life-and-death struggle that they shared alone created an intimacy that bonded them in a special way. Leah knew it was love she felt for Reilly, not just gratitude. But he was convinced that once they reached civilization, the affection they shared would evaporate like the evening dew beneath a morning desert sun.

TO TELL THE TRUTH

Publisher:	Harlequin
Book Number:	236
Publication Date:	May 1978
Setting:	Oregon
Heroine:	Andrea Grant
Hero:	Tell Stafford

Synopsis: Shortly after her parents' deaths, Andrea's boyfriend, Dale, broke their engagement. To make matters worse, the proceeds from the sale of her family home and any money she might have inherited had been depleted by her parents' medical bills.

Feeling deeply depressed and abandoned, Andrea faced a bleak future. Luckily, John Grant, her father's best friend, learned of her unfortunate circumstances. Wise and understanding, he insisted she move into his house until she recovered from her painful loss.

Although Andrea was young and John was confined to a wheelchair, gossip circulated about their relationship. Determined to salvage her reputation, John suggested a marriage of convenience, stipulating that should she fall in love again, their marriage would be annulled. Believing that after loving Dale she would never again be struck by Cupid's arrow, Andrea agreed.

Three years later, at John's suggestion, she was vacationing at Squaw Valley. Prepared for a week of skiing, the last thing on her mind was romance. But that was before

she looked into Tell Stafford's dark eyes and felt awareness quiver through her.

What began as a simple flirtation quickly escalated,
and suddenly she was deeply in love. But even if Tell
shared her feelings, how long would his love last when
she confessed her secret?

Then the unthinkable happened . . . Tell proposed.
Accepting his ring, Andrea knew she must tell him the
truth. Unfortunately, John chose that moment to telephone. When Tell answered and discovered her husband
calling, he didn't stay around for explanations. Bitterly
hurt and sickened by her deception, he checked out of
the hotel.

Devastated, Andrea returned home. Sensing her unhap-
piness and hoping to raise her spirits, John invited house-
guests. When they arrived, Andrea was stunned to see that
Tell Stafford was one of their visitors. Treating her with
nothing but contempt, Tell believed she'd married his
friend for money. She'd lost Tell's respect and trust.
Without those, how could she hope to ever regain his
love?

SONORA SUNDOWN

Publisher:	Harlequin
Book Number:	239
Publication Date:	June 1978
Setting:	Arizona
Heroine:	Brandy Ames
Hero:	Jim Corbett
Occupation:	Film star

Synopsis: As Brandy Ames watched the sun sink over the
foothills, setting the western horizon ablaze with vibrant
color, she decided that she could easily fall in love with the
Sonora Desert every evening at sundown. But, beautiful as

it was, the desert was no place to lose one's way after dark.

Abandoned by her horse, lost and progressively becoming more worried, Brandy stumbled onto a campfire. Ah, the warmth of human companionship. Or maybe not.

The man beside the fire was anything but inviting. Judging from his cold and suspicious manner, she assumed he was a cattle rustler. By the time he administered first aid to her cactus-prickled skin and gave her a hot meal, coffee, and his bedroll, she decided that if he were a thief, he was a rather nice one, despite his gruffness.

When a rescue team found her, Brandy discovered that her new love interest, Jim, wasn't a rustler after all—worse. He was the famous actor James Corbett. A man with his experience would, undoubtedly, prefer more glamorous, sophisticated women, and they were available by the score. He would never be interested in a simple country girl.

If only Brandy could forget the warmth of his body as he had held her in his arms, sheltering her from the storm. If only she could forget the heat of his kiss.

BIG SKY COUNTRY

Publisher:	Harlequin
Book Number:	244
Publication Date:	July 1978
Setting:	Montana
Heroine:	Jillian Randall
Hero:	Riordan

Synopsis: Jill's best friend was engaged, and Jill was thrilled for her. Kerry was such a good person; if anyone deserved to be happy, it was she. Finally, a man had seen past Kerry's plain exterior to the beautiful woman inside. Jill had been blessed with extraordinary good looks, and had often thought it unfair that Kerry seemed to have been cheated in that regard. But the tables had turned for Kerry; her fiancé, Todd, didn't seem to mind. And as long as she was happy, so was Jill.

Then Todd's brother appeared on the scene, demanding that Todd and Kerry break their engagement. Poor Kerry had a difficult time standing up to this domineering, intimidating man. But Jill, spirited and fiercely protective of her friend, had no problem. In fact, she welcomed the challenge to bring this uppity Riordan brother down a few notches.

Jill set a trap for him, figuring that, like every other man she had ever known, he would be easy prey. She soon realized that she hadn't considered all the contingencies. What was she going to do with this man, known only as "Riordan," now that she had caught him?

SOMETHING EXTRA

Publisher:	Harlequin
Book Number:	248
Publication Date:	August 1978
Setting:	Louisiana
Heroine:	Jolie Antoinette Smith
Occupation:	Degree in home economics
Hero:	Steve Cameron
Occupation:	Plantation owner

Synopsis: Now that she'd obtained her degree in home economics, Jolie Antoinette Smith had to make a decision about her future.

After returning to her parents' South Dakota farm, she hoped to find a solution to her dilemma. Instead, she discovered that the adage "You can't go home again" couldn't have been more appropriate.

Turning down her childhood friend John's marriage proposal added to her restless confusion. Although she cared a great deal for him, there was something missing in their relationship.

Sensing Jolie's dissatisfaction, her Aunt Brigitte insisted on financing a trip to Louisiana as a belated graduation gift. Jolie wondered if the ancestral home, Cameron Hall, was still standing. Why not take a vacation and find out?

Soon after reaching her destination, Jolie realized she was in danger of losing her heart to more than the old family plantation. Although the new owner, Steve Cameron, was way out of her league in experience, she was irresistibly attracted to him.

But Steve believed the most precious thing a man possessed was his freedom, and he was certain that a commitment to a relationship would jeopardize his autonomy. Before her vacation was over, could she find some way to change his mind?

THE MASTER FIDDLER

Publisher:	Harlequin
Book Number:	252
Publication Date:	September 1978
Setting:	Arizona
Heroine:	Jacqueline Grey
Hero:	Choya Barnett

Synopsis: Demanding that her parents allow her to live her own life, Jacqueline Grey didn't foresee the consequences of her words. When she left home, she never imagined she'd have a car accident and find herself stranded in Tombstone, Arizona. The moment she collided with widower rancher Choya Barnett, and his young son, Robbie, her life seemed to go from bad to worse. Her wallet was missing, and her parents refused to accept her collect telephone call. How could she pay for the auto repairs?

When Choya paid her bills, Jacquie didn't like the terms of repayment. He expected her to become his housekeeper—and his mistress.

He said she'd had her way too often: now it was time she paid the price.

As Jacquie fell under his spell, she wondered if the price would be her heart.

BEWARE OF THE STRANGER

Publisher:	Harlequin
Book Number:	256
Publication Date:	October 1978
Setting:	New York
Heroine:	Samantha Gentry
Hero:	Chris Andrews

Synopsis: Samantha Gentry's horoscope told her to "beware of the stranger," but she didn't believe in such silliness. Perhaps her instinct should have warned her that the man who appeared at her office and told her to come with him might have a hidden agenda. She believed he was Owen Bradley, an employee of Samantha's tycoon father. Her dad had sent him to whisk her away to a secluded island in the St. Lawrence Seaway, or so he said.

But once she arrived on the tiny island, she discovered that her "host" wasn't Owen at all, but someone named Chris Andrews. Unless he was lying . . . again.

Also, she realized that being lured to this lonely destination had proven to be much simpler than leaving. Soon Samantha realized she was being held prisoner by this stranger who had stolen her away. He insisted that her presence on his island was business, nothing more. But what sort of business? A little investigating told Samantha that his name wasn't Chris Andrews, either. Suspicious whispered conversations in the night caused her to fear that the worst had happened: she had been kidnapped and was being held for ransom.

Samantha intended to confront him, to demand explanations, to know why he was lying to her at every turn. But somewhere along the way, she had stopped thinking of him as her captor and begun looking at him as the man who had kissed her passionately and introduced her to feelings and sensations she hadn't known she possessed.

Beware of the stranger . . . she reminded herself . . . *because he can steal your heart.*

GIANT OF MESABI

Publisher:	Harlequin
Book Number:	259
Publication Date:	November 1978
Setting:	Minnesota
Heroine:	Alanna Powell
Hero:	Rolt Matthews

Synopsis: When Alanna stepped off the plane, she was expecting her boyfriend, Kurt, to be waiting to greet her. Instead, she was met by his brother, Rolt, who promptly claimed his brother's kiss with a ferocity that left her angry, but strangely weak.

From the moment they had met, five years before, Alanna had been wary of Kurt's older brother. Rolt Matthews was of the dark world, and Kurt was of the day. Handsome and charming, Kurt was the antithesis of his older brother. Whenever Rolt even looked her way, with that enigmatic glitter in his blue eyes, Alanna found him more disturbing than she cared to admit.

He took liberties with her that she couldn't allow.

When she reminded him that she was his brother's girl-friend, he said, "Are you? Not that it matters. I've always taught my brother to share."

Rolt angered her, repulsed her, disgusted her. Obviously he had no moral standards at all. What kind of man tried to seduce his brother's girl?

Yet, when she was with him, she found herself wondering what it would be like to be caressed by those strong, capable hands. Their touch would be firm and authoritative, yet teasing and arousing —

How could she even think such things? She despised the man! What was it about him that his mere presence would cause her to lose all sense of decency and self-respect?

THE MATCHMAKERS

Publisher:	Harlequin
Book Number:	264
Publication Date:	December 1978
Setting:	Delaware
Heroine:	Kathleen Darrow
Occupation:	Nurse/nanny
Hero:	Jordan Long
Occupation:	Oil industry

Synopsis: Kathleen wanted a break from the medical field for a while. Nursing could be such a draining profession that she needed something a bit less challenging to recharge her emotional batteries.

As the oldest of seven children and having worked in pediatrics, she had ample experience in caring for children. So caring for two girls, ages twelve and ten, for the summer sounded heavenly. Days at the beach, swimming and lazing in the sun—it wouldn't be much different from playing around with her younger sisters and being paid for it. An intriguing prospect, to say the least. How difficult could it be?

The girls turned out to be a bit precocious, a mischievous, adventurous pair to say the least, but nothing Kathleen couldn't handle. It was the father who was a handful!

From the moment they met, Kathleen knew that she wasn't what Jordan Long had been expecting in the way of a nanny for his precious girls. He had wanted someone much older, matronly, to run his home . . . certainly not a young, sexy woman like herself. He was ready to toss her out on her ear, but the girls interceded, begging him to give Kathleen a chance.

One month, that was his compromise. A thirty-day trial period, and at the end, he would reevaluate his decision.

But Jordan didn't have a chance. His daughters were already plotting against him. They adored Kathleen and were determined to keep her indefinitely. And they were going to make sure that at the end of the month, he felt the same way.

FOR BITTER OR WORSE

Publisher:	Harlequin
Book Number:	267
Publication Date:	January 1979
Setting:	Texas
Heroine:	Stacy Harris
Hero:	Cord Harris

Synopsis: At one time, Stacy and Cord Harris had enjoyed all the best things that life could offer . . . a marriage based on love and respect, a ranch they both enjoyed working, and a beautiful son. Then a plane crash destroyed Cord's body, and their world.

Stacy was just glad to have Cord alive. She didn't mind the extra strain, trying to run the Circle H, raise Josh alone, and cater to Cord's special needs now that he was confined to a wheelchair.

But she did mind his bitterness, his constant self-pity, and the way he lashed out at everyone around him. Cord made no bones about the fact that he would have preferred to have died in that crash than to have been left half a man.

No amount of love and patience could reach inside the hard shell Cord had drawn around himself. As far as he was concerned, life simply wasn't worth living, if he could no longer live it as fully as he once had.

Then Paula arrived, a gorgeous blonde physical therapist who was determined to get Cord back on his feet again. Suddenly, in her capable hands, Cord had found new inspiration, a reason to strive, a purpose for living.

And Stacy was afraid that this time, she had lost him forever.

GREEN MOUNTAIN MAN

Publisher:	Harlequin
Book Number:	272
Publication Date:	February 1979
Setting:	Vermont
Heroine:	Bridget O'Shea
Occupation:	Salesclerk
Hero:	Jonas Concannon
Occupation:	Doctor

Synopsis: Seeing Jonas Concannon again revived all the old feelings of love, passion, and hurt Bridget O'Shea had experienced as a teenager.

She'd spent ten years living with the knowledge that her parents' money was more important to him than her love. She was convinced that this was true, or else he would never have accepted their bribe and left town, abandoning her.

Now Jonas thought he could waltz back into her life and pick up their relationship where it had left off. But he was dead wrong.

Even though he claimed he was still in love with her and wanted her back, Bridget wasn't about to let him break her heart a second time.

SIX WHITE HORSES

Publisher:	Harlequin
Book Number:	275
Publication Date:	March 1979
Setting:	Oklahoma
Heroine:	Patty King
Occupation:	Trick rider
Hero:	Morgan Kincaid
Occupation:	Rodeo stock owner/rancher

Synopsis: Hoping cowboy Lije Masters would eventually see her as a woman, Patty King had followed him on the rodeo circuit and begun her career as a trick rider. She believed herself in love with him and longed for the day when he would discover that he shared her feelings.

But then her world collapsed. Lije married another woman.

Already aware that loving him was hopeless, Patty didn't need stockman Morgan Kincaid with his constant insults as a reminder. Arrogant and infuriating, Morgan refused to let her wallow in self-pity. She hated him. She only put up with Morgan's barbed comments because, for some inexplicable reason, her grandfather seemed to enjoy his company.

When her horses were injured, Patty gritted her teeth and accepted Morgan's offer to board them at his ranch. Surrounded by his family, she reluctantly agreed to a truce. With their feud temporarily on hold, Patty began to view Morgan in a different light.

Gradually, her feelings changed. What she'd felt for Lije had been infatuation. But the stubborn Morgan refused to listen when she told him she was over Lije. How could Patty convince him that she truly was a woman who knew her own mind and heart, that she was deeply in love with him?

SUMMER MAHOGANY

Publisher:	**Harlequin**
Book Number:	**279**
Publication Date:	**April 1979**
Setting:	**Maine**
Heroine:	**Gina Gaynes**
Hero:	**Rhyder Owens**

Synopsis: Nine years earlier, a much younger Gina had fallen hard for Rhyder Owens. At only sixteen years old, she had thought this older man simply the most compelling, sexy, and virile male she had ever encountered, let alone kissed. She had flirted with him playfully, only to find that he wasn't one of the shy local boys she was accustomed to handling with such ease.

She had wanted Rhyder completely, and she offered herself to him. He had refused, but the damage to her reputation had been done. The entire town had seen her running, nearly naked and sobbing, from his boat, the *Sea Witch*.

To avoid scandal, her grandfather had insisted that she marry Rhyder. Young, confused, and frightened, she had agreed.

As might have been expected, the "marriage" was a disaster, lasting only one night. The next day, Rhyder had written her a generous check, buying his freedom, and sent her on her way.

Now, nine years later, an established and successful attorney with another man in her life, Gina considered herself immune to the distress that Rhyder's presence had once caused her. But when he suddenly appeared in town after so long, she was caught with her defenses down. To her dismay, Gina discovered that where her feelings about Rhyder Owens were concerned, she was as vulnerable as ever.

Worse still, Rhyder brought a disturbing fact to her attention. When testifying under oath at their annulment, he had perjured himself, swearing that their marriage had never been consummated.

As an attorney, Gina didn't need him to tell her that their annulment was invalid. She and Rhyder Owens were still married.

Gina hated the thought of being his wife. She hated Rhyder . . . intensely . . . completely. Or so she said. He didn't believe her, and Gina wasn't surprised. She didn't believe herself.

THE BRIDE OF THE DELTA QUEEN

Publisher:	Harlequin
Book Number:	284
Publication Date:	May 1979
Setting:	Mississippi River
Heroine:	Selena Merrick
Occupation:	Department store buyer
Hero:	Chance Barkley
Occupation:	Businessman/gambler

Synopsis: Selena's father, the Reverend Merrick, had often warned her that she embraced life too passionately. But, lust for living aside, Selena led a fairly conservative life; she was hardly a woman to be mistaken for a lady of the evening.

But in the city of New Orleans, where vice was the expected and the darker side of human nature the norm, Selena found it exciting to pretend, just for a moment, that she was one of those mysterious purveyors of sexual delights. Having made her "offer" to Chance Barkley, she was dismayed to find him more than willing to accept. In fact, he insisted.

Having successfully rid herself of Chance once, she met him again aboard the riverboat *The Delta Queen*. This time Selena was in a spot too tight to wriggle out of. And she had only herself to thank.

TIDEWATER LOVER

Publisher:	Harlequin
Book Number:	292
Publication Date:	June 1979
Setting:	Virginia
Heroine:	Lacey Andrews
Occupation:	Secretary
Hero:	Cole Whitfield
Occupation:	Owner of construction company

Synopsis: With her bank account at an all-time low, Lacey Andrews was out of options. Although she would have preferred some tropical island, it seemed she would be spending her vacation at her parents' home in Richmond.

When her cousin Margo telephoned, asking if she would house-sit, Lacey jumped at the chance. The opportunity to be alone for two weeks with the ocean and an uncrowded beach at her doorstep was like a dream come true ... especially after having spent so much time that week on the telephone trying to placate the difficult Mr. Whitfield.

As secretary for the construction engineering firm that was building Whitfield's newest complex, Margo had the unpleasant task of explaining why the project was behind schedule. Unfortunately, Whitfield wasn't a man who accepted excuses; he called repeatedly, checking their progress. Although Andrea had never met him, with each phone conversation, her dislike for the obnoxious, sarcastic man intensified. Thankfully, vacation meant a break from dealing with his rudeness.

Soon after settling at the beach house, Lacey realized that her paradise was less than idyllic. Margo and her husband had made a terrible mistake. Each of them had asked someone to stay in their home, and typically, they had neglected to inform each other.

The identity of her new roommate made Lacey's head spin. Vital and compelling, Cole Whitfield was a far cry from the man she'd imagined during their telephone conversations.

What had she been thinking when she had agreed to share the beach house with him? Each day she found him more attractive. She knew she should leave. But how could she, when her heart was telling her to stay?

STRANGE BEDFELLOW

Publisher:	Harlequin
Book Number:	296
Publication Date:	July 1979
Setting:	Rhode Island
Heroine:	Dina Chandler
Hero:	Blake Chandler

Synopsis: Dina had every reason to believe that her husband, Blake, was dead. Two years earlier he had disappeared in the South American jungles, and no one had seen or heard from him since.

Eventually, Dina had put her grief aside and gone on with her life. In his absence, she had taken over the reins of their hotel chain and done well by the business. For the first time in her life, Dina had been more than merely Blake Chandler's wife. She had been a smart, decisive, effective businesswoman, and had enjoyed meeting the challenge.

In her loneliness she had reached out to Chet, Blake's best friend, for comfort and found a deep affection. Convinced that she was a widow, Dina had agreed to marry again.

Then Blake had reappeared, alive, but so changed that she hardly recognized him. Blake's struggle for survival in the jungle had turned the suave, urbane gentleman into a primitive, emotional, and sexual man who both frightened and intrigued Dina.

Sometimes she couldn't help resenting this stranger's intrusion into her comfortable, controlled life. At other times she wanted their marriage to work. She wanted to get to know this new Blake, know him, understand him, and maybe, just maybe, love him.

LOW COUNTRY LIAR

Publisher:	**Harlequin**
Book Number:	**302**
Publication Date:	**August 1979**
Setting:	**South Carolina**
Heroine:	**Lisa Talmadge**
Hero:	**Slade Blackwell**

Synopsis: Lisa Talmadge adored her Aunt Mitzi and was fiercely protective of her. *Nobody* cheated her favorite aunt and got away with it!

Having traveled from Baltimore to Charleston, Lisa had a mission: to expose the culprit who was taking advantage of her sweet but rather gullible aunt. And as far as Lisa was concerned, that weasel's name was Slade Blackwell.

Rather than confront him directly, Lisa concocted a scheme that she hoped would show her Aunt Mitzi how wrong she was to trust this scoundrel. Of course, Lisa would have to tell a few lies along the way, resorting to a bit of duplicity herself.

But even the best-laid plans can go awry when something as unexpected as love gets mixed into the potion. Lisa hadn't worried about lying to a crook who was cheating her aunt, but how about deceiving a man she loved?

Caught up in these newfound feelings, Lisa had to admit that perhaps Slade wasn't the con man here after all. She was.

Soon he would find out that she had been lying to him. And Slade Blackwell didn't strike her as a man who would take kindly to deception.

SWEET PROMISE

Publisher:	Harlequin
Book Number:	308
Publication Date:	September 1979
Setting:	Texas
Heroine:	Erica Wakefield de la Torres
Occupation:	Owner of dress boutique
Hero:	Rafael Alejandro de la Torres
Occupation:	Businessman

Synopsis: For years, Erica Wakefield had needed her father's love. Unfortunately, he was married to his business and rarely noticed her.

Desperate to have his undivided attention, she persuaded him to vacation in Acapulco with her. But soon after their arrival, it became apparent that to Vance Wakefield, the word *vacation* simply meant conducting business from a locale other than his office.

Feeling hurt and angry, Erica concocted a scheme, determined to repay him for his lack of attention. Hadn't he voiced his disapproval when he'd seen her talking to the handsome Mexican she'd gone sightseeing with?

Rafael de la Torres made his living as an escort for wealthy women. What harm could possibly come from convincing him that she was in love with him, then asking him to marry her?

But once married, Erica hadn't counted on being so physically attracted to her husband. Powerless to resist his drugging kisses, she had willingly consummated their marriage.

After returning to her hotel, she discovered that there'd been a business emergency and her father had rushed back to the States. Alarmed that her dad wasn't there to rescue her from her own impetuous actions, Erica abandoned her husband, then followed, never mentioning her marriage.

The experience had given her a new maturity. Now she accepted the fact that her father loved her in his own way. Their relationship was better than she ever imagined it could be. What would happen if he learned that she'd married Rafael?

Complicating matters, she received a marriage proposal. Although she was in love with Forest and he'd be a wonderful husband, how could she marry him when she was still legally Rafael's wife?

There was no dodging the issue. She had to locate the husband she had abandoned. But before her search began, he found her.

The moment their eyes met, Erica realized Rafael Alejandro de la Torres was not the man she'd thought he was. Shocked, she learned he headed a powerful and wealthy Mexican family . . . a family that didn't believe in divorce.

He threatened to go to her father if she didn't break her engagement and at least pretend she was willing to become his wife.

She hated him. So why, after spending time with him, did she wonder if she was only pretending? And why did it hurt when he agreed to a divorce, then turned to walk out of her life?

FOR MIKE'S SAKE

Publisher:	Harlequin
Book Number:	313
Publication Date:	October 1979
Setting:	Washington
Heroine:	Maggie Rafferty
Hero:	Wade Rafferty

Synopsis: Five years earlier, Maggie Rafferty had forced Wade out of her life. By divorcing him, she had hoped to purge him from her heart forever. Her fiery temper, his black rages, they had been a dangerous combination that was destined for disaster.

The only thing they had ever done right together, the only thing worthwhile, had been to create their son, Mike. He was the living symbol of their dead marriage, a union she hoped would stay buried in its shallow grave.

But Wade returned to Seattle, disrupting their lives all over again, resurrecting old feelings that she had hoped were gone forever.

"He's coming! Dad's coming home to see us!" Mike had shouted when he had read his father's letter.

Maggie knew better. Wade was coming to see *Mike*, not her. There was no "us" anymore. And there never would be again.

Maggie was sure she had done the right thing by divorcing Wade. Absolutely sure. She was doing just fine on her own, and she was determined that he see that.

So determined, in fact, that she had to ask herself: Was she trying to convince Wade that she and Mike didn't need him? Or was she trying to convince her own heart?

SENTIMENTAL JOURNEY

Publisher:	Harlequin
Book Number:	319
Publication Date:	November 1979
Setting:	Tennessee
Heroine:	Jessica Thorne
Occupation:	Advertising
Hero:	Brodie Hayes
Occupation:	Business development

Synopsis: For a kid from the wrong side of town who had started life with nothing, Brodie Hayes had done well for himself. Having been away for years, Brodie returned home in style, a successful businessman, ready to show the old crowd that he had "amounted to something" after all.

He figured his old girlfriend had probably married that rich Harvard law student. But he wouldn't mind running into her just the same.

Instead, he found himself face to face with the image of his previous love, the image he had kept in his heart all the years he had been gone. But it wasn't Jordanna; this beautiful face belonged to Jordanna's younger sister, Jessica. And it didn't take long for Brodie to realize that he might be losing his heart to one of those Thorne girls all over again.

The moment Jessica turned to see that tall, handsome figure, her memory rang a bell. A warning bell. He was someone from the past, and not a particularly pleasant chapter of history, either.

Brodie had pursued Jordanna relentlessly, and now it appeared he intended to do the same with Jessica.

Under other circumstances, Jessica might have welcomed the attentions of a successful, handsome, and extremely charming man. But she was afraid to trust the feelings of love he stirred in her.

Was she the one he was thinking of when he gazed into her eyes—so like her sister's? Was she the one he truly loved? Or was Jessica just a surrogate, a convenient substitute for the woman Brodie really wanted, the one he could never have?

A LAND CALLED DESERET

Publisher:	**Harlequin**
Book Number:	**326**
Publication Date:	**December 1979**
Setting:	**Utah**
Heroine:	**LaRaine Evans**
Occupation:	**Actress**
Hero:	**Travis McCrea**
Occupation:	**Rancher**

Synopsis: With a trail of broken hearts behind her, LaRaine Evans had developed a reputation for being a cold, calculating woman. Whether she wanted to admit it or not, she had begun to act the part with more finesse in her personal life than she had ever displayed on the scene.

Love affairs never lasted long for LaRaine, whether she ended them herself or got dumped. She wanted to get off this crazy carousel, to get married, and show the world and herself that she *was* capable of sustaining a relationship.

It had to be someone outside the movie industry, someone who was unaware of her track record. And who better to dazzle with her status as an actress than a wealthy rancher? On location in Utah, LaRaine discovered that she was only a stone's throw from Travis McCrea's renowned spread. The man was rich, single, and by all accounts handsome. What more could she ask?

But Travis McCrea wasn't what LaRaine had been expecting at all. First, he didn't exactly faint dead away at her charms. In fact, other than finding her slightly amusing, he scarcely noticed her at all.

Then there was his house. If the man was so rich, why did he live in such a rundown old house? Although he was ruggedly handsome, he was dressed like a common cowboy and acted like one, too. Hardly the landowner tycoon she had been anticipating.

Despite her first impressions of the man, LaRaine had to admit that she found him fascinating. He was so much more honest and to the point than other men she had met. With a certain degree of discomfort, she felt he could see right through her; she only hoped he liked what he saw.

For some reason that she couldn't quite understand, it seemed very important to LaRaine that this man like her, approve of her. Probably because LaRaine didn't always like herself.

Unlike her previous Hollywood love interests, this man was real and all male. She wasn't sure how to handle him.

Then LaRaine decided that perhaps it would be best not to try to handle him at all. Maybe she should just enjoy him. And maybe, with practice, she could even learn to love him.

KONA WINDS

Publisher:	Harlequin
Book Number:	332
Publication Date:	January 1980
Setting:	Hawaii
Heroine:	Julie Lancaster
Occupation:	Tutor
Hero:	Ruel Chandler
Occupation:	Sugar plantation owner/cattle rancher

Synopsis: Julie thought she had been offered the chance of a lifetime—a tutoring job in Hawaii! The fanciful paradise lived up to its reputation in beauty and mystique. And the Hawaiian hospitality was everything Julie had hoped. Debbie, Julie's new student, and her family greeted Julie with openness and kindness beyond her greatest expectations. Only one member of the household remained aloof, untouchable . . . Ruel Chandler, Debbie's adored older brother.

His mocking, condescending manner irritated Julie to distraction. But Julie had to admit that wasn't the reason for her inability to concentrate.

Ruel cautioned her about the razor-sharp undertows on the beaches at Haleiwa and Waimea Bay. Perhaps he should have warned her that beneath that cool exterior, Ruel Chandler was a man whose passions burned hotter than any island volcano.

THAT BOSTON MAN

Publisher:	Harlequin
Book Number:	338
Publication Date:	February 1980
Setting:	Massachusetts
Heroine:	Lexie Templeton
Occupation:	Newspaper reporter
Hero:	Rome Lockwood
Occupation:	Business tycoon

Synopsis: Because of her feminist point of view, political reporter Lexie Templeton had been accused of hating men. She didn't hate them, she insisted. Lexie simply wanted to find one who would treat her like an equal.

As far as she was concerned, the rich and famous playboy Rome Lockwood was the epitome of all she disliked in men. In a moment of thoughtless chatter, Lexie confided as much to a gossip columnist. "He isn't man enough to keep one woman satisfied," she said without realizing the trouble her statement would cause.

Rome Lockwood stormed into her office, demanding an apology for her ill-founded accusations. Amused, Lexie challenged him to prove that he was man enough for a truly liberated woman and invited him out on a date . . . which *she* would pay for.

To her dismay, he accepted her dare. The battle of the sexes was on!

BED OF GRASS

Publisher:	Harlequin
Book Number:	343
Publication Date:	March 1980
Setting:	Maryland
Heroine:	Valerie Wentworth
Hero:	Judd Prescott

Synopsis: Valerie wanted Judd; she couldn't help herself. She hadn't been able to deny him all those years ago, when she had been a restless, foolish young woman. And, apparently, she hadn't grown any wiser with time.

Long ago, Valerie had given in to temptation. Saying yes to love, saying yes to Judd Prescott had been one of the greatest mistakes of her life.

In spite of her indiscretion, something lovely had come of their union, her beautiful son, Tadd. But the baby's birth had brought shame on Valerie and her family and the loss of her grandfather's love. She had been thrown out of his house in disgrace and forced to raise her child alone.

Only when her grandfather died did she return home to attend his funeral. It wasn't easy visiting a place that had caused her so much pain, so many unhappy memories.

The most difficult part of coming home was having to face Judd Prescott, to see him again, to talk to him, to continue to deceive him. Judd Prescott had no idea that he had a son. Her son. And if Valerie had her way, he never would.

Considering the amount of misery he had caused her, she had hoped she would have gotten over him. With maturity on her side, she prayed she would be able to resist him, should he pursue her.

But Valerie had no idea how stubborn Judd Prescott could be. He didn't bother to hide the fact that he wanted Valerie again. Badly.

Her mind told her that Judd Prescott was trouble. She should stay as far away from him as possible. But Valerie found herself betrayed by her own heart and body. In spite of her best intentions, some temptations were just too strong to resist.

THE THAWING OF MARA

Publisher:	Harlequin
Book Number:	349
Publication Date:	April 1980
Setting:	Pennsylvania
Heroine:	Mara Prentiss
Hero:	Sinclair Buchanan

Synopsis: The day her father, Adam, left her mother for a younger woman, Mara Prentiss had locked her feelings inside.

She hated her father, blaming his infidelity for her mother's death. Bitterness and anger soon turned her into a cold, aloof woman.

When Adam was injured in a car accident and required constant care, Mara called upon her strong sense of family duty. Reluctantly, she brought him home to look after him.

Although her father strongly opposed the idea, Mara hired an agent to lease out a vacant cottage that was nestled in a wooded area on her property. But the moment she met her new tenant, she knew she should have taken Adam's advice.

Sinclair Buchanan frightened her. Striking and virile, he threatened to reawaken all the emotional and physical responses she had tried so hard to bury. She wanted him off her land—the sooner the better.

But Sin had other ideas. Having glimpsed another side of Mara, he befriended her father, then began a campaign to thaw her ice-encrusted heart.

"The only cure I know for sexual attraction is prolonged exposure," he told her as his mouth explored the side of her neck, sending delicious shivers over her sensitive skin. "Tonight can be the beginning of a series of experiments."

His offer was tempting. But loving meant pain. So why was she even considering his crazy suggestion? After all, she had more sense than that . . . didn't she?

THE MATING SEASON

Publisher:	Harlequin
Book Number:	356
Publication Date:	May 1980
Setting:	Kansas
Heroine:	Jonni Starr
Occupation:	High-fashion model
Hero:	Gabe Stockman
Occupation:	Rancher

Synopsis: After six successful years in New York, establishing herself as a fashion model, Jonni returned home to Kansas—her fiancé, Trevor, in tow. She had been looking forward to seeing Gabe Stockman again. He had been the general manager of her parents' ranch for years, and she eagerly anticipated a reunion with her old friend.

Jonni wasn't prepared for the difference that six years could make. She had been little more than a girl when she had left, and she had remembered Gabe through girlish eyes. But she had returned a woman who was now more than simply aware that Gabe was a virile, earthy man, the antithesis of her urbane fiancé.

Trevor represented all she had worked so hard to attain: prestige, success, sophistication. But Gabe touched that country girl whose heart had never left home. Gabe represented her past, Trevor her present. Jonni couldn't decide which man she should choose to share her future.

LORD OF THE HIGH LONESOME

Publisher:	**Harlequin**
Book Number:	**363**
Publication Date:	**June 1980**
Setting:	**North Dakota**
Heroine:	**Kit Bonner**
Occupation:	**Rancher**
Hero:	**Baron Reese Talbot**
Occupation:	**Owner of Flying Eagle Ranch**

Synopsis: For generations, a member of the Bonner family had been in charge of the Flying Eagle Ranch. Although her grandfather, Nate, was officially the manager, as he grew older, Kit Bonner began running things. The absentee owners rarely interfered, satisfied with their profits and an occasional report.

When Baron Reese Talbot arrived to look over his new inheritance, Kit bristled with anger. He had a lot of new ideas regarding the ranch . . . and, even worse, seemed determined to crack her protective shell and expose her vulnerable, womanly side.

Although Kit found her autocratic new boss attractive, she had every intention of putting up a fight. She didn't want a man—any man—and especially one with a title. She knew firsthand how deceitful the upper crust could be. Didn't the townspeople still refer to her as the baron's bastard daughter?

Reese was her father's distant relative, and falling in love with him would be a fatal mistake. But if she didn't find some way of forcing him from the ranch soon, history might very well repeat itself.

SOUTHERN NIGHTS

Publisher:	Harlequin
Book Number:	369
Publication Date:	July 1980
Setting:	Florida
Heroine:	Barbara Haynes
Occupation:	Airline reservations
Hero:	Jock Malloy
Occupation:	Owner of the Sandoval citrus farm

Synopsis: Barbara Haynes had finally gotten over Jock Malloy; her heart had healed, and she was ready for a relationship with a wonderful new man, Todd Gaynor. Todd was everything Jock wasn't: kind, sensitive, reliable, gentle, and affectionate. Every day Barbara reminded herself how lucky she was to have escaped Jock Malloy's spell. Every day she tried to believe her own admonition.

But when Todd took her to Sandoval, the family citrus ranch, to meet his mother and older brother, J. R., Barbara discovered that Fate had a cruel streak after all. Todd's brother—actually, half-brother—was none other than Jock Malloy.

Barbara was torn between the two brothers. Todd made her feel safe, protected from emotions she couldn't control. Appalled, she realized that Todd's gentle affection couldn't compare to the drugging passion that Jock stirred inside her. Although Todd might have been "good" for her, he wasn't the one her heart and body ached for.

She couldn't imagine choosing one brother over the other, but she had to. Would she break the heart of a gentle soul whose love had healed her deepest hurts? Or would she deny her own heart and turn away from the only man she had ever truly loved?

ENEMY IN CAMP

Publisher:	Harlequin
Book Number:	373
Publication Date:	August 1980
Setting:	Michigan
Heroine:	Victoria Beaumont
Hero:	Dirk Ramsey

Synopsis: As far as Victoria Beaumont was concerned, Dirk Ramsey didn't deserve to use the term "journalist." He had built his career by tarnishing the images of one public servant after another. And now he was coming after her politically minded father, Charles.

Victoria would have loved to have tarred and feathered Dirk Ramsey. It was the least she could do. But her father chose, instead, to invite him to the Beaumont family's summer home on Mackinac Island for a few weeks to "get to know them personally."

Victoria couldn't believe it! Inviting the enemy himself right into their camp! Whatever was her father thinking?

From the moment they met, their contempt for each other was painfully evident. He considered her a snob; she thought him an uncouth bore. The only thing stronger than their dislike for one another was their attraction.

In spite of all his apparent "shortcomings," Victoria had to admit he was the sexiest man she had ever met. And his blatant advances on her left no doubt that he was interested as well.

But was his fascination with her that of a man for a woman? Or that of a journalist for the daughter of a man he was about to destroy in print?

DIFFICULT DECISION

Publisher:	Harlequin
Book Number:	386
Publication Date:	October 1980
Setting:	Connecticut
Heroine:	Deborah Holland
Occupation:	Travel agent/secretary
Hero:	Zane Wilding
Occupation:	Conglomerate controller

Synopsis: Arrogant, with about as much feeling as a stone. That was Deborah Holland's first impression of Zane Wilding. But he wasn't the only pebble on the beach, and having been recently betrayed by a former lover, Deborah wasn't exactly looking for love. All she wanted from Zane Wilding was a job. When he offered her one as his personal secretary, she knew it wouldn't be easy working for such a difficult man.

Once in his employ, Deborah found herself dealing with an even more impossible entity than Mr. Wilding: *Mrs.* Wilding. An unhappy, haunted woman with a serious drinking problem, Sylvia Wilding accused Deborah of cheating with her husband. Even thinking of the acts Mrs. Wilding suggested brought a hot flush to Deborah's cheeks. But was her embarrassment entirely due to the lewd language Sylvia used? Or was it because Deborah knew that those words, crude as they were, simply echoed her own desires, her own hopes . . . and her fears?

HEART OF STONE

Publisher:	Harlequin
Book Number:	391
Publication Date:	November 1980
Setting:	New Hampshire
Heroine:	Stephanie Hall
Occupation:	Bookkeeper at the White Boar Inn
Hero:	Brock Canfield
Occupation:	Owner of the White Boar Inn

Synopsis: Stephanie's brother, Perry, had practically raised her, and he was forever looking out for her best interests. He warned her about Brock Canfield in no uncertain terms. "Brock is smooth and finished," he told her, "like a diamond that's been cut into a perfect stone, hard and unfeeling."

Brock wasted no time living up to his reputation. Within minutes of meeting her, with his girlfriend in the room next door, he made his move on Stephanie.

"If you're smart, you'll slap my face, Stephanie," he advised her.

"I'm smarter than that," she returned. "I'm not going to fight you, or in any way heighten your interest in the chase."

Although he continued to pursue her, Stephanie warned herself that they were from two completely different worlds. He was a jet-setter; she preferred the small-town life in the quiet New Hampshire inn. He was Chateaubriand; she was Yankee pot roast.

In her wildest dreams, Stephanie couldn't have wished for a more ardent or determined lover. He offered her more than she could allow herself to accept. She felt like a child who had just been given a wonderful treat, but was afraid to enjoy it too much. Because she knew the time would come—all too soon—when her happiness would be taken away.

ONE OF THE BOYS

Publisher:	Harlequin
Book Number:	399
Publication Date:	December 1980
Setting:	New Jersey
Heroine:	Petra Wallis
Occupation:	Camera operator
Hero:	Dane Kingston
Occupation:	Entertainment producer/director

Synopsis: As a successful camera operator, Petra Wallis had learned long ago that if she wanted the crew to respect her, she had to avoid romantic entanglements with her fellow workers. And, as usual, she had no problem keeping to her convictions when she found herself being directed by the sexy Dane Kingston. She and Dane had shared a stormy past, a misunderstanding that had turned into a screaming match on set. There was certainly no love lost between them and no sign that he would present any temptation that she couldn't resist.

Professional all the way.

But her high standard of professionalism was difficult to maintain with this difficult man undermining her hard-earned position with her crew at every turn. Soon Pet didn't know which passion he aroused most quickly in her, fury or desire. It wasn't easy to hate a man whose kisses left her weak and wanting more.

WILD AND WONDERFUL

Publisher:	**Harlequin**
Book Number:	**416**
Publication Date:	**March 1981**
Setting:	**West Virginia**
Heroine:	**Glenna Reynolds**
Occupation:	**Freelance writer**
Hero:	**Jett Coulson**
Occupation:	**Owner of Coulson Mining**

Synopsis: Glenna Reynolds refused to stand idly by and wait for the government to shut down her father's mine. Orin Reynolds hadn't fully recovered from two previous heart attacks, and there was a good chance he wouldn't survive losing his company and home.

In light of her father's poor health, the banks refused to lend him the money to make necessary safety repairs that would keep the mine operating. It seemed that the only chance they had to save their business was to merge with a company large enough to absorb their losses. That meant Coulson Mining.

Although the owner, Jett Coulson, was a tough businessman, Glenna found him devastatingly attractive. He was the kind of man she could easily fall in love with. But after reviewing the company's records, he refused to help, stating the obvious: It would be more profitable to purchase the mine after it was seized by the government.

Knowing Jett found her physically attractive, Glenna went to his room, determined to change his mind. She was mortified when he refused to accept her bargain.

She was in love with Jett, but she had cheapened herself in his eyes by making such a demeaning offer.

When he bought the mining company, how would she face him again?

A TRADITION OF PRIDE

Publisher:	Harlequin
Book Number:	421
Publication Date:	April 1981
Setting:	Mississippi
Heroine:	Lara Cochran
Hero:	Rans MacQuade

Synopsis: Lara Cochran knew what it was to be in love and happily married. She also knew how it felt to have her world suddenly collapse around her, leaving her shattered and empty. Having spoken those words, "Until death do us part," Lara couldn't bring herself to divorce Trevor, even after she found out about the other women. She had been raised with a tradition of pride; the Alexander family kept their word. No matter what. And they certainly didn't get divorced.

Besides, Lara couldn't imagine needing a divorce. She certainly wouldn't be falling in love with any other man, not after the way Trevor had treated her. Men, love, marriage . . . she had no use for any of it.

Then Rans MacQuade came along, the virile manager of her father's Mississippi plantation. He stirred feelings in her that she had thought were long dead, emotions she had hoped never to feel again.

Lara began to question her family's standard. She had been taught that if you made a mistake, you had to live with it. But how could she, when it would mean having to live without Rans?

THE TRAVELLING KIND

Publisher:	Harlequin
Book Number:	427
Publication Date:	May 1981
Setting:	Idaho
Heroine:	Charley Collins
Occupation:	Ranch owner
Hero:	Shad Russell
Occupation:	Cowboy

Synopsis: Running the Seven Bar Ranch was hard work and plenty of it. Charley had barely been able to keep on top of things when her older brother had been on his feet. But with his leg in a cast, he was worthless, and Charley needed help. Fast.

Help arrived in the form of Shad Russell, a drifter who was willing and able to take up the slack at the ranch. Soon Charley realized that if anything, Shad had understated his abilities. She didn't know how they had ever gotten along without him. The thought of him moving on, as drifters always did, made her sad; it was only a matter of time.

Shad was shockingly candid about his desire for her. He was equally honest about the fact that he had nothing to offer Charley other than the pleasure of the moment. No future, no commitment. Unlike Chuck Weatherby, her neighboring rancher, who adored her and was more than willing to devote his life to her.

Everyone thought Charley should marry Chuck. Everyone pushed her in that direction, whether she wanted to go there or not. Her friends, family, Chuck, even Shad. They all felt they knew what was best for Charley, and didn't mind telling her so.

But Charley knew what she wanted. She wanted Shad. Even though her common sense told her it was foolish to love a drifter, a loner . . . a traveling man. The voice of logic spoke, again and again. But her heart just didn't seem to be listening.

DAKOTA DREAMIN'

Publisher:	Harlequin
Book Number:	445
Publication Date:	August 1981
Setting:	South Dakota
Heroine:	Edie Gibbs
Occupation:	Rancher
Hero:	Will Maddock
Occupation:	Rancher

Synopsis: Only a week out of high school, young Edie had married Joseph Gibbs. She had put all dreams and plans for her own future aside because Joe had needed her. His wife had recently died in a car accident, leaving him with two small children to raise. Edie loved Joe and his kids and had never felt that she had sacrificed herself by marrying him, by being a mother to his two babies.

But Joe had carried a heavy burden of guilt those eighteen years of their marriage. He had been determined that if anything were to happen to him, Edie would be able to fulfill her dream . . . buying a ranch in the Dakotas. To that end, he had used the occasional monies generated from his home workshop inventions to buy a generous life insurance policy.

As though Joe had entertained some premonition about his untimely death, the worst came to pass. But, as he had planned, Edie was offered a new life, a fresh start with the generous and unexpected payment from his insurance policy.

Although she still grieved her loss, Edie couldn't believe her good fortune. After years of providing caretaking for others, the children were grown and she would have her dream, a spread of her own in the Black Hills.

When Edie saw the land she had bought, she knew that fragile dreams, spun with the delicate hand of imagination, didn't always hold up to the harsh light of day. Her reality consisted of a dilapidated house, rotting fenceposts, and a ramshackle barn. This "fixer-upper" property didn't need a facelift; it required lifesaving major surgery.

Edie wasn't afraid of hard work, and neither were Joe's grown children, Jerry and Allison. This was a family affair, and together they would accomplish miracles. They had a ranch and a future to build.

But hard work wasn't the only obstacle Edie and her family would have to overcome. Another obstruction appeared—their next-door neighbor, Will Maddock. He wanted Edie's land and was determined that she would surrender it to him.

Edie's mind was set. She would never give up her ranch—or her heart—to the likes of Will Maddock.

With time she found that keeping control of her ranch was one thing. Not losing her heart to her handsome, arrogant, and persistent neighbor was quite another.

NORTHERN MAGIC

Publisher:	Harlequin
Book Number:	475
Publication Date:	January 1982
Setting:	Alaska
Heroine:	Shannon Hayes
Hero:	Cody Steele
Occupation:	Owner of Steele Air

Synopsis: Rick had promised Shannon that the minute he had a secure job and a place for them to live, he would send for her. Neither had anticipated it would take so long. Months later, she received a one-way ticket to Anchorage and was quickly on her way to join her future husband.

But when she arrived, Rick was nowhere to be found. Even his landlord was looking for him; Rick had been missing for two weeks.

Cody Steele, owner of Steele Air, denied that he had ever hired Rick Farris. But he generously offered to help Shannon find Rick. After all, he couldn't turn away a lady in distress, leaving her with the impression that Alaska was a cold, unfeeling place. The fact that she was young and beautiful had no bearing on his decision . . . or so he told himself.

As they searched for Shannon's elusive fiancé, Shannon and Cody found more than they had expected— love and fulfillment in each other's arms.

Shannon was overcome with guilt. How could she fall in love with another man? What about loyalty? What of her commitment to Rick?

How could Cody honor his pledge to help Shannon, yet not betray his own heart?

Both lived in constant dread that they wouldn't find Rick Farris . . . and of what would happen when they did.

WITH A LITTLE LUCK

Publisher:	Harlequin
Book Number:	482
Publication Date:	February 1982
Setting:	Wisconsin
Heroine:	Eve Rowland
Occupation:	Music teacher
Hero:	Luck McClure
Occupation:	Works in lumber industry

Synopsis: At twenty-six, Eve Rowland doubted she'd ever marry. With her plain looks and nonaggressive nature, she had given up on the romantic fantasy of being swept off her feet by Prince Charming.

The night she bumped into a handsome stranger and he called her "a little brown mouse" only reinforced her own low opinion of her sex appeal. Mortified, she'd scurried away without learning his name.

A short time later, while vacationing with her parents, she met Luck McClure again. And it seemed that his young son, Toby, was determined to find his widower father a wife. Within moments of meeting her, the eight-year-old was convinced that Eve was the perfect candidate.

How could she disagree? She was falling hard for Luck. The problem was . . . he was still very much in love with his dead wife. How could she ever compete with a beautiful ghost?

When Luck proposed, Eve questioned his motives. Was he simply looking for a woman who could be a mother to his son? Or was he ready to put the past behind him and love again?

THAT CAROLINA SUMMER

Publisher:	Harlequin
Book Number:	488
Publication Date:	March 1982
Setting:	North Carolina
Heroine:	Annette Long
Hero:	Josh Lord

Synopsis: Annette was a flirt and she didn't mind who knew it. What was the harm? All she wanted was a little innocent fun on her vacation at the North Carolina resort.

And who better to have it with than the gorgeous, extremely sexy owner of the resort, Josh Lord?

Annette was accustomed to having the members of the opposite gender respond with typical male interest when she turned on her considerable female charm. Finding a willing participant in her game of flirtation had never been a problem before.

But Josh Lord didn't seem particularly interested. In fact, he was decidedly cool in his lack of response to her advances.

Okay, she thought. So he was probably used to having women come on to him. After all, he was a hunk, a wealthy hunk, owner of a glamorous resort. But Annette had never had to take no for an answer, and she didn't intend to now. This was one prime catch who wasn't going to get away.

Finally she had him on her hook, but Josh Lord wasn't exactly dangling there at the end of her line. Annette had her hands full, trying to reel this one in without being pulled overboard.

THE HOSTAGE BRIDE

Publisher:	Silhouette
Book Number:	82
Publication Date:	September 1981
Setting:	Missouri
Heroine:	Tamara James
Occupation:	Accountant
Hero:	Bickford Rutledge
Occupation:	Entrepreneur

Synopsis: It had been a bad idea. Very bad. But at the time, Tamara had seen no other way to get the money for her invalid mother. As head of the accounting department at

Signet Machines, she had access to the company funds and the trust of its owner, Howard Stein. Tamara didn't think of herself as an embezzler. Far from it. She had taken the money with every intention of paying it back in full. And she would have done so, if Mr. Stein hadn't decided to suddenly sell the business to entrepreneur Bickford Rutledge.

A whiz with facts and figures, it didn't take Bick long to find the discrepancy in the company books. And it took him even less time to figure out who was responsible.

Tamara knew she was at his mercy and prepared herself for the worst. Exposure, humiliation, prosecution, even imprisonment. But Bickford Rutledge had another plan for the beautiful accountant . . . one that, even in her wildest imaginings, she hadn't anticipated. He promised to keep her secret on one condition: that she marry him.

Prison or marriage to a man she hardly knew. Tamara didn't know which choice frightened her most. But the moment Bick kissed her, she knew which made her pulse race fastest.

When he touched her, Tamara knew that Bick wanted her. Maybe he even loved her. But after what he had discovered, Bick didn't believe he could ever trust her. She had to find a way to convince him otherwise.

THE LANCASTER MEN

Publisher:	Silhouette
Book Number:	106
Publication Date:	October 1981
Setting:	North Carolina
Heroine:	Shari Sutherland
Occupation:	Student
Hero:	Whit Lancaster
Occupation:	Owner of tobacco plantation

Synopsis: The men Shari Sutherland dated paled in comparison to her stepbrother, Whit Lancaster. Although at times he was as autocratic as her stepgrandfather, she considered him the perfect big brother.

Unfortunately, Whit and his grandfather were firm believers in male superiority. In the Lancaster household their word was the law. Even more infuriating, they harbored some very old-fashioned ideas about a woman's role in life.

Three years earlier, Grandfather Lancaster had forbidden her to attend college. Rebelling against his edict, she had packed her bags and run away to school.

Her independence had been hard-won. Shari was determined that the Lancaster men would never regain control of her life.

When her mother suffered a stroke and needed someone to care for her, Shari returned home.

The constant arguments with her grandfather made her life nearly unbearable. Adding to the stressful situation was Whit's shocking revelation.

"I can't pretend to be your brother anymore," he said just before he kissed her. "This charade had to end sometime."

The safe, secure relationship she thought she and Whit had always possessed was shattered into a million pieces. Was it possible that she was more interested in him as a man than a brother?

He told her they were being married. But this time if he wanted to have his way, he'd better stop commanding . . . and learn to ask.

FOR THE LOVE OF GOD

Publisher:	Silhouette
Book Number:	118
Publication Date:	December 1981
Setting:	Arkansas
Heroine:	Abbie Scott
Occupation:	Legal secretary
Hero:	Seth Talbot
Occupation:	Minister

Synopsis: If only that cantankerous old car that Abbie had named Mabel hadn't broken down on the side of the road ... if only that gorgeous hunk hadn't stopped to offer a helping hand ... if only the hunk *hadn't* turned out to be Eureka's new minister. . . .

Abbie cursed her luck! Of all the men in the world whom she could have fallen head over heels for, why did he have to be a man of God?

As far as Abbie was concerned, ministers were supposed to be old, staid, paternal types. But Seth Talbot was anything but fatherly. And the feelings that this virile man stirred in her were far more of a fleshly nature than Abbie would ever want to admit. He had no business looking that good in a T-shirt and cutoffs. And all those muscles—what kind of pastor had a body like that? Seth Talbot was all flesh and blood, hard male sinew and bone. Not even the cloth could conceal that.

Rebellious, unorthodox, and, by his own admission a "bad boy," this preacher was all Abbie had ever wanted in a man ... or a lover. But she felt guilty even thinking those thoughts about a servant of the Lord.

The last thing she wanted was to lead him into sin, or so she thought. But once he had kissed her, Abbie wasn't sure exactly who was leading whom.

WILDCATTER'S WOMAN

Publisher:	Silhouette
Book Number:	153
Publication Date:	May 1982
Setting:	Louisiana
Heroine:	Vanessa Cantrell
Occupation:	Interior decorator
Hero:	Race Cantrell
Occupation:	Oil wildcatter

Synopsis: Although Vanessa had divorced Race Cantrell four years before, she had maintained a close relationship with his father, Phillip. Orphaned at the age of sixteen, Vanessa had come to think of Phillip as her own father. So when she received the telephone call that he had suffered a heart attack, she didn't hesitate before rushing to his side.

As well as being concerned about Phillip, Vanessa was worried about having to see Race again. She wanted to believe that she had put him, their marriage, and the pain of their breakup behind her. But if she had, why did she shake at the very thought of speaking to him?

Once they had been happy together. Race's courage and his rebellious, free spirit had been some of the things she had loved about him. But he had been impossible to live with. His reckless speculation in the oil industry had left them financially devastated, and Vanessa had finally reached the limit of what she could endure.

Now, four years later, Vanessa had it all: a successful interior design business, a luxury apartment in the French Quarter of New Orleans, material possessions, and financial security. Unfortunately, she also had an enormous void that it seemed no man could fill. For all of his obvious faults, Race Cantrell was a hard act to follow.

When they were reunited, when she saw him, when she touched him, Vanessa remembered all the reasons she had loved him to distraction. He was still as virile, as sexy, as passionate as ever, capable of stirring those old feelings, and new ones as well.

But some things never change. Race Cantrell was still a wildcatter, a gambler who lived on the edge. And Vanessa was determined not to spend the rest of her life balanced on that precipice beside him.

The problem was, after seeing him again, after reexperiencing the joy of his touch, she wasn't sure she could live anywhere else.

THE SECOND TIME

Publisher:	Silhouette
Book Number:	177
Publication Date:	September 1982
Setting:	Florida
Heroine:	Dawn Canady
Hero:	Slater MacBride

Synopsis: Slater MacBride had made it big, finally. Around the Florida Keys he was known as a bit of a tycoon, a self-made man who had worked hard at the task. He had it all now: the power, the money . . . all those things that *she* had wanted.

Eleven years earlier, he had been in love with a beautiful girl named Dawn, and she with him. But Dawn Canady had wanted to marry money, and at that time, all he had to offer her was his heart.

Slater no longer hated her as he had when she had first left him. But he couldn't help but feel sick with the old bitterness when he heard that she had returned to the Keys, a recent widow.

"I made up my mind a long time ago that I was going to marry a rich man," she had told him the morning she had walked away from him. "The second time, I'll marry for love."

Rachel MacKinley could hardly believe it was hers to enjoy.

Going on a cruise alone at the age of thirty-two was hardly the way Rachel had planned her life, but not everything had turned out the way she had intended.

She and her husband Mac had never had children—an unexpected void in her life—and Mac had died young, leaving her a widow before she was even forty.

With a lot of love to give and no one to receive it, Rachel had poured all of her energies into her thriving furniture business. At least one aspect of her life seemed successfully under her control.

With a major ad campaign beginning, now was hardly the time for Rachel to go on a holiday, but her friends convinced her that it was a vacation she sorely needed and that the business wouldn't collapse just because she had taken a week off.

The idea of being pampered, basking in the sun, and eating sumptuous food held a certain appeal, Rachel had to admit. Just an uncomplicated week of self-indulgence.

Her fairytale cruise lacked one important element, a Prince Charming, but that was the way Rachel wanted it. No entanglements, nothing so frivolous as a shipboard affair.

But apparently Cupid sailed the *Pacific Princess* as well. A misunderstanding by the ship's crew landed her in the same cabin with a gorgeous guy who could easily assume the role of prince, if Rachel would let him. The error was easily explained: Rachel and Gardner MacKinley had the same last name. Gard was convinced they had even more in common than surnames and wanted to explore the possibilities.

Rachel couldn't deny her body's desire to do as he suggested. But the last thing she needed was a casual fling. She had guarded her heart too long to simply throw caution aside and take the plunge.

When he held her and kissed her, Rachel could feel his sincerity, the genuine affection and longing. But she knew she was lonely and vulnerable, and that could corrupt her judgment. How could she be sure that this charming prince was truly interested in living happily ever after once the cruise was finished?

WESTERN MAN

Publisher:	**Silhouette**
Book Number:	**231**
Publication Date:	**June 1983**
Setting:	**Colorado**
Heroine:	**Sharon Powell**
Occupation:	**Rancher**
Hero:	**Ridge Halliday**
Occupation:	**Rancher**

Synopsis: If there had been a course in adolescent crushes getting out of hand, Sharon Powell would have qualified as an expert. Ridge Halliday was a fellow rancher and a friend of her brother. He was also the embodiment of every woman's fantasy. It wasn't fair to any impressionable teenage girl to be exposed to a man like him.

As a girl, Sharon had been helplessly in love with her sexy neighbor. And now that she had grown into a woman, she had put all childish things aside . . . like her adolescent fantasies of romance. As a full-grown female, her fantasies concerning Ridge Halliday were far more vivid and had progressed from mere hazy romance to unadulterated, fleshly lust.

Sharon liked to think that she had outgrown her starry-eyed adoration of the man. She had certainly worked hard enough at it. So why did her body still respond to Ridge's own particular brand of lazy sensuality? If she were truly over him, why did those fantasies spring so easily and so often to mind?

Almost against her will, she found herself playing coy

with him, encouraging him, then denying him. When he accused her of playing hard to get, she had to admit it was possible. After all those years of longing for him, chasing after him and never catching him, Sharon had to admit: It felt *great* to have him do the pursuing for a change.

TERMS OF SURRENDER

Publisher:	Silhouette Special Edition
Book Number:	1
Publication Date:	February 1982
Setting:	Texas
Heroine:	Angie Hall
Occupation:	Electronics
Hero:	Deke Blackwood

Synopsis: His broken marriage, his father's death in a plane crash, his mother's passing . . . Deke Blackwood had lost so much in such a short time. He was still reeling emotionally from the shock.

In his life, he had only one light remaining to shine into his darkness, but what a wonderful glow she gave. His daughter, Lindy. Angie's daughter. The only remaining symbol of what they had once had together, but had somehow lost along the way.

After everyone else had disappeared, leaving him alone and shaken, Deke had become obsessively protective of his little girl. Nothing would happen to her. No one and nothing would ever take her from him. Deke Blackwood simply wouldn't allow it.

When he heard that Angie was back in town after nearly seven years, he felt like the breath had been knocked out of him. And she had visited Lindy's school, spying on the girl behind his back. Deke wasted no time hunting her down and confronting her. He demanded to know what she wanted, while assuring her that—whatever it was—she wasn't going to get it. She had run out on him, on their baby, years ago. Who did she think she was, barging into their lives like this?

Angie knew exactly who she was and what she wanted. She was that beautiful little girl's mother. The child with her hair and Deke's eyes. And Angie realized, more than ever before, what a terrible mistake she had made when she had relinquished control of her daughter to the all-powerful Blackwood family.

Seventeen years old, pregnant, broke, and scared, Angie had thought it best to allow Deke to raise the baby. He had money, a stable family life, the Blackwood power behind him. Surely he would be better suited to provide for their child. And he had done an excellent job. Angie couldn't fault him for that. Even if he hadn't been the perfect husband, he was an excellent father, and she was grateful.

But Angie knew what she wanted. She wanted . . . needed . . . her daughter. And more than ever before, Angie realized that the girl needed her mother.

What Angie didn't realize was that she also wanted and needed Deke. Once before she had captured his heart, and now the stakes were so much higher. Could she do it again?

FOXFIRE LIGHT

Publisher:	Silhouette Special Edition
Book Number:	36
Publication Date:	July 1982
Setting:	Missouri, California
Heroine:	Joanna Morgan
Hero:	Linc Wilder

Synopsis: Joanna needed to get away from Los Angeles for a while, and her Uncle Reece's invitation to visit the Ozarks seemed like a welcome diversion. She had always been fond of her uncle, and the Ozarks were known for their peaceful, soul-soothing beauty.

When Joanna arrived at her uncle's stomping grounds she had her first surprise. The location of his cabin was described to her by a local as, "Take the second gravel road on yore left. Every time the road branches, stay to the left. As the crow flies, it's probably no more than four miles, but you'll have to go 'bout eleven mountain miles 'fore you get there."

Not exactly easy access, she had decided.

Then there had been the team of mules that had run her off the road and into the ditch. And the broad-shouldered, tawny-eyed man who had offered to help, but had found her bad temper more amusing than threatening. Maybe this Ozark paradise and its natives were a bit more primitive than she had been expecting.

Her uncle was determined for her to meet his neighbor, Linc Wilder, but Linc seemed reluctant to make an appearance. When he finally did, Joanna was dismayed to see that he was the golden-eyed guy who had witnessed her mishap with the mules. He hadn't forgotten her temper tantrum, and neither of them was especially eager to renew their brief acquaintance.

In a short time, both forgot their original differences, and felt the attraction beginning to grow between them. But Linc wasn't so sure about this California girl. Was it the real thing, this romance they shared in the Ozark wilderness, lit by the mysterious glow of the foxfire? Or was he nothing more than a hillbilly, a momentary diversion, to be cast aside when she decided to return to the golden coast?

THE BEST WAY TO LOSE

Publisher:	Silhouette Special Edition
Book Number:	132
Publication Date:	November 1983
Setting:	Mississippi
Heroine:	Pilar Santee
Hero:	Trace Santee

Synopsis: When Pilar had married Elliott, she had realized that the day might come when she would have to say goodbye to her husband who was so many years older than she. But she hadn't expected that terrible day to arrive so soon. Only fifty-five years old, in seemingly perfect physical health, Elliott Santee had collapsed from a massive coronary on the tennis court. And all the high-tech medical intervention that Santee power, money, and influence could buy hadn't saved him.

Pilar had never dreamed that losing her beloved husband could hurt so badly, or that she would feel so cold afterward, her heart encased in icy grief, hard and impenetrable. She would never love again. She was sure of it. Not when loving meant that you could lose, and hurt this badly.

Pilar hadn't considered that there was another Santee man in her life—Trace Santee, Elliott's son from a previous marriage. He embodied all the qualities she had loved in his father: pride, strength, a passion for living. Plus Trace had his own unique qualities that she couldn't deny, in spite of her self-imposed solitude.

At first she felt that she would betray Elliott's memory by allowing his son to take his place. But Trace was determined to find his own niche in Pilar's heart, a place that not even his father had touched.

LEFTOVER LOVE

Publisher:	Silhouette Special Edition
Book Number:	150
Publication Date:	February 1984
Setting:	Nebraska
Heroine:	Layne MacDonald
Occupation:	Newspaper reporter
Hero:	Creed Dawson
Occupation:	Rancher

Synopsis: For Layne MacDonald, some things were more important than even the career she loved. And one of those was finding her birth mother. Taking a personal and indefinite leave of absence from her newspaper job, she headed for a Nebraska ranch, seeking answers.

She was hoping to find the woman who had given her away at birth, she was hoping to find the key to her unknown past, but she wasn't expecting to find love.

Creed Dawson might have been accused of many things in his life, but he had never been called a pretty boy. With a well-over-six-foot frame and a hard, lean physique, he would have been expected to have a "Marlboro man" face. But Creed's features were blunt, ruggedly male, outlaw-tough; some might even say ugly.

Creed had never fooled himself into thinking he was a ladies' man. Quite the contrary. His manners were as simple as his face. If he had nothing to say, he didn't bother. If he didn't think something was funny, he didn't laugh. Plain as that.

Layne found him wonderfully intriguing, this big bear of a man with a gruff exterior and a wounded, but gentle, heart. Maybe he didn't see himself as desirable, but she did, and Layne was determined to show him just how valuable he truly was.

But Layne had entered Creed's life under false pretenses,

and it was only a matter of time before her secrets, her lies, were revealed. Creed Dawson had been hurt so deeply by so many people. Layne hoped her love would heal him, but for all she knew, her deception might be his destruction.

TOUCH THE WIND

Publisher:	Pocket Books
Publication Date:	May 1979
Setting:	Mexico
Heroine:	Sheila Rogers
Hero:	Rafaga

Synopsis: In a blaze of gunfire, Sheila Rogers had been ripped from her comfortable, if not fulfilling, life. She found herself in the hands of a ruthless bandido, a man whose people called him Rafaga, The Wind.

Considered an outlaw by society, Rafaga lived by his own code of honor, fighting his war against injustice any way he could.

At first, Sheila considered him a savage, violent and greedy. Why else would he kidnap her and hold her for a ransom of gold? But as she got to know him, to know his people and their ways, she realized that his actions were based on compassion, a love for those unfortunates around him who were starving, depending upon him to provide sustenance.

Sheila had been brutalized by a man before, but that man had been her own husband, taking her through the act of rape. In the arms of her outlaw lover, she experienced pleasures she had never known before. Her body and spirit blossomed beneath his gentle ministrations, opening fully to him.

But cold reason appeared on wings of fear. She lived in terror that he would discover how completely she was enthralled by him. There was no future for her love. Sheila knew she had to flee from Rafaga ... while she still had the chance to forget him.

THE ROGUE

Publisher:	Pocket Books
Publication Date:	February 1980
Setting:	Nevada
Heroine:	Diana Somers
Hero:	Holt Mallory

Synopsis: Diana had always been the boss's daughter, his only child, and that position had brought with it privileges that she had long taken for granted. As the princess of his empire, Diana bowed her proud head to no man ... except the Major, as she and everyone else called her father. She needed only her dad, and he needed only her. Their world was complete.

Then the Major hired a new man, Holt Mallory. A whipcord-lean, sun-leathered man with steel-gray eyes, Holt radiated an arrogance and sexuality that both attracted and threatened Diana. She made it clear to her father that she didn't approve of his choice. Unfortunately, the Major had a mind of his own and wasn't inclined to take her opinions into consideration. He argued that he wasn't getting any younger, and Holt Mallory would make a good manager when he retired someday soon.

This didn't sit well with Diana, who felt that, her gender aside, she should be the one to take over the ranch when the Major stepped aside, not some new Johnny-come-lately.

But Diana couldn't help feeling affectionate toward Holt's adorable nine-year-old son. In Diana's opinion, the boy embodied all the charm and charisma that the father lacked. Having recently lost his mother, the boy cried out to be loved, and Diana's maternal instincts answered his need.

The father had needs of his own, which he made abundantly clear. Diana resisted him as long as she could, knowing the day would come when she would lose the battle.

When a rogue stallion raided their ranch, ravaging the brood mares, Diana and Holt found they had a common mission—to hunt down the ghostly white stallion. But Diana soon discovered that she was the prey, and Holt was relentless in his pursuit.

RIDE THE THUNDER

Publisher:	Pocket Books
Publication Date:	July 1980
Setting:	Idaho
Heroine:	Jordanna Smith
Hero:	Brig McCord

Synopsis: Wild and willowy, Jordanna Smith was the offspring of a dashing, prominent New York banker and a glamorous socialite mother.

More her father's daughter, Jordanna preferred to travel the world in search of big game with her dad than to attend her mother's dull society balls.

No man could even come close to living up to her father's flamboyant image ... at least, in his daughter's adoring eyes. She preferred the pursuit of big game to the world of her mother's parties ... until the night she met a handsome stranger. In a moment, the huntress became the hunter's oh-so-willing prey, glorying in being captured. His touch stirred a feral desire in her that she hadn't uncovered on her wildest safaris.

Unsettled by the stranger and his effect on her, she fled

to the Idaho mountains with her father's hunting party. But Jordanna and her mystery lover were destined to meet again, to hunt together, and to clash in a welter of jealousies and ambitions.

By day, Jordanna and the party's guide, Brig McCord, shared the lust of the hunt, by night, their passion for one another.

But soon their newfound love was put to the ultimate test. Other, darker passions and deeds—jealousy, betrayal, murder—threatened to destroy them.

Jordanna's world crumbled as she had to face the disturbing secret about her father and brother. A secret that broke her heart, that had already caused one death, a secret that could cost Jordanna her life . . . and her love.

NIGHT WAY

Publisher:	Pocket Books
Publication Date:	July 1980
Setting:	Arizona
Heroine:	Lanna Marshall
Hero:	Hawk

Synopsis: Young, beautiful Lanna Marshall met J. B. Faulkner by chance one evening and an affection like that between a father and daughter developed. Not knowing J. B. was one of the wealthiest men in Arizona, Lanna was astonished to discover at J. B.'s death that he had left a large portion of his vast estate to her.

And so was the rest of J. B.'s family, so much so that his wife, son, and daughter conspired to trick Lanna out of her inheritance.

The only person who seemed not to care was the mysterious half-breed ranch hand Hawk. Yet Hawk's reasons to care were even stronger than Lanna's, and the passion that grew between them could lead only to an explosive ending.

THIS CALDER SKY

Publisher:	**Pocket Books**
Publication Date:	**August 1981**
Setting:	**Montana**
Heroine:	**Maggie O'Rourke**
Hero:	**Chase Calder**

A sky of sunshine,
A sky of change,
This sky that covers
The Calder range.

A sky of justice,
A sky so strong,
This sky that pays for
A Calder's wrong.

A sky of challenge,
A sky of right,
This sky that strikes with
A Calder's might.

A sky of parting,
A sky in two,
This sky that carries
A Calder through.

A sky of union,
A sky complete,
This sky that watches
Two Calders meet.

A sky of promise,
A sky so grand,
This sky that carries
The Calder brand.

Synopsis: The code of the West was pretty simple: Women were scarce and treated with respect, unless they showed they didn't deserve it. Men settled their own problems and didn't take them to anyone else. There was no place for weak individuals in the West; sooner or later, they were weeded out.

The Calder family had the strength, the land, the authority in Montana. No one bothered to dispute that fact. Webb Calder was a tough character who expected only the best a man could give, and even more from those he loved. His son, Chase, had been raised to appreciate the hard work and sacrifice that had made the Triple C what it was, the finest spread in Montana.

Angus O'Roarke, the Calders' neighbor, envied the Calders—their wealth, their power. But Angus was more of a dreamer than a doer, and he was one of the weak who was destined to be left by the wayside. He refused to take responsibility for his own mistakes, for his shortcomings and failures. Everything was the Calders' fault. As far as O'Roarke was concerned, it was greedy bastards like them who kept him from having all the good things in life that he deserved.

Maggie O'Roarke was Angus's daughter, and she displayed all the fire and ambition that her father couldn't. Having watched her mother literally work herself to death, Maggie had decided early in her young life that things would be very different for her. Maggie didn't hold anything against her mother for the woman's self-effacing attitude. Maggie figured her mom just didn't know any better. But Maggie did! She would never allow any man to have dominion over her! For years she had been saving money, hoarding it away, waiting for the day she could escape her stifling world and make her own dreams come true.

Before Maggie had the chance to put her plans into motion, her father embarked upon a path of his own. Rustling Calder beef, his decision could only lead to violence and, eventually, death. A gentle affection, fired by the heat of youthful passion, had begun to grow between Chase and Maggie. But no love could survive the hatred that resulted from their families' feud. In spite of her feelings for Chase, Maggie was still her father's daughter. And when tragedy struck, like him, she blamed the Calders.

With no reason to remain in Montana, Maggie decided it was time to go to California, to pursue the goals she had set aside for her family. But in her heart, how could she be sure if she was following her dream or running from Chase, running away from love?

THIS CALDER RANGE

Publisher:	**Pocket Books**
Publication Date:	**April 1981**
Setting:	**Texas/Montana**
Heroine:	**Lorna Pearce Calder**
Hero:	**Chase Benteen Calder**

Free grass for the taking —
My luck's gonna change,
'Cause there's nothing left in Texas
To match this Calder range.

Get them cattle movin'.
Honey, dry your eyes,
'Cause that Calder range is waiting
Under blue Montana skies.

From right where you're standin'
As far's you can see,
That's Calder range you're lookin' at,
And all for you and me.

From free grass to fences,
A lotta things have passed,

But one thing that's for certain
This Calder range will last.

We built this Calder range
To last five times a score.
It's a legacy we're leavin' —
Of pride and something more.

Synopsis: In September 1878, Chase Benteen Calder sat on his horse and scanned the immense landscape of Montana, so different from the crowded, overrun plains of Texas. He had found what he had been looking for for so long. In his mind's eye he could see the future, his future. Herds of cattle would grow fat on the native grasses. He would have barns walled with thick wood beams, and a big house sitting on a knoll from which he could view his empire. Not that day, but someday.

Benteen knew all about hard work, and he knew he would have to work like hell to make his dream a reality. But, standing there, surveying the empty canvas upon which he would create his world, he never questioned the cost. Sweat or blood, he would gladly pay the price.

Young, sheltered, innocent, and naive, Lorna Pearce was frightened when she heard of her fiancé's plans to build his dream ranch in Montana. Benteen had told her that he wanted a magnificent spread of his own, but she had believed he would locate in Texas, not some faraway, godforsaken place.

In spite of her fear, Lorna believed that a wife's duty was to follow her husband, and she resolved to be at his side wherever the journey took her.

Neither Benteen nor Lorna had any idea what obstacles lay between them and the culmination of their dreams. Trials and calamities that would daunt weaker souls blocked their path. The monotonous desert trail, the searing sun and driving wind, thorny thickets and the threat of rattlers were only the beginning. Further along the road, they encountered a killer stampede, violent

storms, Indian attacks, and the temptations of the bawdy
Dodge City.

Only then did Lorna and Benteen Calder realize that, in
the end, this dream of theirs might cost them their love,
even their lives.

STANDS A CALDER MAN

Publisher:	Pocket Books
Publication Date:	January 1983
Setting:	Montana
Heroine:	Lillian Reisner
Hero:	Webb Calder

Stands a Calder man,
Young and proud is he,
Wanting to decide
What he's born to be.

Stands a Calder man,
Flesh and blood is he,
Longing for a love
That can never be.

Stands a Calder man,
Lonely now is he,
Turning to the land —
To the Triple C.

Stands a Calder man,
All alone is he,
Passing to his son,
The Calder legacy.

Synopsis: Webb Calder knew all that his parents, Benteen
and Lorna, had endured to establish the empire that was

his. The Calder legacy had been bought with blood and pain, and Webb found that he must pay the same price if he were to hold on to the family's land.

Fleeing the poverty and overcrowding of the Eastern cities, homesteaders invaded the Montana ranchland by the hoards. They were determined to turn the cattle-grazing lands into wheat fields. Webb Calder and the other ranchers were equally determined that they wouldn't. The ensuing battle erupted with gunfire and arson, and the equally devastating behind-closed-doors treachery and betrayal.

Webb Calder wasn't sure who to call enemy or friend. But he knew one thing for certain: He was deeply in love with Lilli Reisner. She was one of "them," one of the new settlers who were making his life a living hell. She was also beautiful, spirited, and made his blood burn hotter than a prairie fire.

No matter how much Webb might desire her, Lilli wasn't his and never would be. Not only because she was an outsider—he would have been willing to overlook that—but because she was another man's wife.

More than once Webb had asked Lilli to leave her husband and be with him, but she couldn't. The only two people in her life who mattered were Webb and Stefan. But when Lilli dared to be with Webb, as her heart and body insisted, Webb was nearly killed and Stefan was left a broken man. She vowed it would never happen again, no matter how Webb begged her for the occasional stolen moment together.

But at night, when she lay beside her aging husband and ached for Webb's touch, she wondered: Was she being incredibly strong . . . or merely foolish?

CALDER BORN, CALDER BRED

Publisher:	**Pocket Books**
Publication Date:	**October 1983**
Setting:	**Montana**
Heroine:	**Jessy Niles**
Hero:	**Ty Calder**

Wanting to belong isn't easy
When they're making it rough instead.
And the hardest of all is knowing
They're all Calder born—and Calder bred.

It's not that I'm wanting to hurt you,
I just can't walk the path that you tread.
Don't stand between me and what I can be
'Cause you're Calder born—and Calder bred.

Loving is something like dreaming
When it comes to the woman you wed,
So why does your mind keep turning
To one who's Calder born —
and Calder bred.

Trouble's got a way of picking its time
To keep you from mourning your dead.
Look to the land for the answer,
'Cause now you're Calder born —
and Calder bred.

Together you'll face the future,
All the sunlight and shadows ahead,
And you'll raise your children knowing
They'll be Calder born—and Calder bred.

Synopsis: Ty Calder had been born a Calder, but he
hadn't been raised one. Problems between his parents had

driven them apart, and his mother, Maggie, had reared him far from the land that was his birthright.

At the age of sixteen, Ty found himself on the Triple C Ranch, his family's pride and joy. But Ty didn't know the first thing about ranching, a fact that was a constant source of shame for him. He would never live up to his father's larger-than-life image. There was no point in even trying.

Jessy Niles *had* been raised on the ranch, and she could ride, rope, herd, and deliver a calf with the best of the cowboys. She tried to share her knowledge with Ty, but taking advice from a skinny girl was difficult for the proud, young Calder, who already felt woefully inadequate.

As he matured, Ty realized that even if he spent a lifetime learning the business of running a ranch, there would always be men—many men—on the Triple C who would know more than he. Unlike him, they seemed to have been born knowing it. Rather than fight a losing battle, Ty decided to take a different path; he would attend the university. Perhaps there he would learn ways to help the Triple C, methods that were exclusively his own. His father, Chase, adamantly opposed Ty's decision, insisting that no professor could teach him what he needed to know. Only the land could do that.

While away, Ty learned more than he had intended—about women, not ranching—thanks to the sexy, irresistible Tara Lee Dyson. Tara knew better than to chase a man she wanted, so she allowed him to pursue her, choosing exactly the right moment to let him catch her. With his ring on her finger, Tara was next in line to be queen of the Calder empire.

With Tara to influence him, Ty began to change his ideas of what was best for the Triple C. When tragedy struck and Ty found himself at the helm, he felt he had only one course to steer: To save the ranch, he would need to exploit every asset the land had to offer. And, as Tara had pointed out to him so clearly, a fortune lay beneath the soil in the form of coal.

Jessy insisted that his plan made no sense. Even if he saved the ranch financially, the land would be raped by the process of digging for the coal. What was the point in saving it, only to destroy it?

Ty found himself torn between the two women and all they represented. Tara was his wife, the glamorous mistress of his manor. But he had long suspected that the Calder name was what she had wanted from him, the wealth, the power, the potential. Tara had a terrible hunger that could never be satisfied; the more he gave her, the more she would demand. At first she had been all heat in his arms, a fever, burning hot. But, like a flare, it was quick to blaze and quick to cool, leaving him in a cold darkness.

In Jessy, Ty found a true warmth that stayed with him long after he had left her arms. She embodied all that was Calder, in the truest sense of the name. Her love of the land, her quiet strength, her sincere and deep affection for him . . . just as when they had been teenagers, she had a lot to teach him about what it really meant to be Calder born, Calder bred.

SILVER WINGS, SANTIAGO BLUE

Publisher:	Poseidon Press
Publication Date:	August 1984
Major Characters:	Cappy Hayward
	Marty Rogers
	Mary Lynn Palmer
	Eden Van Valkenburg

JANET: The parodies of song lyrics . . . are the actual songs the Women Air Force Service Pilots (WASPs) sang while they marched to and from the flight line, their classes, and their barracks. In their own way, the songs tell much of the girls' story.

We are Yankee Doodle pilots
Yankee Doodle do or die.
Real live nieces of our Uncle Sam
Born with a yearning to fly.
Keep in step to all our classes
March to flight line with our pals
Yankee Doodle came to Texas
Just to fly the PTs.
We are those Yankee Doodle gals.
Oh, I'm a flying wreck, a-risking my neck,
and a helluva pilot too —
A helluva, helluva, helluva, helluva,
helluva pilot too.
Like all the jolly good pilots, the
gremlins treat me mean;
I'm a flying wreck, a-risking my neck,
for the good old three-eighteen.
I just called up to tell you that
I'm rugged but right!
A rambling woman, a gambling woman,
drunk every night.
A porterhouse steak three times
a day for my board,
That's more than any decent gal
can afford!
I've got a big electric fan to
keep me cool while I eat,
A tall, handsome man to keep me
warm while I sleep.
I'm a rambling woman, a gambling woman,
and BOY am I tight!
I just called up to tell you that
I'm rugged but right!
HO-HO-HO—rugged but right!
We wanted wings,
Then we got those goldarned things
They just darned near killed us,
That's for sure.

They taught us how to fly
Now they send us home to cry
'Cause they don't want us anymore.
You can save those AT-sixes
To be cracked up in the ditches,
For the way the Army flies
Really clears them out of the skies.
We earned our wings,
Now they'll clip the goldarned things
How will they ever win the war?

Synopsis: The Women Air Force Service Pilots, the first WASPS, risked their lives, their ambitions, and their dreams to help the war effort during World War II. Determined to win their wings in a man's world, four young women were united by their fearless passion for flying.

Cappy Hayward—an Army brat torn between love and hate for military life, she savored the freedom and power of flying and fought an ever-growing attraction to a career Army man.

Marty Rogers—a working-class girl whose flying expertise was her ticket to glory, she longed for a chance to outshine her brother and win her parents' love.

Mary Lynn Palmer—a Southern belle with a husband flying overseas, her soft-voiced manners contrasted with her steely courage in the skies.

Eden Van Valkenburg—a New York socialite looking for wartime excitement, she discovered a love that even beauty, glamor, and money couldn't buy.

From the rigors of military flight to their turbulent romances with fellow officers, they fought their own private wars for love and respect in a world where life, time, and love were never more fleeting, and never more precious.

THE PRIDE OF HANNAH WADE

Publisher:	Pocket Books
Publication Date:	February 1985
Setting:	New Mexico
Heroine:	Hannah Wade
Hero:	Jake Cutter

Synopsis: As the wife of cavalry officer Steven Wade, Hannah dutifully accompanied her husband to the wild and rugged deserts of New Mexico, where his regiment was stationed. Despite the precaution of a constant guard, Hannah was kidnapped by an Apache warrior. Although she was forced to submit to inhumane treatment and cruel humiliation as the warrior's slave, Hannah was determined to survive.

Hannah knew that under the circumstances, the "honorable" thing to do was to commit suicide. She had been taught by society that no respectable woman would allow a savage to touch her, even if it meant taking her own life.

But life had never seemed more precious to Hannah than when it appeared to be in such mortal jeopardy. Even at the risk of being a "soiled" woman, Hannah did whatever she had to day by day, praying for the moment when her beloved Steven would rescue her.

When help did finally arrive, it wasn't in the form of her husband at all, but in Captain Jake Cutter. Anxious to resume her life as it was before, Hannah was reunited with her husband.

Soon Hannah realized that although she had returned alive and well, her life would never be the same. Not only did the other officers' wives regard her with suspicion, but Steven too began to treat her differently.

Though restored to her own world, Hannah faced her greatest and most painful challenge of all, not that of capture and slavery at the hands of savages, but the bigotry and prejudice of her own "civilized" friends and family.

THE GLORY GAME

Publisher:	**Poseidon Press**
Publication Date:	**June 1985**
Setting:	**International**
Heroine:	**Luz Kincaid Thomas**
Hero:	**Raul Buchanan**

Synopsis: Wealthy, a member of high society, happily married—or so she thought—Luz Kincaid Thomas had it all. She believed her life to be a fairy tale come true, until her husband left her for a younger woman. Thrown into a maelstrom of confusion and insecurity, Luz thought she had lost everything. Her teenage daughter rejected her; her son presented problems of his own.

Amid the glitzy, glittering world of polo and "beautiful" people, Luz found herself with a very middle America sort of problem: She was a forty-two-year-old woman whose life had been swept away. Now she had to make a new life for herself, rather than depend on a man to give it to her. She needed to find out exactly who she was, not the woman who had always been defined by those around her. She wanted to get to know and grow to love that woman, whoever she turned out to be. And maybe, just maybe, after all that was accomplished, Luz might find the courage to love again ... when the right man came along.

THE GREAT ALONE

Publisher:	**Poseidon Press**
Publication Date:	**June 1986**
Setting:	**Alaska**
Major Characters:	**Tasha Tarakanov**
	Zachar Tarakanov
	Marisha Blackwood
	Wylie Cole

Synopsis: Alaska. Harsh and pitiless, yet rich and magnificent. Throughout its history ran the lust for gold—the "soft gold" of the sea otter pelts that lured the Russians across the Bering Strait, the "black gold" of the oil strikes, the numerous gold rushes that drew adventurers from the "lower 48."

The stark, white, often barren land of the Big Freeze was peopled by colorful characters, some native-born, some who had come from afar to seek out and claim its hidden treasures.

Concubine of a Russian fur hunter, White Swan was a native who saw her culture wiped out by the brutal Russians.

Tasha Tarakanov—offspring of a conquering Russian and his conquered Aleut woman—had to choose between her beloved Russian Cossack, Andrei, and the safety of her Aleutian tribe, and in choosing founded a dynasty of native Alaskans.

Zachar Tarakanov had the misfortune of falling in love with the fiery, dangerous Raven and of betraying his tribe's greatest secret.

Walks Straight, a noble native, chose his own death rather than reveal the mystery of the island of the sea otters to the Russian trappers.

A woman of mixed ancestry, Nadia managed to keep her heritage secret. But when her "shame" was discovered by her American husband, Gabe Blackwood, he reacted by torturing his wife.

Nadia's daughter, Marisha Blackwood, fled the island of her forebears with a handsome Klondike prospector in search of gold. She found it in her persona of Glory, the most famous whore in Alaska. Glory lived for the day she could take revenge on "Pa" Blackwood.

Wylie Cole, a restless man, carried the burden of tradition he couldn't keep. He defended his homeland from the Japanese invaders during World War II, at last finding his home in the love of a good woman.

Alaska. A land as rich in human emotion and high drama as its natural resources. There, in the Great Alone, unfolded stories of heroism and tragedy, greed and nobility, the lives of Alaska's builders and plunderers.

HEIRESS

Publisher:	**Little, Brown**
Publication Date:	**1987**
Setting:	**Houston, London, Cairo**

Major Characters:

Abbie Lawson—Spoiled, pampered and beautiful, Abbie had it all: her father's name and its accompanying power, the money, the social status, the best schooling, the possessions. Dean Lawson had given her everything, except the heartfelt assurance that he truly loved her. And without that, the rest was meaningless.

Rachel Farr—Equally beautiful, also the daughter of the powerful Dean Lawson, Rachel had been denied all that Abbie had taken for granted. His illegitimate love child, Rachel had never been able to claim those privileges that had made Abbie's life so comfortable. Lonely and shy, Rachel had waited, envying her sister, longing for the day when she, too, would take her place in the world as Dean Lawson's daughter. When he died, Rachel found her chance . . . and clasped it with eager hands.

MacCrea Wilder—A self-made, passionate man, he loved the spoiled and equally fiery Abbie. When it came to stubbornness and a lust for life, they were the perfect match. Perhaps too perfect, too alike to ever be together.

Lane Canfield—Before Dean Lawson's death, Lane had been the man's close friend and advisor. But Lane was in love with Lawson's daughter. Dean's *other* daughter. Lane longed to save the delicate Rachel from herself, from the fires of jealousy that threatened to consume her and those around her.

Synopsis: Two beautiful sisters with a mysterious past, forever rivals for their father's love, their social heritage, and their rightful claim to the large family fortune, Abbie and Rachel were bound by a fateful secret. Born on the same day, only one was legitimate, the other Dean Lawson's bastard.

From Houston's glamorous River Oaks and the cherished family ranch, "River Bend," to the teeming capitals of London and Cairo, to the empires of Texas Oil and Arabian horses, each sister was confronted with a shattering succession of betrayals and revelations. The two women were compelled to either duplicate the misdeeds of the past or create their own true identities.

The struggle appeared to be a contest for wealth, power, social standing, and men. But, off the glittering battlefield, beneath the glamorous trappings, Abbie and Rachel were simply two sisters, each trying to answer the question their hearts demanded to know: "Whom did Daddy love best?" In the end, only one of them could truly be the Lawson heiress.

RIVALS

Publisher:	**Little, Brown**
Publication Date:	**1989**
Setting:	**San Francisco**
Heroine:	**Flame Morgan Bennett**
Occupation:	**Advertising executive**
Hero:	**Chancellor ("Chance") Stuart**
Occupation:	**Real estate magnate**

Synopsis: Flame Morgan Bennett was a woman of contrasts: as fiery as her red hair, she was as cool as the green of her eyes. Although penniless, her beauty, her family's name, and her job as a high-flying advertising executive allowed Flame to move in San Francisco's most glittering circles.

At a glitzy cocktail party, she met Chancellor "Chance" Stuart, a real estate magnate with all the finesse, subtle charm, and rakish good looks of the skilled gambler. From that moment, the die was cast as Flame and Chance embarked on an extraordinary love affair.

But Flame discovered her family roots and learned about all the previous deceptions and intrigues between the Morgans and the Stuarts. She realized that history would irrevocably repeat itself.

Having been hurt too often before, Flame had decided never to love again. But, helpless to resist her need for Chance, she had decided to gamble everything for the opportunity to be with him. She didn't realize until later that "everything" was exactly what she stood to lose.

For, despite the love and desire they felt for each other, Flame and Chance were destined to become the bitterest of rivals.

MASQUERADE

Publisher:	**Little, Brown**
Publication Date:	**1990**
Setting:	**New Orleans**
Heroine:	**Remy Jardin**
Occupation:	**Daughter of shipping magnate**
Hero:	**Cole Buchanan**
Occupation:	**President of family shipping business**

Synopsis: Determined, courageous, and intelligent, Remy Jardin had to employ every resource at her disposal to unravel the circumstances surrounding an accident involving her family's shipping company. In the process she risked forever losing the man she loved, and possibly even her own life.

After a mysterious attack at the carnival in Nice, Remy was stricken with amnesia. For reasons she couldn't explain, Remy was equally mystified by the charms of Cole Buchanan, president of the family's international shipping company—and Remy's former lover.

Cole was obviously furious at the Jardins, but Remy could no longer recall why. Returning to her family's New Orleans mansion, Remy embarked on a search for the truth. Her journey drew her deep into Mardi Gras New Orleans and raised questions she had never dreamed she would have to face.

What had really caused the wreck of the *Dragon*? What was her family trying to hide—not only from her but from the rest of the world? Had Cole, the man she loved and trusted, betrayed her?

Remy soon realized that in that dark world of passion and deception, power and intrigue, anyone might be wearing a mask, and nothing was what it seemed.

ASPEN GOLD

Publisher:	Little, Brown
Publication Date:	1991
Setting:	Aspen, Colorado
Heroine:	Kit Masters
Occupation:	Film actress
Hero:	John Travis
Occupation:	Film producer and actor

Synopsis: Beautiful, vivacious Kit Masters, an "urbane cowgirl," had to choose between a film career and the man she had secretly loved all her life.

Born and raised on an Aspen cattle ranch, Kit discovered her love and talent for acting at an early age. She had starred in many productions at the Aspen Repertory Theater before leaving Colorado to seek brighter lights in Hollywood.

After a stint on a soap opera, she was offered a movie lead opposite heartthrob actor-producer John Travis—a role that would make her a star. And to top it all off, Kit captured the dashing Travis's fancy, not only on screen but off as well.

Only one thing stood between Kit and happiness: the memory of her old flame Tom Bannon, who had grown up on the adjacent ranch. Kit had always assumed that she would marry Tom someday, but he had married someone else. So much for childhood dreams, she had decided.

Back in Aspen with Travis and the rest of her Hollywood entourage to shoot her movie, Kit was reunited with Bannon, and they discovered that they were still irresistibly drawn to one another.

But both Kit and Bannon were haunted by the past, he by the memory of his dead wife, the tempestuous, raven-haired Diana, and she by the fact that Bannon had once betrayed and abandoned her.

To further complicate matters, Bannon was currently involved with his dead wife's sister, Sondra, a scheming real estate mogul. Sondra would stop at nothing to get Kit out of Aspen and away from Bannon.

When Sondra's attempts to convince Kit to sell her childhood home to greedy real estate developers failed, she formulated a new and far more deadly plan that would get rid of Kit for once and for all.

Kit faced not only a bitter rival in Sondra but a difficult dilemma: She had to choose between Travis and Bannon, between fame and love, between her Colorado past and a Hollywood future.

TANGLED VINES

Publisher:	Little, Brown
Publication Date:	1992
Setting:	Napa Valley, California
Heroine:	Kelly Douglas
Occupation:	Television news personality
Hero:	Sam Rutledge
Occupation:	Vintner

Synopsis: As the hostess of a successful prime-time magazine show, Kelly was on the threshold of accomplishing her lifelong dream of becoming a news anchor.

Kelly was self-made, with no one to credit for her rise to stardom but herself. Years before, she had exorcised herself from a miserable childhood in Napa Valley, California. With courage and determination, she had left behind decades of accumulated painful memories, along with an abusive, alcoholic father.

Her journey hadn't been an easy one, but in the end, she had managed to transform dowdy little Lizzy Dougherty into the chic and successful Kelly Douglas.

By chance, Kelly was assigned to do a feature story on Napa Valley, where she became entangled in the lives of Katherine Rutledge, the matriarch of the famous Rutledge Estate Winery, and her grandson, the ruggedly handsome vintner Sam Rutledge. Sam epitomized the family motto: If you're a Rutledge, *wine,* not blood, runs through your veins.

When a murder on the Rutledge estate was linked to Kelly's ne'er-do-well father, her entire world was turned upside down. She was forced to confront the past she had so long tried to hide and the emotional pain she had so long repressed.

Amid the turmoil of these events, Kelly and Sam discovered passion and love—but could Kelly afford to let Sam see the battered child within? Would she jeopardize her promising new life and career, or risk losing the one man she loved in order to protect her secret past?

THE PROUD AND THE FREE

Publisher:	**Little, Brown**
Publication Date:	**1994**
Setting:	**Georgia, 1830s**

Major Characters:

Temple Gordon—young, pampered daughter of a wealthy plantation farmer. Passionate and idealistic, she believed that her idyllic world would last forever and would fight to see that it did.

"The Blade" Stuart—Temple's lover and husband. His passion for life burned just as hot as Temple's. But The Blade had seen and done more than she, and he knew what the future held. He had fought enough battles to know: His people's war was lost before it had even begun.

Eliza Hall—a schoolteacher in search of adventure. She had left her comfortable home to live among the "savages" and teach them about the finer things of civilization. As the Cherokee Nation dissolved, Eliza stayed and endured the hardships with those she had learned to love. She knew they had much to teach her about loyalty and courage.

Will Gordon—Temple's father. He had lost everything: his land, his life's work and possessions, children, the woman he loved. But he retained his honor and spirit and was willing to begin again.

Nathan Cole—a minister of God, torn between his mission and a government that would prevent him from answering that sacred calling.

Jed Parmelee—had loved Temple from the first moment he had seen her. But he was, first and foremost, an officer, and he would fulfill his duty, even if it meant destroying the life of the woman he adored.

Synopsis: The Gordon family had all the prestige, monetary success, education, and gentility of any other Southern plantation owner. But, no matter how hard they had worked to carve their dreams into reality, their world was in jeopardy of being swept away: The Gordons were Cherokee.

Although they considered themselves citizens of the Cherokee Nation, with their own government and laws of society, the powers in Washington had different ideas. With the strength of Andrew Jackson's presidency behind them, Georgia had decided to evict the Cherokee from their ancestral lands, seize their homes and fertile farmlands, and relocate them in the West.

From the covert actions of the vigilante Georgia Guard to the more sophisticated, but equally damaging, decisions made by Congress and the Supreme Court, the

United States government systematically robbed the Cherokee of their rights and properties.

With its society eroding beneath it, the Cherokee Nation resisted as best it could. Some chose to fight with words in the political arena, hoping for justice. Others felt the only way was to take up arms and resort to violence. Passions ran deep, no matter what the chosen method of battle. And the differences of opinion as to how to wage the war caused internal conflict among the people, which was, in many ways, even more painful than the external pressures.

Temple Gordon and "The Blade" Stuart were two people caught in the web of this conflict. The daughter of a wealthy plantation owner, Temple was full of fire and spirit, believing that her people would eventually win the war with the government and retain their precious land. But the man she loved knew it was a lost battle. He, too, wanted what was best for the Cherokee Nation, and he believed that the only way to survive was to submit to the oppression—at least in action, if not in spirit.

Their love for each other and for their people was the light that lit the dark days of terrorism and betrayal that preceded their evacuation. It was the fire that warmed them on the bitter Trail of Tears as they trudged the frozen path to the West and their new lives. It gave them the strength to bury their dead and defend their loved ones who were still clinging to life.

But how could that love—strong though it was—survive in a world of treachery, disease, deprivation, and cruelty? How long could they cling to each other when their support and loyalty lay with such different courses of action?

LEGACIES

Publisher:	**Little, Brown**
Publication Date:	**1995**
Setting:	**Boston, 1860s**

Major Characters:

> *Diane Parmelee*—One of Boston's most exquisitely beautiful young women, daughter of a Union army officer.
> *Lije Stuart*—A natural-born leader and Harvard graduate who must join his father in fighting for the Confederacy.

Synopsis: At a time of social uncertainty and political unrest, the country is on the brink of Civil War. Since her childhood, Diane Parmelee has only ever had eyes for one man, the dashing Lije Stuart. After his graduation from Harvard, Lije and Diane are united by a burning passion that promises to endure forever. But promises are easily broken, and with the outbreak of the Civil War Lije feels compelled to join his father and family on the side of the Confederacy.

Diane is pulled in the opposite direction by her own father's role in the Union army, and where there was once a promise of marriage, peace and a charmed life, Diane must now watch as Lije defies her appeals and leaves for war. In a story of fierce loyalty and devotion to ones past and heritage, the love between Diane and Lije threatens to survive against insurmountable odds.

NOTORIOUS

Publisher:	HarperCollins
Publication Date:	1996
Setting:	Northern Nevada
Heroine:	Eden Rossiter
Occupation:	Rancher
Hero:	Kincade
Occupation:	Rodeo champion

Synopsis: *Notorious* returns to the wild ranch country of northern Nevada, where a determined woman must fight against her neighboring ranchers, her own ne'er-do-well brother, and the ruthless elements of the western prairie to protect her family's land. Eden Rossiter owns Spur Ranch, located thirty miles north of the small town of Friendly, Nevada. Her strength is as memorable as her beauty, and she struggles in a world of cattle runs and prairie dust where a spirited woman is not generally welcome. Eden is notorious in Friendly for having eluded a first-degree murder charge some years before, and she is also widely admired for not selling off the family ranch after her grandfather's death. But now Eden is in *real* trouble—Duke Depard, owner of the neighboring two-and-a-half-million-acre Diamond D Ranch, is ruthlessly determined to drive her out of business. Depard is too powerful an enemy for anyone to stand up to alone, and Eden's only family is her brother, Vince, whose gambling habits make him unpredictable and dangerous.

Then a stranger drifts into Friendly. Kincade is a soft-spoken, ruggedly handsome man who takes up Eden's cause and becomes her ally against Depard and his band of crooked ranchers. Their union is strictly business, and Eden, who deeply distrusts affairs of the heart, is determined to keep it this way. But Kincade has never felt for another woman the way he feels for Eden. As they struggle together through danger and adversity, Eden realizes the depths of Kincade's devotion, and her reserve gives way to the untapped passions of her heart.